SLAVERY, FREEDOM, AND DEVELOPMENT

In this innovative reinterpretation of the economic history of Africa and Europe, Warren C. Whatley argues that freedom from Western-style slavery is at the origin of modern Western economic growth. Such freedom was achieved around the thirteenth century in Western Europe by making enslavement among European Christians a sin yet still a recognized property right and form of wealth. After 1500, the Triangular Trade in the North Atlantic integrated the slave and free sectors of expanding European Empires, spreading freedom and development in Europe and slavery and underdevelopment in Africa. Whatley documents when the slave and/or free sectors drove the expansion of empire and how exposure to slave trades in Africa spread institutions and norms better suited to capturing and trading people – slavery, polygyny, ethnic stratification, and inherited aristocracies – some of the mechanisms through which the past is still felt in Africa today.

Warren C. Whatley is Professor Emeritus of Economics at the University of Michigan. His scholarly research in economic history spans Africa, Europe, and the Americas. He served on the editorial boards of the *Journal of Economic History* and *Explorations in Economic History* and as president of the National Economic Association.

Figures

Maps

Tables

Preface

This book is about the economic history of slavery and freedom, underdevelopment and development. This history begins when war captives are taken as slaves. War is as old as human history, and captives were taken as slaves as recently as two centuries ago. The liberal philosopher John Locke referred to the taking of slaves as "a continued state of war."

What you did with your captives made all the difference in the world. Since they were now in your possession, you could release them, sell them to the highest bidder, or take them home. If you took them home and introduced them into your community, then the members of your community would have to decide who was a slave and who could possess them, who was free and who was not – what Orlando Patterson calls "the first problem of slavery." How this problem gets solved, especially for the second generation and beyond, has given rise to at least five different slave cultures in world history. Emerging out of Western slave culture is one of human history's greatest achievements – the abolition of slavery and the unleashing of freedom dividends, what Deirdre McCloskey (2016) calls the "Great Enrichment." Abolishing slavery is a necessary ticket to board the train to modern enrichment.

This book is my telling of this story. It is not the typical telling, but I hope to show you how the view from here reveals a fundamental determinant of economic development, underdevelopment, and world inequality even today. In the final act, but by no means the first, the chief protagonist is the transatlantic slave trade between Africa and the Americas. Modern economic development spreads where slavery is abolished – in Britain, Western Europe, the United States of America north of the Mason–Dixon Line, and wherever freedom was the established social norm for all. Underdevelopment sets in where this was not the case – south of the Mason–Dixon Line, along the color line that W. E. B. Du Bois predicted would be "the problem of the 20th century," in Africa, and beyond. In Africa most of all, because Africa was where the enslaved people – the captives of war – originated. A close look at the economic history of slavery and freedom in Europe and Africa reveals how Africa became the mirror image of Europe.

In this book, I take up this and many related issues, like the economic role of identity, the inefficiencies of slavery, and the distinction between social norms and institutions. In many ways, these intellectual seeds were planted more than fifty years ago for me, during my undergraduate days at Shaw University in Raleigh, North Carolina. Those years, 1968–1972, were turbulent ones, socially and personally. Revolution was in the air, and we felt invincible. I felt invincible, invincible enough to take the movement to Baghdad! Yes, Baghdad, as in Baghdad, Iraq, as in Saddam Hussein and the Gulf War. It was here that I got my first glimpse beyond my veil.

My journey began shortly after the conclusion of the Yom Kippur War in 1973, when I became an exchange student at the University of Baghdad. There were five of us. Many agreements must have been concluded behind closed doors to make it possible to go to Baghdad, but known to me was my admiration for a man named Bob Moses, a soft-spoken leader of the 1964 Freedom Summer in Mississippi and Alabama, a founder of the Black Panther Party, and eventually a recipient of a MacArthur Fellowship for innovative teaching. We first met in the early 1970s when I was a student at Shaw and he was organizing with Stokely Carmichael's All-African People's Revolutionary Party. Both had been organizers in the South, where political study groups, like the one that brought us together at Shaw, had been training grounds for leadership in the effort to register Black voters. Stokely Carmichael would give a fiery speech with crescendos of "Black Power" and a raised fist. If the crowd returned the call, they were receptive to the next step in mass mobilization. In the South, the goal became nationalist in aspiration, eventually leading to the formation of the Black Panther Party (see the last installment of the Public Broadcasting Service documentary series *Eyes on the Prize* for details).

A decade later, the aspiration would be pan-nationalist, and we would deploy the same strategy in Baghdad. Why? Because the political philosophy of the Ba'ath Socialist Party (the party in power in Iraq, Syria, and Egypt at the time) was Pan-Arabism – one Arab state or confederation, it wasn't obvious which. *Our* political philosophy was Pan-Africanism – the All-African People's Revolutionary Party – one African state or confederation of states – again, not obvious which. We read and passionately debated scholar-activists like Eric Williams, Walter Rodney, George Padmore, Kwame Nkrumah, and Stokely Carmichael. In our minds, the Ba'ath Party was waging cultural warfare for the hearts and minds of sub-Saharan African students and the future African elite, and they were winning, appealing to their Muslim identity, not their African identity. "Your assignment, if you choose to accept, is to start a study group about Pan-Africanism in Baghdad, and like in Mississippi and Alabama, Stokely Carmichael will come to town and address the students. See you then." I was unsure what to do next in Baghdad, but it was for the cause. And I felt invincible. And what an adventure!

To make a long story short, the study group was indeed formed. We met many times. They became my friends and confidants. Saving my life when I contracted food poisoning. Very rich, eye-opening conversations among smart and eager students from many different cultures worldwide. I was known as Mohammed Ali Clay, the American.

As I said, I cannot tell you what I was supposed to do with my study group. Certainly not start a Baghdad chapter of the Black Panther Party, but by the time Stokely Carmichael and Bob Moses came to town (and they did come to town), the movement had taken on a life of its own.

It happened one evening in a well-lit room with a low ceiling. It must have been the basement of one of the student houses. There were many student houses, one for each country, where we would huddle, debate, and share cigarettes in large, open spaces with intimate seating. Many students from many countries. That night, it felt like thousands, from Ghana, Ethiopia, Somalia, Eritrea, Nigeria, Senegal, Mali, Morocco, and more.

The issue was whether or not to form a Pan-African Student Union at the University of Baghdad. Some of the members of my study group were front and center. "Wow, this stuff really works," I remember thinking. "But how did it come to this?" It had taken on a life of its own. Spontaneous and organic. Evolving out of open and passionate conversations across cultures. By now, I was a passive observer in awe of what I was seeing unfold.

As you can imagine, the issue was identity. "Are we African, Muslim, or Arab?" In the end, a Pan African Student Union was indeed formed. I could not vote, but before my professionalism got the better of me, I would list on my CV, "Co-Founder of the Pan African Student Union, University of Baghdad, Baghdad, Iraq."

My most vivid memory of my year in Baghdad, and the reason I am telling you this story, happened during the final chapter of that meeting, or at least the students who eventually carried the day. To my surprise, they were Berbers from North Africa. Fair-skinned, straight hair, and maybe blue eyes – I was too stunned to tell. They looked Greek or Roman to me. They argued that they were African, not Arab, from the continent of Africa, and that they had never been "Arabized" by the Muslim forces coming from Arabia. As a consequence, Islam was not their defining identity. African was! The continent of Africa.

For a young African-American kid from inner-city Philadelphia, this was a serious challenge to my worldview. "This identity thing is more complex than I thought." It is obvious to me now that identity motivates people to do many things, perhaps most things. Your race. Your mate. Your church. Your political party. Even the meaning of life. Individualistic identity, Western liberal identity, has unlocked secrets of the universe and created technologies that can solve world hunger, increase peace, and even preserve this remarkable and beautiful planet we live on. The key to unlocking these secrets was cultivating a high degree of cooperation among diverse people with highly individualistic identities. To my surprise, in writing this book, I have come to believe that the historical origin of Western norms of freedom and liberty are rooted in the emergence of a Western European Christendom identity that declared slavery among them sinful but still legal.

African identity? That is a relatively recent identity, emerging out of the many diasporic Afro-creole slave communities around the world – Afro-American, Afro-Cuban, Afro-Brazilian, and eventually Pan-African along DuBois' color line, or Stokely Carmichael's All-African People's Revolutionary Party. I have also learned that the identity of their captors was nearly half a millennium old by then – European Christians, as in Catholic, Protestant, and many other denominations, but European Christians, among whom enslavement was a sin – a freedom not extended to others.

This is my telling of the story: the abolition of slavery in Western Europe unleashing freedom dividends and modern economic development. It may at first sound like the typical telling of the story, what J. M. Blout (1993) calls the "Eurocentric" telling, where modern economic development emerges first in Western Europe in isolation from the rest of the world. The Eurocentric view is still the dominant view among economic historians, so my question becomes "When was slavery abolished in Western Europe?"

As an exercise, I suggest you ask a friend from Europe. They will probably give you what I call the empire answer: 1807 or later. But if you ask them about the metropole, about Western European nations, you will get the strangest look of puzzlement, perhaps a nod to the fall of the Roman Empire, but nothing much beyond that.

Why? Because Western Europe never legally abolished the *institution* of slavery until they abolished it in their overseas colonies. It became a *sin* in thirteenth-century Europe for one Christian to enslave another, but slavery remained a legally recognized property right until that right was repealed beginning with nineteenth-century abolitions of the transatlantic slave trades and the origins of international human rights laws. More importantly, it became a sin to enslave captives in thirteenth-century Christendom precisely when western economic development began what van Zanden (2009) calls "the long road to the Industrial Revolution."

That is the view from here. The customary law, or norm, called *sin*, allowed Western Europe to have its cake and eat it, too. It unleashed freedom dividends at home while feeding them with the exploitation of enslaved people in their colonies. Those enslaved people came from the continent of Africa, not yet Africans, but Wolof, Akan, Bambara, Fon, Igbo, and others.

My telling of this story has reminded me of my conversations and experiences in Baghdad in 1974, so I wish to dedicate this book to those friends and comrades, wherever they may be today. That early glimpse beyond my veil has always helped me see the other side of things, especially during the writing of this book. Ann's nickname for me is "the wander," but I am easy to find.

Back to the story behind the book. Over time, and with the protection and motivation of many scholars and mentors, I became an economist. To be more precise, I became an economic historian primarily because Donald J. Harris, one of my mentors at Stanford University, advised me not to transfer to the anthropology department or even seek a joint degree. Luckily, I took that advice and studied under the tutelage of Harris, Gavin Wright, and Paul David. Much of this book is about the comparative economic history of Africa, Europe and the Americas. I am convinced that one cannot explain how Africa became a mirror image of Europe without an economic perspective on history.

However, I did take those anthropology classes, and when I turned my attention to Africa, I found anthropology to be center stage in the data sources and the debates. I discovered a revolution underway in African economic history and development. Central to the reconstruction of that history was the availability of new data and methods that make a book like this possible. I am referring to the Trans-Atlantic Slave Trade Database, with its high-frequency counts of African slave exports (1500–1860) and the georeferenced anthropological observations on "precolonial" African societies found in George Murdock's *Ethnographic Atlas* (published in 1967, but with the median date of anthropological observations compiled within circa 1900). These are core collections used throughout this book. When the two are combined using new estimates of travel times to the nearest international slave port, one begins to see how exposure to international slave trades altered the institutions and norms of African societies. By spreading slavery in Africa, exposure to international slave trades produced an Africa that was a mirror image of Europe, the Africa that Europeans recorded on the eve of colonial occupation.

Acknowledgments

My intellectual debts are many, most of them documented in the bibliography at the end of this book. I wish to express special gratitude to the many students at the University of Michigan I have had the distinct pleasure of working with. I also want to take this opportunity to express special thanks to several friends and colleagues who were gracious enough to read some or all of this manuscript in various stages of its completion: William Darity, Jr., Deirdre Nansen McCloskey, Paul Rhode, John Thornton, Ann Cooper Whatley, Carmen Ann Baker Whatley, Jan Luiten van Zanden, and Gavin Wright. Last, but not least, I want to thank Michael Watson of Cambridge University Press, without whose encouragement over many years this book would not have been written.

CHAPTER 1

Reinterpreting African Economic History

A SHOCKINGLY SIMPLE IDEA

This book advances a shockingly simple idea: that the Age of Revolution in Western Europe was also an Age of Revolution in Africa. When I say Africa, I mean sub-Saharan Africa. The period stretches from the thirteenth century to the dawn of the twentieth. Western European economies developed from backwater farmers into empires that colonized most of the world. Africa, on the other hand, developed in the opposite direction. This book explains why.

The Eurocentric narrative emphasizes technological and institutional advances across the Eurasian continent that accelerated the growth of population and the size of economies. Transportation and gunpowder technologies were transformed into empire-building machines of colonial expansion across the globe. The military, cultural, political, and economic expansions of Muslim empires in the Middle East and Christian empires in the West spilled over into the Indian and Atlantic oceans, and beyond, while China withdrew from the high seas to manage its vast internal dynasties.

In Western Europe, in the meantime, individual freedom became the cultural norm, and moneymaking a virtue. In the Middle East and China, not so much. Economic growth in Western Eurasia outstripped economic growth in Eastern Eurasia, and as Western European empires expanded into the Americas and beyond, the political, economic, and cultural configuration of our modern world came into view. World events seemed to march inexorably toward the creation of our modern world – events that, in hindsight, appear revolutionary in their totality. Capitalism and democracy were unleashed on the world.

That is the dominant narrative for three-quarters of the world's population. But what about Africa? What was happening in Africa when all of this revolutionary change was occurring worldwide? Africa typically enters the picture as the source of the enslaved labor needed by Western European empires to colonize the Americas. We will have much to say about the contributions of slavery to the European take-off and its impact on subsequent economic growth and inequality worldwide. But what about Africa?

At the beginning of our period, Africa was the primary source of the world's supply of gold, not slaves. Sprawling empires had already been built in both East and West Africa. Islamic empires in India had already extended trade networks as far south as the Zambezi River to trade for the gold of Zimbabwe. Islamic empires on the Mediterranean coast had already extended trade networks across the Sahara Desert, deep into the West African goldfields at Bure, Bambouk, and eventually to the Gold Coast on the Atlantic. When the Islamic Ottoman Empire seized Christian Constantinople in 1453, seafaring Christians from Portugal accelerated their search for an African way around the enemy, reaching the Gold Coast of Africa (in present-day Ghana) in 1471, two decades before Columbus sailed into the Atlantic. Vasco da Gama rounded the Southern Cape of Africa and reached India in 1498, a mere six years after Columbus stumbled upon what would become known as the West Indies. The African Kingdom of Kongo, at the mouth of the mighty Congo River, converted to Christianity *before* the Protestant Reformation in Europe.

Perhaps the Great Divergence between Eastern and Western Eurasia can be best understood as a comparison of different paths of development in China and Europe (Pomerantz 2000; Frank 1998), but the Great Divergence between Africa and the West is best understood in terms of changes in the relationship between the two regions. The most significant change was European colonization of the Americas. The growing trade with the Americas turned the economic gaze in Europe *and* Africa from east to west.[1] The growing Triangular Trade between Europe, Africa, and the Americas integrated the slave and free sectors of European empires and sealed the deal for capitalism as the dominant economic force for change worldwide. And while we know a great deal about the contributions of Africans and African Americans to the Rise of the West, we know far less about how the triumph of capitalism impacted Africa. I can think of no better way to make this point than to call attention to the fact that this period of unprecedented and revolutionary change worldwide is still called the *precolonial* period of African history, as in before colonization by Europeans in the late nineteenth century.

So how did this Age of Revolution impact Africa? That is the central question of this book. International trade statistics suggest that African economies benefited from their growing trade with the world. Africa's export trade increased dramatically during this period, with the terms of trade moving decidedly in Africa's favor (Gemery and Hogendorn 1990). Maize and other New World crops increased African farmers' capacity to support larger urban populations,[2] and net exporters of gold became net importers of gold, some argue to circulate larger African national products.[3]

This book argues that international trade statistics like these do not tell the most important part of the story, because the fastest-growing African export was enslaved people. The book explains how the adverse effects of increased slave *production* swamped any positive benefits of increased *trade*, and why these adverse effects were large, significant, and touched every aspect of the ways exposed Africans related to each other – economically, politically, and culturally.

Why? Because enslaving people and marching them to the coast required the systematic use of violence to strip people of their freedom and dignity, hold them against their will, and sell them to the highest bidder. By the time an enslaved person left the continent of Africa, the social process I call slave production had already left behind a trail of violence and aggression that did not leave with the slave. As Walter Rodney (1972: 95) succinctly put it, "When one tries to measure the effect of European slave trading on the African continent, it is essential to realize that one is measuring the effect of social violence rather than trade in the normal sense of the word."

FREEDOM AND SLAVERY IN AFRICAN ECONOMIC HISTORY

This book documents the fate of African societies as they became exposed to international slave trades (the transatlantic, trans-Saharan, Indian Ocean, and Red Sea trades). It traces the ripple effects of the associated unfreedom and documents how the Age of Revolution in Western Europe was also an Age of Revolution in Africa.

What happened inside Africa has long remained obscure because, until recently, scholarship contained few quantitative measures that could trace the effects, and many of the firsthand observations were tainted by the racism and self-interested fantasies of greedy slave traders, sensationalizing explorers, and proselytizing missionaries. These biases have persisted and metastasized because Africans left behind little alternative evidence. To the victor goes the spoils, and when the victors are far-flung empires ruling over diverse people in far-off places (and monopolizing the written record of what transpired), the histories of the vanquished can fade, or worse, become justifications for their subjugation.

Fortunately, there has been a renaissance in the economic history of Africa that has shed new light on this period, and this book falls squarely within that renaissance. A recent book by Joseph Fourie (2021), *Our Long Walk to Economic Freedom*, is a highly readable interpretation of some of this new research from the perspective of South Africa. It interprets human history as a long walk to economic freedom, often a long meandering walk. The present book also interprets and reinterprets some of the new economic history of Africa, and with similar lessons about freedom being the source of economic growth and development.

The book, however, digs deeper to explore the historical origins of freedom as an emerging social norm in *Western Europe*. Orlando Patterson, in his twin volumes *Slavery and Social Death* (1982) and *Freedom in the Making of Western Culture* (1991), argues that the histories of Western slavery and Western freedom are connected in fundamental ways. Why the close historical connection? Because, according to Patterson, once an enslaved person is introduced into a society, that society must decide what it means to be free and what it means to be enslaved – what Patterson calls "the first problem of slavery."

Economic historians seldom consider this first problem of slavery, yet enslaved people represent wealth to their owners, which lends the problem to economic analysis. Chapter 2 identifies at least five solutions to Patterson's first problem of slavery found in recorded history, each with a different set of institutions and norms for preserving and growing slave wealth. Western-style slavery has been the most effective at preserving slave wealth. It also occupies two important placeholders in Western economic history – Greco-Roman slavery and modern racial slavery. Out of the tension between freedom and slavery in the West emerged the Western norm we call freedom, literally defined as "freedom from slavery."

The historical question, then, is this: How did Western Europe abolish the most persistent form of slavery the world has ever known? They did it by establishing the norm that it was a sin to enslave a fellow Christian captured in war. Since slavery is, by definition, an inefficient economic system compared to a free one, abolition unleashed economic dividends throughout the land.

But norms and institutions are very different animals. Freedom from slavery became a widespread social norm in Western Christendom, but slavery and slave wealth remained legal property protected by law. As a consequence, Western European empires, often called mercantile empires, were able to feed the emerging freedom dividends at home with the products of slave wealth held offshore. That slave wealth was originally "produced" in sub-Saharan Africa, and slave production, by definition, is the abrogation of freedom. The famous Triangular Trade integrated the slave and free sectors of European empires, reinforcing freedom and development within Western Christendom and its offshoots, while spreading slavery and underdevelopment in sub-Saharan Africa.

The spread of these fundamentally different social norms (slavery and freedom) explains why Africa and Europe became mirror images of each other by the end of the slave trade era. Freedom in Europe and slavery in Africa. Monogamy in Europe and polygyny in Africa. Rule of law in Europe and customary law in Africa. Nation-states in Europe and ethnic diversity in Africa. Patrilineal descent in Europe and an array of descent rule in Africa. Development in Europe and underdevelopment in Africa.

The book explains why sub-Saharan Africa became the hunting ground for the enslaved labor of Eurasian empires – Islamic and Christian. The Eurocentric narrative claims that a tradition of African slavery was as ancient as time, rooted in a feature of the African landscape called land abundance or low population density. Slavery was indeed widespread in Africa when first observed close up by Europeans in the late nineteenth and early twentieth centuries. It is another matter altogether to conclude that slavery was an ancient African tradition rooted in stubbornly low population densities, especially since population density is as much an outcome of institutional choice as a cause, and data on African populations before the twentieth century are notoriously poor, and the international slave trades did not help the population grow.

This book reinterprets this history, too. It begins by documenting the impact of two environmental constraints on African agricultural productivity and population growth. Tropical areas of the world have long suffered from soil erosion, long before the effects of climate change, not because their soils are particularly susceptible to erosion, but because tropical downpours create runoff that erodes topsoil. The second environmental constraint is the tsetse fly, an insect unique to sub-Saharan Africa that seriously constrained the development of draft animals as a source of nonhuman power in agriculture and transportation, but also herds as a store of wealth.

Together, these two environmental constraints produced pockets of poverty across Africa, but they did not produce slavery as an institution. Instead, the evidence presented here documents how international slave trades essential "attacked" tsetse fly infested areas and left behind the institution of slavery. The twentieth-century view that low population density *caused* African slavery stems from seeing these two outcomes (slavery and low population density) as confirmation of the Nieboer–Domar hypothesis, a theory popular among economists that argues that low population density encourages slavery (Nieboer 1900; Domar 1970).

EVIDENCE

Such a radical reinterpretation of precolonial African economic history requires evidence. Was the impact of the international slave trade significant enough to transform African societies in this way? This is a complex empirical question, but it goes to the heart of the matter and so must be addressed empirically.

First, a growing international demand for enslaved Africans created new economic opportunities for some Africans and the loss of freedom for others. I document changes in the size of this new economic incentive to enslave by comparing the export price of enslaved Africans to the export price of gold – an important alternative export in gold-producing regions of Africa.

Data on the real value of gold bullion date back to 1253, to the beginning of our period, and offer a long view of economic development in gold-producing regions of Africa. Across the continent, and around the world, gold was a medium of exchange and a regulator of the value of other currencies, like silver, copper, and cowrie shells. By comparing the export price of enslaved Africans to the export price of African gold, one can measure the magnitude of the new economic incentives to capture slaves in gold-producing regions of Africa – some of the most prosperous regions in sub-Saharan Africa.

The evidence points to the late seventeenth century as the time when the export price of slaves outstripped the export price of gold. By the end of the eighteenth century, the export price of slaves exceeded the export price of gold by a factor of ten. In regions without a valuable alternative like gold to export, economic incentive to reallocate resources toward slaving and away from other economic activities was significantly larger, and experienced significantly earlier. Important examples include Kongo and Benin, two kingdoms that fell into chaos because of earlier exposure to external demands for slaves.

Second, technology shocks like the flintlock gunpowder technology amplified political-economic responses to the new trade incentive. An analysis of the eighteenth-century British slave trade documents a systematic gun–slave cycle at the heart of the British transatlantic slave trade, one that often evolved into an explosive regional arms race of raid-or-be-raided that few African societies could escape. As the gunpowder technology diffused across the African landscape, it disrupted regional balance of power that fueled social conflict, enslavement, and the export of captives.

Third is the question of social transformation. Did sustained exposure to slave trades alter African social relations and cultures, and if so, how? Can we consider these changes to be revolutionary in character? The answer here is an emphatic yes. Chapter 8 takes us inland, in search of a precise measure of exposure. Nineteenth-century explorers like David Livingstone and Henry Morton Stanley carried portable chronometers that recorded their precise locations on the face of the earth. Feeding these and other data into GIS computer software allows us to measure variations in travel times across the Africa continent, with travel times to the nearest international slave port measuring exposure to international slave traders on the coast.

Chapter 9 then documents some of the ways African societies responded. International slave traders and their agents often attacked poverty-stricken regions and intensified existing tensions and power relations between and within societies. Exposure to *capture* often militarized societies with the resources to mount a defense, and the prerequisite was often captured slaves to exchange for the latest imported weaponry (guns, horses, and iron). Decentralized kinship societies in catchment zones struggled to find ways to defend themselves without calling into question their norm that freedom meant belonging to kin. A solution was often the incorporation of enslaved women as wives in polygynous matrilineal societies and as concubines in polygynous patrilineal ones.

Exposure to the *trade* of captives as they made their way to the coast encouraged the spread of a bundle of institutions that preserved and concentrated slave wealth: the institutions of slavery and polygyny, but also inheritance rules that concentrated wealth (slaves, land, and capital) in patriarchal male-headed households. On the west coast of Africa, this bundle of institutions tended to emerge under the protection of an inherited aristocracy.

There is also evidence that exposure altered the fundamental constitutional order of some lineage societies. Theoretically, if a society's lineage system changes, so does its corresponding kinship terminology, but with a lag. Disequilibrium between the two indicates recent changes in lineage-based practices and belief that the kin terminology has yet to catch up with (Murdock 1949). In Africa, this kind of disequilibrium correlates with proximity to slave ports, calling into question interpretation of African lineage systems as social systems frozen in time. Exposure to slave trades disrupted them, and the adaptation was not completed when the *Ethnographic Atlas* took its snapshot.

An interesting related question is "who was winning?" before indirect colonial rule increased the political power of aristocracies. Also, was the salience of kinship in precolonial Africa (as opposed to occupational castes, guilds, or classes) intensified by exposure to slave trades?[4] However one interprets these finding, we know that exposure to slave trades intensified gender oppression, with increasing shares of the population having no kin other than their husbands, masters, and owners. Collective property weakened, replaced by extended nuclear families of polygynous slaveholders who came to inherit both economic wealth and political authority. It was as if the only constant was change.

DOCUMENTS

Most of the supporting evidence comes from sources widely used by economic historians and development economists, some developed by the author. Listed here are descriptions of some of the most important collections. This book, and many other books and articles on this and related topics, could not have been written without these pioneering efforts in collecting, digitizing, and disseminating historical documents.

THE TRANSATLANTIC SLAVE TRADE DATABASE (TSTD), CIRCA 1500–1860. This is perhaps the most critical collection. As early as the 1960s, historians began collecting archival records on slave voyages across the Atlantic. By the late 1980s, several independent efforts had collected records on approximately 11,000 voyages in sixteen separate datasets. Starting in 1991, various grants from various sources coordinated these efforts. The resulting dataset is now generally available for easy query and download at www.slavevoyages.org. The version used in this book contains data on 34,948 transatlantic slave voyages with 276 variables for each voyage – like dates of travel, port of origin, national flag, African port of embarkation, numbers of enslaved people embarked, port of disembarkation in the Americas, and much, much more. Most modern studies of the transatlantic slave trade rely heavily on these data, including this study. The existence of so much historical documentation on one market speaks to its importance at the time.

THE ETHNOGRAPHIC ATLAS (EA), CIRCA 1900. The EA was initially published in the journal *Ethnology* in twenty-nine installments between January 1962 and July 1980 by George P. Murdock. The goal was to create a quantitative database from existing ethnographic monographs on the far-flung cultures of global empires as they existed in the late nineteenth and early twentieth centuries. Murdock used both primary sources – ethnographic and anthropological studies based on direct fieldwork – and secondary sources, which were themselves based on the archives of missionary societies, field notes, and special communications by anthropologists and colonial officials. The final dataset codes ethnographic information on 1,267 societies worldwide, digitized and published in 1999 by J. Patrick Gray.

Murdock claimed confidence in his coverage of Africa, stating, "The author has reason to believe that a completely exhaustive survey of the literature would reveal ... in Africa a few new societies but probably no additional clusters" (Murdock 1967: 115). There are over 100 variables in the EA. Most are categorical codes created from descriptions found in the ethnographies. Some codes are anthropological – such as sex taboos, marriage and family structures, kinship terminology, dominant lineage myths, and more. Murdock's book *Social Structure* (1949) explains his approach, the variables he sought to code, and why. Other codes are more sociological, political, or economic – like the organization of local communities, the levels of executive political authority above the local community, whether or not the society practiced slavery, the dominant patterns of property inheritance, and more.

MERGING TSTD AND EA. Nunn (2008) merges the TSTD and the EA, which has allowed researchers to analyze the relationships between the two. He accomplishes this using two additional pieces of information. The first is the Murdock map of the locations of African societies found in the EA (Murdock 1959). The second is a collection of fifty-four samples of African-American slave populations. The American samples contain information on 84,656 enslaved people with 229 distinct African "ethnic" designations. These ethnic designations are used to allocate slave exports (found in the TSTD) to coastal and interior ethnicities (found in the EA). Nunn does the same for the Indian Ocean slave trade. These are the data used in recent econometric studies of the long-term effects of the slave trades on African development. They help identify slave "catchment" zones.

Efforts to separate cause from effect in cross-sectional correlations typically rely on instrumental variable estimation techniques. The most common instrumental variable is Euclidean distance. In this context, distance measures transport and communication costs or the inland reach of international slave demand. Distance has been measured in various ways, sometimes as inclusion within an arbitrary buffer around an international slave port, but most often as a mixture of straight-line distances by land and sea, with mixed results.[5]

This book replaces straight-line distance with estimates of travel time between each society in the EA and the nearest major international slave port, estimates developed by the author (Whatley 2022a). Travel time outperforms straight-line distance in a statistical sense and identifies social outcomes of the slave trades that straight-line distance misses. Travel time includes the effects of groundcover type (e.g., jungle vs. plains), terrain (uphill or down), river velocity, headload, and local knowledge about the best path forward. Parameters come from hydrological studies, survey maps, hiking and headload studies, and travel times recorded by early British ambassadors, missionaries, and explorers. The Index of Tsetse Fly Suitability (Alsan 2015) accounts for spatial variations in the availability of horses and camels for travel. Together, these data are used to evaluate, in great detail, how exposure to international slave traders on the coast altered African norms and institutions.

THE ANGLO-AFRICAN TRADE STATISTICS. These are annual estimates of the value of trade between Britain and Africa. Observations run from 1699 to 1807.[6] The original data were recorded by customs officers working in the eighteenth-century British Customs Office and were later housed in the British Archives and digitized by Marion Johnson et al.[7] Being an aggregate annual time series, the Anglo-African Trade Statistics allow us to investigate the dynamics of the eighteenth-century British slave trade. They do not record slave purchases because enslaved Africans were shipped to the Americas and never entered Britain, so they were never recorded in the British Customs Office. The Anglo-African Trade Statistics allow us to estimate the annual value of *net* exports to Africa or the value of British cargo used to purchase enslaved people on the African coast. These data reveal the dynamics of the eighteenth-century British slave trade in Africa, including the dynamics of a gun-slave cycle operating at the very heart of the trade.

SANKOFA

In Twi, *Sankofa* means "go back and take." It is an aphorism of Akan clans who predate the transatlantic slave trade – inquisitive and innovative West Africans who carved dynamic agricultural civilizations out of the forests of what is now part of the nation-state of Ghana. They discovered gold in the forests behind what would become known as the Gold Coast of Africa. Almost immediately, they exploited the opportunity to trade on the world bullion market, but not by sea. Sea trade with Eurasia did not yet exist. The gold flowed northward, carried overland by a coalition of traders called Wangara, who transported the gold more than 1,000 miles from the Atlantic coast to the edge of the Sahara Desert (Wilks 1982a, 1982b; McIntosh 1981). From there, the gold was loaded onto camel caravans for the trek across the Sahara to the Mediterranean, centuries before Portuguese traders intercepted the trade by sea. In the interim, the Akan adopted a set of political and economic institutions that facilitated an impressive degree of trust, social order, and economic growth (Kea 1982; Wilks 1993).

In this dynamic and rapidly changing world, *Sankofa* symbolized critical thinking – the idea that wisdom comes from looking back to learn from the past. At the dawn of the eighteenth century, several Akan clans joined forces to form the Asante Federation to protect themselves from raider agents of the growing transatlantic slave trade. *Sankofa* was appropriated as one of the *Adinkra* symbols to express the new Asante nation's proverbs and philosophical ideas.

For a variety of reasons, *Sankofa* captures the spirit of this book. Quantitative history can reach deep into the Akan past, deeper here than many other places, so the case of the Akan and Asante will be illustrative throughout. True, the current understanding of Africa's past is well beyond Trevor-Roper's and Hegel's claims that Africa had no history before the White man came. Quite the contrary. The pendulum seemed to swing to the opposite extreme in the twentieth century, when scholars began to argue that African social structures were largely unaffected by world events until colonial occupation in the late nineteenth century.[8] While the new economic history of Africa is rewriting some of this history, development economists still tend to interpret what came before colonial occupation as a kind of static, primordial origin of African *traditions*.

This book argues emphatically against this view. It documents too much change to ignore. At one level, it is part of the recent empirical reconstruction of Africa's past. Generally, the book is about the globalization of trade and its impact on the evolution of African economies and societies. The international value of gold offers a new window into medieval Africa, at least in gold-producing regions of Africa. These are among the best-documented histories precisely because these areas were among the first to be integrated into the global economy.

In this sense, the reinterpretation has a Eurocentric flavor. I do not shy away from this fact. My premise is that the globalization of trade and empire during this period was the prime mover of social changes worldwide, and Africa was no exception. The international terms of trade turned decidedly in Africa's favor, primarily because the growing international demand was for enslaved Africans. I argue that this turn of events holds the key to understanding the origins of the Africa that Europeans encountered on the eve of colonial occupation.

By the end of the book, all of this might seem obvious to the reader, and if so, the book will have accomplished some of what I set out to achieve. Not much is generally known, even among scholars and students. I used to ask my undergraduate students at the University of Michigan to tell me what they knew about the transatlantic slave trade, and I was always struck by how little they knew about what transpired *inside* Africa and why.

And how could they? People tend to know of the Triangular Trade between Europe, Africa, and the Americas. They know of the Middle Passage and the ships that carried enslaved Africans across the Atlantic to the Americas. They have some knowledge of the horrible conditions on the slave ships and the lives lost at sea. They know something about the slave auctions in the New World and the exploitation of enslaved African Americans on plantations in the US South, the Caribbean, and perhaps Brazil. All of this is vividly portrayed on TV, in Hollywood films, and in popular books.

However, when I ask, "Where did these enslaved Africans come from?" I get the kind of pause that teachers love and dread – a sign that the class is either poised to learn something new, is lost, or – worse – uninterested. It turns out that the students are not bored but anxious, so I relax and let *Sankofa* do some work.

The first to speak are typically the "faithful" (like me in my youth), who believe Europeans sailed to Africa and stole unwitting Africans as they went about their daily lives.[9] Indeed, there was some of this, mostly in early coastal encounters in the fifteenth and sixteenth centuries. Other students, however, may have visited Africa or hail from an African country, and have seen the slave forts that dot the coast and know something of their history. They know that Europeans mostly restricted themselves to coastal strongholds as protection from rival European powers and hostile Africans. Today, these castles and forts attract millions of tourists seeking a glance out a "gate of no return."

I persist. "So, how were these slaves produced?" The first response is always (and I mean always), "What do you mean produced? That is a strange term to use. Slaves are not produced." "Then where did they come from?" After delicate and sometimes apologetic comparisons of African and American slavery, a student will blurt out, "Africans enslaved other Africans and sold them to Europeans. How could they do that?" Even a scholar as renowned as Henry Louis Gates was compelled to ask this question on the streets of Africa (*The Wonders of Africa*, PBS).

The gaze now turns to me as if to check my credentials. Where will the professor go from here? Milking the moment for as much as I can, I resist the temptation to speak and wait for *Sankofa* to do some work. Following some debate, which can become quite heated, the class comes to agree that Africans somehow enslaved Africans – some reaching the conclusion reluctantly, some with relief, depending primarily on which side of the trade their ancestors happened to fall. And when asked how and why Africans enslaved other Africans, most students admit they have not a clue. Nation-building gets mentioned, as if enslaving was part of the grand march of history. Some students mention famine, judicial slavery, and families selling family members into slavery.

Sankofa? Not quite. What starts out blaming Europeans for the slave trade ends up blaming Africans. It is one of the slipperiest slopes I have encountered in the classroom.[10] A well-developed sense of justice seems to compel students, even scholars, to blame someone for the crime – someone for the original sin. This is a natural inclination for thinkers steeped in Western liberal traditions. Even John Locke, the great liberal philosopher of democracy and self-evident truth, was compelled to view it this way, as were the British abolitionists of the eighteenth century.

In Locke's philosophy, if enslaved Africans were captured in "justified" wars among African peoples who were caught in the natural struggles of nation-building, then the victors had every right to enslave the vanquished because they had justly chosen to spare their lives. Thomas Clarkson (1786; 1839), the intellectual leader of the British abolition movement, turned this logic on its head and argued that if "it was the slave trade which was the cause of the wars (in Africa)," then nobody had a right to the victims, not their African captors nor their British trading partners.[11]

Historical schools of thought also tend to line up on one side of this slope or the other. Were the significant determinants of growth in African slave exports internal to Africa or external? One school of thought emphasizes external shocks and how they increased slave exporting. This view is most forcefully argued by Walter Rodney in *How Europe Underdeveloped Africa* (1972, chapter 4).[12] An alternative approach emphasizes the contributions of preexisting African conditions like low labor productivity, drought, and an African tradition of slavery and slave trading. The strongest modern proponent of this view is John Thornton in *Africa and Africans in the Making of the Atlantic World, 1400–1800* (1998).[13] A third approach tends to be more theoretical and seeks to understand the dynamic interaction between external shocks and internal conditions. Jack Goody's *Technology, Tradition and the State in Africa* (1971) is a good example.[14]

This book falls within this third tradition, but it is an empirical study rather than a theoretical one. In that sense, it subsumes the other two. What further distinguishes it from previous studies is the grounding of African institutions in environmental conditions unique to Africa and then systematically adding the impact of historical episodes like exposure to international slave trades. The story that emerges is one of path-dependent change, but in the end, Africa as a mirror image of Europe.

FROM WALTER RODNEY TO PATH DEPENDENCE

Walter Rodney was a soft-spoken, outspoken, and prolific scholar-activist who was politically assassinated at the young age of thirty-seven in his homeland of Guyana, a small country on the north coast of South America. For more than half a century, his scholarly writings have been a source of controversy in the field of African history. His 1970 book, *A History of the Upper Guinea Coast, 1545–1800,* remains a standard reference. His debate with Professor John Fage on the relationship between the international slave trades and African slavery is antecedent to the transformation of slavery debate.

His most famous book, *How Europe Underdeveloped Africa* (1972), is a critique of the Eurocentric view of world inequality, what J. M. Blaut calls *The Colonizer's Model of the World* (1993). It spoke passionately to the newly emerging post-colonial third world and described how the transatlantic slave trade and colonial occupation underdeveloped Africa. I re-read the book after following a trail of evidence that claimed to debunk it, only to find that the evidence did no such thing. I found in Rodney's words a brilliant and stimulating conception of how the transatlantic slave trade and colonial occupation transformed African economies and societies. It is hard for me to know if I saw so much in those pages because the truth is so obvious or because the book had made such a lasting impression on me in my youth. I suspect the reality rests comfortably in between.

Rodney (1972) argues that the European slave trade was a "basic factor in African underdevelopment prior to 1885" (pp. 95–102). For him, the basic factor was the African production of enslaved people for export. He placed blame squarely on the growing external demand for enslaved Africans and how it encouraged the expansion of slave production and slavery *inside* Africa. Rodney, however, knew that violence did not necessarily impede economic progress. European exceptionalism was not peaceful co-existence. Instead, the true culprit was the external demand for enslaved people, and primarily because it discouraged the capture of land and the cultivation of a citizenry to be taxed by an elite.[15] Like many scholars of his time, Rodney's model of development (his counterfactual) was the European path through feudalism, a pathway that the slave trade blocked.[16] However, Rodney was a good enough historian to acknowledge the diversity of African economies and how that diversity mediated the impact of external forces.[17]

On the question of impact, it turns out that Rodney mainly was right. The international slave trades did discourage the capture of land and encourage the proliferation of small African ethnicities, what I call the "fundamental impact" of the slave trades. Recent econometric research also supports Rodney's view that the international slave trades had long-lasting negative effects on African development and economic growth.

That econometric literature continues to grow.[18] It is not without controversy. The primary evidence consists of cross-sectional correlations between regional slave exports in the past and "bad" social outcomes decades, even centuries, later. The only notion of historical time is the time that elapsed between the two cross-sections. Confidence in the findings is as good as the data and the identification strategy, which are often not as good as one would like.

This line of research has been criticized for "compressing" history because it glosses over historical details (Austin, 2008), like whether or not the slave trade was significant enough to leave indelible marks on African societies for so long. If so, what were the mechanisms by which the impact persisted? The econometric literature is good at identifying cross-sectional correlations between past events and future outcomes but bad at telling the historical story.

Economic historians must tell the story. This book aims to meld these two sources of information, the econometric and the historical. Econometric history is expressly designed to statistically identify and estimate "causal" relationships between past events and subsequent outcomes.[19] This line of research often produces the first salvo in the search for historical legacies, and institutions and culture often take center stage as carriers of legacies.

Like a pulling guard in American football, causal history suggests that some paths forward are more likely than others. The actual historical play, however, unfolds on the ground. Greif (2006) has theorized about the "path of play" in historical settings and has focused attention on how self-enforcing norms and institutions foster social cooperation that can order how the play unfolds (the shared playbook in the football analogy or shared norms in the real world). In the econometric literature, inserting a new player would be a treatment. Comparing average outcomes over many replays with and without the new player can identify the causal impact of the new player on the outcome of the play.

In historical time, unfortunately, there are no replays, so econometric studies utilize various statistical strategies to pseudo-randomize assignment of the treatment and identify its impact on outcomes. These methods are less effective at telling us how or why the treatment affects the outcome or whether historical persistence is a figment of the data, the dates of the cross-sections, or the historical context of the pseudo-experiment (Kelly 2021).

This is definitely a weakness of the case. As Paul David (1985) put it in his classic article on the economics of QWERTY, "it is sometimes not possible to uncover the logic (or illogic) of the world around us except by understanding *how* it got that way" (p. 332). Brian Arthur et al. (1983) in what can be considered one of the earliest statements of path dependence in economic science, modeled the underlying probability structure as a Pólya Urn process, where a colored ball is drawn from an urn followed by the addition of identical colored balls (feedback) so that over time the probability of drawing a particular color (a particular outcome) can approach one or get locked in. From this perspective, lock-in is more likely if the feedback is large relative to the size and diversity of the initial set of possible outcomes, like beginning play with one black and one white ball in the urn. Outcomes of non-ergodic processes like these are not predictable but require an accounting of how the outcomes came to be (the sequence of play).

This book is a historical account of how Africa became the mirror image of Europe. The impact of international slave trades was large, and the options to defend against it were that limited, especially on the Atlantic coast. Other coasts and other slave trades exhibit similar affects, but with differences that reflect the different histories. The Christian transatlantic slave trade was fueled by what Harari (2015) calls the trifecta of science, empire, and capitalism. The Muslim slave trades lacked the capitalism, which explains why the economic records are not as good. Still, there is evidence that they, too, encouraged the spread and evolution of institutions and norms suited for capturing and trading people, in other words, underdevelopment.

CHAPTER 2

Going Behind the Mirror Image

THE SOCIAL CONSTRUCTION OF THE MIRROR IMAGE

At the dawn of the twentieth century, W. E. B. Du Bois (1903) predicted: "The problem of the twentieth century is the problem of the color line." A bold prediction, and to Du Bois's credit, there is no indication that the color line has stopped haunting Western democracies, democracies now entering their third century. But Du Bois goes further. Like most famous quotes, this one is typically shortened. Du Bois actually wrote, "The problem of the twentieth century is the problem of the color line – the relations of the darker to the lighter races of men in Asia and Africa, in America and the islands of the sea" (p. 10). It should be no surprise that the father of Pan-Africanism had a global take on the problem.

So, what was this international color line – what the philosopher Olúfẹ́mi Táíwò calls the "world racial order" of the time (2022)? This book argues that it is the modern manifestation of a social stratification that has been fundamental to Western development and growth for a very long time – the line that runs between slavery and freedom, from the Roman Empire to the United States of America.

For this reason alone, Du Bois's quote is significant, but Du Bois is also critiquing the widely held view at the time that the racial order was a natural order. To Du Bois, the color line was a problem that Western civilization had to solve. Like most social scientists at the time, Du Bois had only recently acquired "evidence" (instead of just guessing) that the norms and institutions of non-Western societies and economies were fundamentally different from the West, especially Africa. This also makes the moment significant, for nothing satisfied the unenlightened mind more than evidence that racial differences were real. Du Bois is also challenging this view – a view that was informing Jim Crow policies in his country, the United States of America.

It is important to note that this twentieth-century view of Africa was actually a relatively enlightened one. Back in the eighteenth and nineteenth centuries, when most of the action in this book takes place, most Western empires were still slave societies, where the buying and selling of enslaved people was still a legal right for free people. That right created all kinds of wealth – in the trading of slaves, in slave-based production of raw materials, and in slaves as an investment and store of wealth. As we shall see, modern Western slavery preserved slave wealth better than any other in recorded human history. Even Britain, home of the Magna Carta and the Industrial Revolution, took a bite. Eighteenth-century British laws and customs had so dehumanized Africans that a contract to trade their bodies, the *Asiento de Negro*, sparked a national imagination of riches that drove the South Sea Bubble of 1720 and helped underwrite Britain's public debt, and with little consideration of the fact that it was human beings being traded (Price and Whatley 2021a, 2021b).

By the end of the eighteenth century, abolitionists like Thomas Clarkson (1786) and liberal political economists like Adam Smith (1776) would voice serious and effective criticisms of slavery on moral and economic grounds, but they too had little knowledge of life inside Africa. Even British abolitionists like Alexander Falconbridge once believed "the kings and principal men breed Negroes for sale as we do cattle" (1788, p. 15). Some thought polygyny was widespread in Africa because Africans birthed more females than males. Malthus would eventually correct some of these misconceptions, but even he had little empirical knowledge of demographic life inside Africa (Reniers 2011). Back then, information about Africa consisted primarily of reports from slave traders who were happy to spread tall tales while profiting handsomely from the idiosyncratic information they acquired on the coast (Rediker 2008). Even they knew very little about what lay behind the coast, let alone any changes brought by their presence on the coast.

The flow of information began to change in the nineteenth century. In 1807, the British Empire withdrew from trading enslaved Africans across the Atlantic Ocean and negotiated the first known international human rights treaties among nation-states (Martinez 2012). To be more precise, Britain extended to the larger world the human rights customs that had governed Western Christendom for half a millennium. British naval superiority policed the treaties on the high seas, and equipped with the latest technology, including quinine protection against malaria and gunpowder protection against people, European explorers, missionaries, and traders began to venture inland, reporting back what they observed about Africa and its people. Famous and infamous explorers like Mungo Park (2000), Henry Barth (1890), David Livingstone (1858), and Henry Morton Stanley (1878, 1879) published and lectured widely in Europe and America, for both popular and academic audiences.

We will have occasions to consult these texts because they contain early scientific observations made by educated people committed to documenting the continent's interior. As subsidized explorers, they carried the latest technology for recording their exact location on the face of the earth (portable chronometers), primarily because they wanted to know how to return to anything deemed valuable. They collected the kind of data that modern computers can turn into useful information about proximity. Their recordings have helped reveal how proximity to international slave ports altered the norms and institutions of African societies and economies – everything from family structure and property rights to gender relations and the centralization of executive political authority.

Computer technology did not exist in Du Bois's time, but the number of African ethnographies was exploding. As one might expect, a characteristic feature of this early literature was its inability to assess the effects of the exposure of Africans to international slave trades. The best example is the influential book by the Dutch anthropologist H. J. Nieboer, *Slavery as an Industrial System*, published in 1900, three years before Du Bois made his prediction. Nieboer is known among economists for the Nieboer–Domar hypothesis, the idea that the profit motive in a land-abundant, low-capital economy encourages the choice of slave, not free, norms and institutions. Nieboer inferred this after studying 466 ethnographies of "pre-modern" societies. I have tabulated and summarized his findings in Table 2.2. Later, we will discuss some of his selection biases. Here, I want to draw attention to the worldwide occurrence of slavery found in these ethnographies, reflecting the general state of knowledge among scholars at the time, including Du Bois.

After discussing several factors that might explain the distribution of slavery around the world, Nieboer (1900) ventures another hypothesis:

> There is another circumstance we have already hinted at, which may partially account for the existence of slavery amongst some of these tribes: the slaves are often Negroes. And Negroes have always and everywhere been enslaved; they seem to be more fit for slaves than most races of mankind (p. 290).

Nieboer never offers the hypothesis that the international slave trades could be a factor.

As the twentieth century progressed, so did the number of ethnographies, culminating in the statistical compendium called the *Ethnographic Atlas* (1967), compiled by George Murdock and associates. The *Ethnographic Atlas* is used throughout modern historical and comparative social science, especially the new economic history of Africa. When Europeans began to trek into the interior of Africa, they noticed three institutions that were the mirror opposites of their own: slavery, polygyny, and decentralized political systems. Map 2.1 shows the spatial distribution of these institutions, as recorded in the *Ethnographic Atlas.*[1] Slavery (85 percent), polygyny (80 percent), and decentralized political systems (67 percent) were indeed widespread in Africa at the end of the slave trade era.

Table 2.1 summarizes what else stands out in the atlas's more comprehensive comparison of African and Western societies at the dawn of the twentieth century.

1. The West was the land of the free. Africa was mired in slavery.
2. In the West, monogamy was the family structure, cultural norm, and law of the land, based on moral precepts and a matchmaking ritual called "courtly love." In much of Africa, polygyny was the norm and custom, also with its moral precepts and matching mechanism – the strategic deployment of family bride wealth.
3. Western societies were governed by the rule of law – criminal and civil – where rules were written and adjudicated by an independent judiciary. In Africa, rules were customary and unwritten, with the authority to judge concentrated in ancestral lineages and their elders. As such, most African societies were governed by the amalgamation of lineages into ruling aristocracies, chiefdoms, kingdoms, and empires.

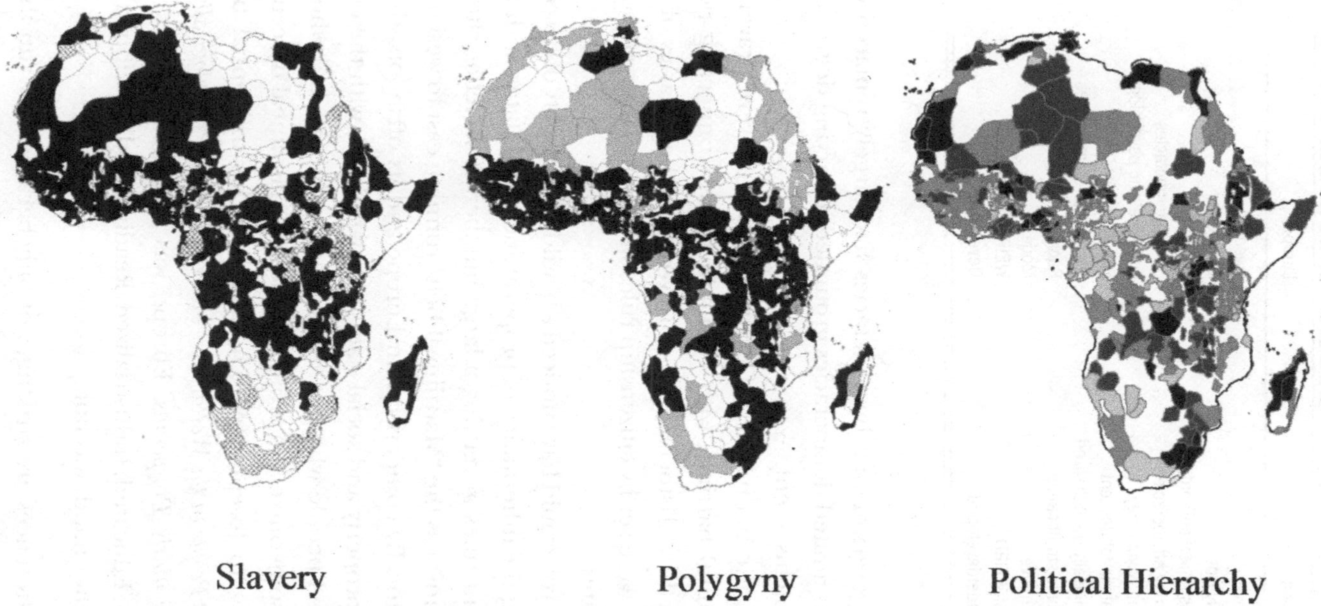

Map 2.1 The mirror image, circa 1900. Data source: The *Ethnographic Atlas.*

Table 2.1 The mirror image in black and white, circa 1900

Africa	Europe
Slavery	Freedom
Polygyny	Monogamy
Customary authority	Rule of law
Strong aristocracies	Strong democracies
Clan psychology	Individualistic psychology
Matrilineal descent	Patrilineal descent
Politically decentralized	Centralized nation-states
Ethnic stratification	Racism
Primitive	Modern
Not WEIRD	WEIRD
Underdeveloped	Developed

Western governmental bureaucracies had largely replaced clan lineages with limited democracies grounded in varying degrees of political enfranchisement.

4. In Africa, the boundaries of political authority were drawn primarily by natural barriers, with ethnic identities connecting people to lands ruled by aristocracies. In the West, the boundaries of political authority were set by citizenship rules within the surveyed borders of nation-states.
5. In Africa, you would have noticed a bewildering variety of descent rules governing the inheritance of property and social status, with matrilineal descent rules governing a large number of societies clustered in what is known as the "Matrilineal Belt" running east to west just below the equator. By comparison, in Europe and its offshoots, the inheritance of property and social status was patrilineal, with the exception of enslaved people who had no property to inherit and whose social status as someone else's property followed matrilineal descent.
6. According to Joseph Henrich (2020), in his influential book *The WEIRDest People in the World: How the West Became Psychologically Peculiar and Particularly Prosperous,* Europe was, tongue in cheek, WEIRD (Western, Educated, Industrialized, Reading, and Developed). Africa, on the other hand, was not.

These differences are striking, not only because they run the gamut from family organization to governance structure, but also because, as a package, they have strikingly different implications for the pace and pattern of economic growth. They predict development and growth in the West and underdevelopment and stagnation in Africa.

So, what explains this greatest of modern divides – the one between Africa and the West at the dawn of the twentieth century, and today? That is the central question of this book. I will try to convince you, the reader, that the fundamental explanation, and the one that also explains the mirror image quality of the comparison, is the first difference listed in Table 2.1 – freedom as a widespread social norm in the West and slavery as a widespread social norm in Africa. This starting point, of course, runs the risk of stumbling down a dark rabbit hole into a deep pile of Eurocentric goo. More on that later, too. For now, let's see what it gets us.

SLAVERY AND FREEDOM AS SOCIAL NORMS

It is not hard to think of slavery and freedom as social norms that can alter, even order, social structures and development paths. Nor is it hard to believe that slavery and freedom are opposite norms. If I ask, "What is slavery? What is freedom?", the immediate intuitive answer is, "An enslaved person is owned or possessed by another human being, while a free person is not." Right off, we see the dialectical nature of the categories. It is difficult, if not impossible, to define one without reference to the other. Orlando Patterson (1982) calls this *the first problem of slavery*. As soon as slaves are introduced into a society ("socially dead" people in his terminology) that society must somehow decide what it means to be free to enslave another.

We tend to think of slavery as an institution, not a norm, but that is because slave societies preserve slave wealth, a readily observable legal institution and store of value. The value of freedom, on the other hand, is more diffused and not directly observable, so we tend to think of freedom as a norm. Hornbeck and Logan (2023) measure the value of freedom as the foregone surplus product from the misallocations of resources in a slave economy, a useful theoretical device for estimating the value of freedom from slavery, but it is not readily observable. Nor is there anything called an institution of freedom like that for slavery.

Greif (2006) distinguishes norms from institutions, where norms are beliefs that hold sway even when societies are off their equilibrium path. They are mechanisms that help societies select one equilibrium (or set of institutions) from many possible equilibria. Burke and Payton (2011) offer a game-theoretic definition:[2]

> The key property of a social norm from a modeling standpoint is that *it induces a positive feedback loop between expectations and behaviors*: the more widely that members of a social group practice a behavior, the more it becomes expected, thus reinforcing adherence. In its simplest form, this type of feedback loop can be modeled by a coordination game. (p. 314)[3]

Consider one of the simplest coordination games: reaching consensus on which side of the road automobiles should drive on. The benefits of coordination are apparent. Left or right does not matter. The mechanism that holds the norm in place is internal and self-enforcing – a matter of life and death. Police issue very few traffic citations for driving on the wrong side of the road.

Another coordination game, one that we will encounter throughout this book, is the choice of descent rules, like matrilineal or patrilineal. On the surface, unilineal descent rules appear as innocuous as the side of the road we drive on. Each divides society into one of two tracks. Patrilineal societies track lineage through men and not women; matrilineal societies track lineage through women and not men. We should be careful to distinguish matrilineal from matriarchal. Matrilineal societies are still patriarchal in that men still dominate in most social spheres. However, in matrilineal societies, men inherit their wealth and status from their mothers, not their fathers. As we shall see, this distinction has important implications for the structure of slave cultures and the preservation of slave wealth.

Unilineal descent rules like these divide societies into institutionalized groups of people, where the groupings facilitate internal and external cohesion and stability. Internally, commonly perceived lineage establishes the boundaries of belonging and identity. One can think of belonging as the expectation of certain rights (like rights to property, inheritance, and mates) and responsibilities (like child rearing or old age assistance). With membership comes expected behaviors, like obeying authority, choosing appropriate marriage partners, and performing public services like collective labor and defense.

Unilineal rules can enhance intergroup cohesion if they divide societies into many related kin groups, each with relative autonomy in adjudicating internal conflict and punishing abnormal behavior. Abnormal behavior toward members of one's group can bring punishment or banishment from the group. Moscona, Nunn, and Robinson (2020) investigate a special case: unilineal kin groups that are also territorial – meaning places where unilineal rules also enforce unilocal post-marital location (matrilocal or patrilocal) and where political allegiance is to the lineages' hereditary aristocracy only. Unilineal groups like these are naturally territorial, where we tend to see recurring social conflict and "feuding," like among the Hatfields and McCoys along the Tug Fork of West Virginia and Kentucky in the late nineteenth century. An overarching religious and political authority can help reduce intergroup conflict, but only if it has acquired the authority to do so. In European Christendom, banishment was like excommunication from all kin groups, left alone to fend for oneself.

Think of Patterson's first problem of slavery as a coordination problem that arises the moment enslaved people are introduced into society. Society must reach consensus concerning who can possess another and the rules and mechanisms that enforce the social stratification. Economic models do not address the first problem of slavery, but focus on the "second problem of slavery" – its profitability (Conrad and Meyer 1958), viability (Yasuba 1971) and efficiency (Fogel and Engerman 1974; Wright 1978; David et al. 1976). These were the issues at stake in the slavery debates in the 1960s and 1970s about the structure and performance of American slavery. At a general level, they are also the issues at stake in the New History of Capitalism literature (Johnson 2013; Baptist 2014), with important differences in evidence and interpretation, prompting Morris (2020) to quip "It's Déjà Vu All Over Again." These debates, like most, assumed the first problem of slavery was solved sometime before time, primarily because they study Western slave systems, which share a common solution to the first problem of slavery.

But how do norms like slavery and freedom get established in the first place? Burke and Young (2011) restate Patterson's first problem as follows: "If they (norms) represent equilibrium behaviors in situations with multiple equilibria, how does society settle on any particular norm starting from out-of-equilibrium conditions?" (p. 318). Their formal answer is as follows:

> Consider, for example, a two-person interaction in which the rules can take *m* different forms. Before they can interact, the players must agree on the rules that will govern their interactions. If they agree on the kth set of rules, they play the game and get the expected payoff (a^k, b^k). If they fail to agree, their payoffs are zero. A population-level equilibrium in which everyone plays by the same set of rules can be viewed as a social norm. It can be shown that, under a fairly wide range of stochastic best response rules, such a process (a pure coordination game) will select an *efficient* norm: an equilibrium whose payoffs are not strictly dominated by the payoffs in some alternative equilibrium. (p. 320)

You might think this class of solutions could not possibly apply to the first problem of slavery. Perhaps free people can agree that slavery benefits them, but what about enslaved people? How could they decide to be a part of this?

This question brings us face-to-face with the conditions of slave supply. An enslaved person might "agree" to be a part of this *if the alternative is death,* which is why Patterson calls slavery "social death," a condition that originates in war or extreme poverty. If two people agree to recognize slavery as a form of property to be traded, they receive a payoff in the form of slave wealth, a form of wealth created out of the abrogation of someone else's freedom. If they disagree, which is an option, they get zero, and no wealth is created. "A population-level equilibrium in which everyone plays by the same set of rules (trading captives) can be viewed as a social norm," usually an efficient one in that the payoff of some alternative equilibrium does not strictly dominate. Traders receive slave wealth. For enslaved people, social death is the alternative to actual death. Slave trading and slavery normalized the violent abrogation of freedom, which is why John Locke (1690) called slavery "the state of war continued" (Chapter 4, section 24).

When exposed to the possibility of trading enslaved people, societies must choose to interact or not. Sometimes, like in Africa, where societies were often exposed to international slave trades on many sides, people had little choice but to interact, and raid or be raided became the name of the game. Even under these conditions, societies arrived at different institutions and practices for solving the same coordination problem, this due to chance events and the vagaries of history. An example is the impact of a society's lineage system on the growth of slave wealth. Burke and Young (2011) call this prediction "local conformity/global diversity" (p. 322).

This is not to say norms never change. We belong to the modern age that abolished slavery, although the business is unfinished,[4] so we know intuitively that norms can change. Today, slavery is abhorred, an abnormal behavior that almost the entire world condemns.[5] Norms can shift due to accumulated small changes in behaviors and expectations (like the impact of sex selectivity in slave exports on the ability to track lineage). Norms can change in response to an external shock that suddenly changes agents' payoff functions (like introducing gunpowder technology into the African context). Norms can be changed by coordinated social action or movements (like Islamic Jihad). Norms are typically stable until a certain threshold is crossed. The linkage between behavior and expectations can create a nonlinear feedback effect (like the gun–slave cycle). If enough people change their behavior (or how they expect others to behave), everyone will want to follow suit (like the raid-or-be-raided arms race). That is, norms have staying power but can change rapidly. This is the notion of punctuated equilibrium.

A few words about crossing normative boundaries. What is normal often escapes notice. Normality usually feels natural, especially if the cost of obliviousness is negligible. In slave societies, free people often face the insignificant cost of ignoring the fact that they are free. Enslaved people do not have that luxury. The cost of ignoring the facts of enslavement includes corporal punishment, sale, even death. Enslaved people are always more aware of their situation than free people.

This is one of the reasons widespread debt slavery – where free people sink into slavery – tends to destabilize slave systems. Previously free people become aware of the value of breathing free air. Between the eighth and late-seventh century BC, the population of Athens was on the verge of rebelling against large-scale and growing debt bondage. To avert the rebellion, Solon the Liberator abolished debt bondage, creating a labor crisis for the elite. The solution was the large-scale importation of alien slaves. Edmund Morgan (1972, 1975) describes a similar dynamic at work in colonial Virginia, where fear of rebellion among free-but-dependent Englishmen encouraged the importation of enslaved Africans to avert another crisis like Bacon's Rebellion. Charles Beard, in *An Economic Interpretation of the Constitution of the United States* (1913), argues that a similar fear motivated the Founders to structure government with extensive balances of power that could resist a takeover by rebellious Englishmen.

Finally, if norms tell us what we should do, taboos tell us what we should not do. Taboos are behaviors that society considers to be highly abnormal, unthinkable behaviors that carry extreme and harsh judgments and penalties. But taboos, like norms, are socially constructed. What is considered taboo in one society can be widely accepted in another. For example, a free woman cohabitating with an enslaved man is considered taboo in patrilineal societies but perfectly acceptable and normal in matrilineal ones.

DEFINING SLAVERY

At this point, it is helpful to clarify some terminology. What is slavery? What is freedom? How might the two be related? We often take slavery to be a more straightforward norm to define because slave wealth and the institutions that support it have been observed in many places around the world and throughout history. That fact, in and of itself, is cause for pause. How could many societies choose the same institution at different places and times? And then, there is the issue of a slave mode of production. Does an isolated household "slave" in a late medieval household have the same rights and face the same denials as a field "slave" in the antebellum South of the United States? Or a "slave" in precolonial Asante? Or an urban "slave" in the Greco-Roman world?

There are stark differences in these cases, differences that have implications for freedom and economic development. A Greco-Roman slave might have the right and expectation to acquire freedom through either self-purchase or manumission. That was rarely the case in the antebellum South of the United States, where it could also be illegal. In the nineteenth-century Sokoto Caliphate in northern Nigeria, a slave could pay a *Murgu* for the right to work independently of his master and eventually purchase his "freedom." A slave concubine was "freed" upon the death of her master if she had borne him a child, and her children were "free" by birth (Lovejoy 1988; Lovejoy 2005).

When we think of slavery as denying freedom, we run into similar and perhaps more complex problems of classification. While a free Roman citizen may have had rights similar to a free citizen in twentieth-century New York (to be all you can be), freedom in precolonial Africa often meant a sense of "belonging" to a kinship network, a clan, or an ethnic group.

Still, we can only proceed with a definition that we can all agree on, at least most of us. The goal is to settle on a definition of slavery that is restrictive enough to capture standard features across a broad class of slave systems, yet flexible enough to adapt to different environments and technologies. Nieboer (1900), the Dutch anthropologist, took up precisely this challenge. He did more than state the Nieboer–Domar hypothesis. He wanted to infer the hypothesis from the observed distribution of slavery across societies. To do so, he surveyed the ethnographic literature that existed in 1900 and set out to document the institution of slavery among the "savage" people of the world, as distinct from the "semi-civilized and civilized" (p. 8).

Notwithstanding his terminology, documenting the institution of slavery worldwide would require a definition. Nieboer began by defining slavery as "one man possessed by another," going to great lengths to explain that his "scientific" definition of slavery excluded kindred phenomena that might be considered slave-like. In his view, "feminists make a very great use of the term slavery to define the condition of wives" (p. 8), but according to Nieboer, this fell outside his definition of slavery, as did all kinship relations. He also excludes principal–agent relationships between a king and his subjects, like the relationships between lord and serf in late medieval Europe; even tributary "domination of one group or tribe over another," regardless of how the lower ranks are treated.

Heuristically, Nieboer's approach is a good start because it improved the accuracy of the social relation captured by his coding, which is precisely what we are looking for. Some slave systems might influence family structure, others not. Some might establish tributary relationships that force the subordinate group to supply slaves as tribute, others not. Nieboer ignores this variation and codes a common denominator. As he surveys the existing literature, he looks for descriptions of "one man possessed by another" and codes that as "slavery." His method is no different from Murdock's, just coding fewer cases and variables. Being a functionalist, Nieboer eventually imposes another restriction and defines slavery as "one man possessed by another and forced to labor for him." Thus, the title of his book, *Slavery as an Industrial System,* although his definition of slavery is neither industrial nor large-scale. It is slaveholding.

Nieboer's classification scheme has many flaws. This last restriction (to labor) allows Nieboer to exclude cases where all slaves were women, because if labor was the basis of the master–slave relationship, there would also be male slaves. A priori, I see no reason to exclude these cases. Nieboer does not mention he encountered any. Harems of enslaved concubines in the Muslim world come to mind, but Nieboer excludes these societies because he considers Muslim societies to be "semi-civilized." He also does not include cases where slavery was introduced through contact with "civilized" or modern societies, like some Native American societies in the US South. He also excluded societies that kept slaves for trade only. And Nieboer never mentions the possibility that African slavery was introduced through contact with civilized societies (as in the transatlantic slave trade) or contact with semi-civilized societies (as in the trans-Saharan slave trade).

Nieboer's findings are tabulated in Table 2.2. The first column describes the broad regions of the world to which the numbers apply. The second column tabulates the number of societies in each region that allowed slavery as "one man possessed by another and forced to work for him." The third column lists the number of societies in each region that did not allow slavery – nominally "free" in their own way. The fourth column tabulates the number of uncertain cases in each region, where Nieboer was unable to determine status one way or the other.

Table 2.2 Nieboer on slaveholding

Region	Slave	Not	Uncertain	Slave (percentage)	Certain (percentage)
North America	19	51	5	27	93
Central and South America	13	29	4	31	91
Australia	0	20	0	0	100
Melanesia	5	13	4	28	82
Polynesia	2	6	2	25	80
Micronesian	0	5	0	0	100
Malay Archipelago	66	11	10	86	89
Indochinese Peninsula	7	3	0	70	100
India, Afghanistan, Himalayas	10	8	0	56	100
Central Asia	3	8	0	27	100
Siberia	3	8	4	27	73
Caucasus	3	5	2	38	80
Africa: Bantu	37	18	17	67	76
Africa: Sudan Negroes	26	10	6	72	86
Africa: Hamitic people	12	3	0	80	100
Africa: "light-colored South Africans and African Pygmy"	3	0	5	100	38

Source: Nieboer (1900), pp. 47-165.

The next column reports the percentage (or density) of slave societies in each region. The last column reports a measure of the degree of confidence in the coding – the degree to which slavery was clearly distinguishable from "free."

According to Nieboer, slavery was found in every region of the world except Australia and Micronesia. The highest density was found in southern Africa at 100 percent, but with an extremely low degree of certainty (38 percent). It is unclear that these societies were slave societies, but rather something that might occasionally look like slavery to a Western observer. The next highest concentration is found in the Malay Archipelago, at 86 percent, with a high degree of certainty (89 percent). Following Malay are three African regions, what Nieboer calls Bantu, Hamitic, and Sudanese, ranging from 67 percent to 80 percent slave and with a high degree of certainty. High concentrations were also found on the Indochinese Peninsula (70 percent), and India, Afghanistan, and the Himalayas (56 percent), each with an extremely high degree of certainty. This was the dominant view of slavery at the turn of the twentieth century, in Du Bois's time.

DEFINING FREEDOM

Freedom, by definition, literally means freedom from slavery. According to the *OED*, the word means "Exemption or release from slavery or imprisonment." It is of Frisian, Dutch, and German origin, first appearing around 1225 AD. The word *liberty*, a closely related but distinct word, means "Freedom from bondage or dominating influence of sin, spiritual servitude, worldly ties, etc.," and is of Latin origin, first appearing around 1384 AD, a century and a half later.[6] It is understandable why "freedom" rings loudly in the literature on freedom from slavery, as in African-American history and literature, while the words "liberty" and "liberalism" refer to expanded rights for people who are already free. Thus, we find the word *liberty* in the American Declaration of Independence from Britain, not the word *freedom*. It simply would not have played in 1776 to declare "that all men are ... endowed by their Creator with certain inalienable rights, that among these are Life, *Freedom* and the pursuit of Happiness."

There are other definitions of freedom we should consider. Patterson, in *Freedom in the Making of Western Culture* (1991), defines Western freedom as a tripartite social norm consisting of personal, sovereign, and civic freedoms. "Personal freedom, at its most elementary, gives a person the sense that one, on one hand, is not being coerced or restrained by another person in doing something desired and on the other hand the conviction that one can do as one pleases within the limits of the other person's desire to do the same" (p. 3).

This is the kind of liberal *Bourgeois Dignity* (2010) and *Equality* (2016) that Deirdre McCloskey argues is the source of the Great Enrichment of modern economic growth – that unprecedented increase of 16 to 100 times more stuff per capita in a little over 200 years. It is also consistent with, though less developed than, Amartya Sen's (1999) notion of material freedom, where people have the means and the opportunities to "live the life they have reason to value." It is also consistent with Burke and Payton's (2011) definition of norms as expectations with feedback.

The second note of freedom is what Patterson (1991) calls sovereign freedom:

> This conception of freedom is always relative. At one extreme stands the person who is absolutely free with respect to another, namely the slave master or absolute ruler or God; at the other extreme is the person who has no freedom with respect to another, namely the slave in relation to his master. Between the two are other human beings with more or less power or freedom, with respect to others. (p. 4)

This notion of freedom closely aligns with the libertarian notion of freedom, as the freedom to act regardless of the wishes of others or the impact on others. This is a note of freedom that rings loudly in the USA. The recent controversy over wearing masks during the COVID-19 pandemic is a case in point. Libertarians argued that they had the sovereign freedom not to wear masks, regardless of the impact on others. Kingship, divine right, and possibly state-mandated death penalty are examples of sovereign freedoms, like Hobbesian Leviathan.

Patterson's (1991) third note of freedom is civic freedom:

> the capacity of adult members of the community to participate in its life and governance. A person feels free, in this sense, to the degree that he or she belongs to the community of birth, has a recognized place in it, and is involved in some way in the ways it is governed. The existence of civic freedom implies a political community of some sort, with clearly defined rights and obligations for every citizen. (p. 4)

This is the kind of civic equality that Prak and van Zanden (2023) describe for fourteenth-century Dutch society. It is the kind of belonging that Darity, Mason, and Stewart (2006) show can reproduce racial identity in a competitive racialistic world. The political community need not be a full-blown democracy with full-blown enfranchisement. However, in Sen's conception, broad participation in the processes that govern the life of a community justifies and promotes "the life that people have reason to value," and is best achieved in a full-blown democracy with full enfranchisement.

According to Patterson, the people excluded from slavery inhabit a world where the normal expectation is freedom from slavery. A slave society, by definition, is one where freedom and slavery coexist, like two social norms in opposition to each other. One need not be Hegelian to appreciate the social, ideological, and psychological tensions this creates. As Patterson (1991) puts it: "It may indeed be illogical and immoral to desire for oneself the absence of obstacles, only to be able to restrain others, but, as this work will demonstrate, it is a socio-historical *fact* that human beings have always sought to do just that, and have frequently succeeded in doing so" (p. 3).

In this sense, it may be no accident that the word *freedom* has Germanic origins. Germanic tribes practiced an extreme form of slavery, the freedom from which, according to Acemoglu and Robinson (2019), also introduced "assembly politics" into the Frankish Kingdoms, allowing Europe to enter the narrow corridor between liberty and Leviathan that is essential for sustained economic development (pp. 152–64).

THE INEFFICIENCIES OF SLAVERY AND FREEDOM DIVIDENDS

A defining feature of an enslaved person is a *natal alien* person, *possessed* by another who has total *control* over life and labor and the most basic social bonds of kinship and *family*, and is *forced* to work for someone else. It is not hard to see how slavery chocks anything that might be considered a freedom dividend. That is not to say enslaved people have no human agency. The most basic evidence of agency is the fact that slaves must be motivated to work.

The economist Ronald Findlay (1975) models slave agency in a way that allows us to identify some of the inefficiencies of slave systems. To get enslaved people to work, enslavers used carrots (incentives) and sticks (the whip). Harsher methods of supervision can be applied to enslaved people, so the stick will get more from slaves than from free people. "On the other hand, the desire for freedom on the part of the enslaved can elicit a greater response to incentive payments if these can be accumulated for the eventual purchase of freedom – manumission" (Findlay 1975, p. 928).

Both management practices (the greater use of the stick and the dream of eventual freedom) reduce slave labor costs, a source of *profit* in slave systems. Labor costs are reduced because enslaved people have fewer rights and powers to resist the stick, and since freedom is worth more to them than anyone else, slaves are willing to pay more for freedom than the market will pay their owner. Both incentives extend the use of slave labor to the point where the marginal cost of labor exceeds the marginal benefit, a misallocation of resources that emanates from the normalization of slavery.

Slave systems with a high probability of manumission recoup some of these losses. By this metric, Virginian slavery was becoming more wasteful in the antebellum era. Babcock (1974) calculates that the odds of achieving freedom through manumission in the 1790s were 20 percent, but only 2 percent in the 1850s. Temin (2017) compares the frequency of manumission in five slave systems (Classical Greece, Early Roman Empire, Southern United States, the Caribbean, and nineteenth-century Brazil) and finds frequent manumission only in the Roman Empire:

> slaves often were able to purchase their freedom if they could earn the necessary funds in a peculium, which served as a tangible measure of slave productivity. The right of slaves to accumulate and retain assets was an important part of the incentive structure of slaves that brings their conditions closer to free men ... There was nothing like the peculium in modern American slavery. Brazil offered a partial modern exception. (p. 124)

Future research on manumission will focus on Brazil, where abundant data exist on slave prices and where manumission was more frequent than in the United States. Mattoso, Klein, and Engerman (1986) were able to report average manumission prices for 13,127 recorded cases in Bahia, between 1818 and 1888, with information on date, gender, and age (90 percent being urban workers). Unfortunately, they do not analyze the data. Recently, Mann and Andrade (2023) published an online database of 5,648 individual manumissions in Bahia between 1831 and 1840, also by age, date, and gender. Soon we should learn a great deal more about the processes involved and the prices slaves were willing and able to pay for their freedom.

Bodenhorn (2011) uses variations in the age at manumission to document some of the factors that influenced manumission prices in antebellum Virginia. The lower the age at manumission, the lower the price paid, price being the length of life spent enslaved. Many personal factors reduced the price of freedom – skin tone, whether or not the slave owner was female, being manumitted as part of a group or family, and lower fear of slave insurrection. Sample selection must have been enormous. Completed manumissions must grossly underestimate the actual prices paid, as many negotiations must have fallen apart after slaves had invested significant sums and services to improve the probability of being manumitted (Brana-Shute and Sparks 2009). Whitman (1997) describes the scene in Baltimore, where freedom contracts were more enforceable than elsewhere in the South. An 1817 law required that the sale of a slave for a *term of years* be registered in court, although this was not often done (pp. 93–118). Still, the possibility of entering a market where more enforceable contracts were possible was attractive to enslaved people, who sometimes asked to be sold into the Baltimore market "to get free" (p. 111).

Shawn Cole (2005), finds that enslaved people who purchased their freedom paid a premium of 19 percent over the market price. John Moes (1960), in an insightful comment in the *Journal of Political Economy* criticizes the idea that a slave society cut off from outside supplies (like the USA after 1808) could sustain itself over the long term, arguing that masters would realize they could negotiate a better deal with their slaves by offering them eventual freedom and splitting the difference. Moes believed economic rationality like this explains the decline of slavery in Rome during Pax Romana, and cites several studies, including Westermann (1955), claiming that "manumission prices were in excess of the usual market prices for slaves" (p. 183).

Waste like this raises a serious question: Why do we not see more self-purchase and manumission in the antebellum Slave South of the United States? According to Fogel and Engerman (1974) and Engerman (1973, p. 50), infrequent manumission might be explained by scale economies in the slave labor system that was unavailable in the free sector, where plantation management could drive slaves in gangs larger than sixteen, well beyond the scale achievable by the typical family farm. Evidence of this kind of scale economy on American plantations has been challenged (Sutch 2018; Wright 1978), and it does not explain why manumission was illegal in some places and times. Moes (1960) concludes that "Racial prejudice and concerns with white supremacy undoubtedly were basic underlying factors" (pp. 186–87). In other words, modern *racial* slavery was more wasteful than Roman slavery.

What about the full value of loss freedom caused by *social death*? What would be the loss if we included the slave's value of loss freedom, an externality that a slave society cannot recoup? Hornbeck and Logan (2023) use estimates of the statistical value of life to estimate the value of social death from the slave's perspective. They estimate that emancipation from slavery in the United States generated aggregate economic gains equal to 7 to 60 years of technological innovation for the *entire* US economy. According to Hsieh et al. (2019), a similar occupational reallocation of talent among women and Blacks following the civil rights legislation of the 1960s explains 20 percent to 40 percent of the growth in aggregate output per worker between 1960 and 2010. And Chapter 42 of Deirdre McCloskey's *Bourgeois Dignity* (2016) is entitled "Dignity and Liberty for Ordinary People, in Short, were the Greatest Externalities," and explains the Great Enrichment of 16 to 100 times more stuff per capita since 1700.

SERFDOM IS NOT SLAVERY

Summarizing what would become the Nieboer–Domar hypothesis about the relationship between land abundance and slavery, Nieboer writes:

> we shall find that slavery is not likely to exist in those countries where all the land is held as property. And as this has been the case in Western Europe for some centuries, we discovered one of the principal causes, perhaps the main cause, why slavery (and serfdom, which is a mitigating form of slavery) have long since disappeared in these countries. (p. xxii)

First, notice that Nieboer never considers the possibility that the causation ran in the opposite direction, that the abolition of slavery could unleash freedom dividends that help populate the land. Second, it is important to point out that serfdom is *not* a mitigating form of slavery, a distinction too often overlooked, but one that has important implications for understanding the relationship between slavery and freedom. Economists as influential as North and Thomas (1971), Evsey Domar (1970), and Acemoglu and Wolintzky (2011) have modeled this hypothesis. The basic idea is this: If land is abundant, as in wilderness or frontier, then landowners cannot attract employees for less than employees can make on their own, leaving little surplus for landlords after paying workers their opportunity wages. One way to make a profit is to close off access to land. Slavery and serfdom, as methods of coercion, accomplish this, but in fundamentally different ways.

An important historical test was the Black Death (1346–1353), a plague pandemic that reduced the population of Europe by 30 to 60 percent. According to the hypothesis, it should have increased slavery and serfdom throughout Europe, but it did not. In some places, like Western Europe, laborers' market power increased, which incentivized the spread of an independent peasantry. Domar (1970) in the conclusion of his essay, criticizes Nieboer for thinking land abundance was a necessary *and* sufficient condition for slavery or serfdom (pp. 31–32), having overlooked political power and the elites' ability to collude to close off the frontier.

Acemoglu and Wolintzky (2011) resolve the issue by explicitly modeling coercive and free sectors that compete for workers. Labor scarcity will increase freedom if labor demand in the free sector dominates, which might have happened in Western Europe during the Black Death, where plague-related deaths were greatest in cities. The model, however, requires assumptions about mobility between the coercive and free sectors that do not apply to slavery – like the opportunity to pay freedom dues or the high probability of escaping coercion and finding a non-coercive employer, or having any power at all to defend oneself during migration and search. Rather than assuming these kinds of intersectoral mobilities, it seems more likely that different classes of coercion (slavery and serfdom) exhibit different responses to labor scarcity. The difference between the rights and obligations of slaves and serfs makes all the difference in the world.

Compare two familiar cases – African-American slavery and Western European serfdom. The trade of captured Africans across the Atlantic and into a land-abundant America, where the native population had been decimated by disease, is a labor-scarce environment ripe for slavery as the institution of coercion. Escape back to Africa was virtually impossible, and race-based restrictions on mobility closed off local escape. The outcome of slavery is not hard to explain. By contrast, serfs in medieval Europe were not enslaved aliens brought from a distant land but were local farmers with bundles of rights "purchased" from local lords in exchange for the payment of feudal dues. Plague-induced deaths improved serfs' power to expand the bundle of rights their feudal dues could purchase.[7] The distinction is why slaves could be sold and serfs not. One was alienable wealth, the other not.

Natal alienation is what distinguishes slavery from serfdom, and applies to enslaved people regardless of the society or historical context being considered. The names of the major slave trades in world history drive home the importance of distance by land and water: the Indian Ocean slave trade; the Black Sea slave trade; the Mediterranean slave trade; the medieval European slave trade, mainly on the North Sea and across the English Channel; the trans-Saharan slave trade; and the transatlantic slave trade.

In his book *Ancient Slavery and Modern Ideology* (1980), Sir Moses Finley writes about this in ancient Rome: "This totality of the slave owner's rights was facilitated by the fact that the slave was *always* a deracinated outsider – an outsider first in the sense that he originated from outside the society into which he was introduced as a slave, second in the sense that he was denied the most elementary of social bonds, kinship" (p. 75). In his 1799 book *Travels in the Interior Districts of Africa*, the Scottish explorer Mungo Park observes the same in Africa: "the value of a slave in the eye of an African purchaser, increases in proportion to his distance from his native's kingdom: for when slaves are only a few days journey from the place of their nativity, they frequently affect their escape" (p. 258). Pierre Bonnassie, in *From Slavery to Feudalism in Southwestern Europe* (1991), notes that "in antiquity, the slave was *always* a stranger, brought from afar (from the barbarian countries), entirely removed from his place of origin, ignorant even of the language of the land of his captivity" (pp. 36–37).

Slavery is not serfdom.

CHAPTER 3

Lessons from Slavery in World History

LARGE-SCALE SLAVERY IN WORLD HISTORY

Nieboer's 1900 definition of slavery is useful, but it does not go far enough. Fast forward three-quarters of a century and we get a radically different picture. In *Slavery and Social Death* (1982), Orlando Patterson surveyed the literature as it existed in 1982. He also recorded societies where "one man is possessed by another and forced to work for him," but only for "large-scale slave societies" where enslaved people constituted more than 20 percent of the population. He not only estimated the slave percentages of the populations but also the approximate dates. He included all societies that meet this criterion – ancient, premodern, modern, civilized, or semi-civilized, on any continent, at any time. He had access to the *Ethnographic Atlas,* but he consulted a much larger literature (see Appendix C, pp. 352–64, 458–76). His results are reported in Table 3.1, where I sort the data by century to convey a sense of the history of large-scale slavery in world history.

Before the fifteenth century, large-scale slave systems were widespread in Europe. As early as the fifth century BC, Greek city-states like Athens and Corinth were large-scale slave systems, where approximately 30 percent of the population was enslaved. The same applies to Rome, from as early as 225 BC to the end of the Roman Empire around 476 AD. After the collapse of the Roman Empire, large-scale slavery thrived in Spain and the islands of the Mediterranean. In the ninth to eleventh centuries, large-scale slavery flourished in Iceland and western England and began to spread into northern Africa with the spread of Islam. In Asia, large-scale slavery thrived in Korea as early as 660 AD, in both the Unified Silla Period and the Koryo

Table 3.1 Patterson on large-scale slave systems in world history

Name and location of society	Approximate dates	Slave percentage
Before the fifteenth century		
Greek states (Athens, Corinth, Aegina, and Chios)	Fifth century BC–early Roman	30–33
Roman Italy	225–200 BC	10
Roman Empire	1–150 AD	16–20
Roman Italy	100 BC–300 AD	33–35
Sicily	150 BC–150 AD	>66
Visigothic Spain	415–711 AD	>25
Muslim Spain	756–1492 AD	>20
Mediterranean Spain	Thirteenth century	>20
Central Crete	1350–1500	>20
Southwestern Cyprus	1300–1500	>20
Majorca	Fourteenth and fifteenth century	>18
Iceland	870–950	>20
Western England	Ninth century to 1080	>20
Islamic Ghana	1076–1600	>30
Mali	1200–1500	>30
Wolof and Sereer states of Senegambia	1300–1630	>30
Iraq, Lower Mesopotamia (ninth–tenth century)	Ninth to tenth century	>50
Korea		
Unified Silla period (660–918)	660–918 AD	50?
Koryo Dynasty (918–1392)	918–1392	>33
Fifteenth century		
Atlantic Islands (Madeira, Canary)	1450–1600	30–50
Songhay	1462–1720	>40
Korea (early Yi Dynasty)	1400s	30–37
Sixteenth century		
Algiers	1500–1700	> 25
Cape Verde	1500–1878	>50
Sao Tome	1506–1864	32–66
Borno and Bagirmi	1580–1890	40–50
Española	1560–1570	90–92
Cuba	1500–1861	30–90
Trajin, Central American slave portage system	1510–1620	90
Coastal mining area of Venezuela	1510–1600	90
European-dominated urban Mexico	1570–1650	50
Mining Mexico	1590s	13.5
Brazil (as a whole)	1530–1872	50–66
Seventeenth century		
Darfur	1600–1874	40
Kamen	1600–1800	30

Table 3.1 (cont.)

Name and location of society	Approximate dates	Slave percentage
Housa City-States	1600–1800	30
Wolof post-Jolof	1630–1900	33
Yoruba Empire (Oyo, city-states of Ife and Benin)	1600–1897	30–50
Banda Islands	1621–1860	>80
Jamaica	1658–1834	24–91
Barbados	1643–1834	24–81
Antigua	1678–1834	48–94
St. Kitts	1678–1834	48–92
Nevis	1678–1834	52–92
Montserrat	1678–1834	27–99
Bahamas	1671–1831	40–68
Bermuda	1670–1833	24–49
Martinique	1664–1848	50–84
Haiti	1681–1789	35–90
Guadeloupe	1609–1834	64–84
French Guiana	1665–1830	33–94
USA South as a whole	1690–1860	15–40
Panama City	1607	>90
Thailand	1600–1880	25–33
Korea (Northern Seoul, Kumhwa, and coastal Ulsan)	1663–1810	17–75
Eighteenth century		
Fulani Jihad States (Fouta-Jalon, Masina, etc.) and Sokoto Caliphate (Housaland)	1750–1900	30–66
Segou	1780–1861	>40
Asante and Gayman Kingdoms	Eighteenth and nineteenth century	33
Dahomey	Late eighteenth and nineteenth century	>33
"House" city-states in Niger Delta	Eighteenth and nineteenth century	>50
Portuguese Mozambique	1750–1910	50–80
South Africa	1701–1820	41–54
Mascarene Islands (Reunion, Mauritius, Seychelles)	1730–1848	54–88
Decadent Kongo Kingdom	1700–1900	>50
Columbian Choco	1763–1808	20–39
Surinam	1790–1862	20–91
Curaçao	1700–1862	29–65
St. Eustatius	1786–1829	53–71
St. Martin	1770–1816	72–84
Barbuda	1790	83–87
Anguilla	1790	84
Guyana (Dutch and British)	1701–1834	88–93
British Virgin Islands (Dominica, St. Vincent)	1756	84
Granada	1777–1834	90–96

Table 3.1 (cont.)

Name and location of society	Approximate dates	Slave percentage
St. Lucia	1772-1834	86-92
Tobago	1770-1820	93-98
Trinidad	1797-1834	50-69
British Honduras	1745-1832	42-71
Minas Gerais (Brazil)	1735-1872	18-98
Bahia (Brazil)	1702-1870	12-50
USA (VA, SC, NC, GA)	1708-1860	24-57
Nineteenth century		
Waidai (Central Sudan)	Nineteenth century	50
Tuareg of Sahara and Sahel	1800-1965	33
Sherbro and Mende (Sierra Leone)	Nineteenth century	>40
Vai paramount Chiefdoms	1826-1920	50-60
Temme chiefdoms	Nineteenth and early twentieth century	>50
Duala of Coastal Cameroon	Nineteenth century	>50
Gabon River Kingdoms	1820-1856	50-70
Decadent Kasanje Kingdom of Angola	Late eighteenth and nineteenth century	>50
Luvale Chiefdom of Zimbabwe	Nineteenth century	>50
Lozi state	1864-1906	50-75
Arab-Swahili Slave System of East Africa (Zanzibar, Pemba, Mombasa, Malindi, Madagascar)	1811-1895	50-90
Portuguese settlement in Angola and Mozambique	1830-1900	>75
USA (MS, AL, LA)	1810-1860	33-55
Norsus (Lolos) of Yunnan Province (SW China)	Late nineteenth century-1940s	47
Burma (Hukawng Valley and Triangle Area)	Late nineteenth-early twentieth century	>30

Source: Patterson (1982), Appendix C, pp. 352-64, 458-76.

Dynasty. It spread to the salt mines of southern Iraq in the ninth and tenth centuries, where the "Zanj" rebellions put brakes on expansion.

By the fifteenth century, large-scale slavery in Europe remained only in Muslim Spain, Central Crete, southwest Cyprus, and Majorca – the outskirts of Christendom. It then spread to the Atlantic islands of Madeira and the Canaries off the coast of Spain, Portugal, and Africa. In Africa, following the collapse of the Mali Empire, Songhay emerged in 1462 as a large-scale slave state along the bend of the Niger River. Slavery in Korea continued to thrive during the Yi Dynasty of the fifteenth century.

By the sixteenth century, large-scale slavery was spreading to the islands off the west coast of Africa, serving as entrepôt for the emerging transatlantic slave trade. By the seventeenth century, as the slave plantation complex took hold in the New World, we begin to see the effects in Africa. Exposure to the trans-Saharan and transatlantic slave trades spread large-scale slavery in the western Sudan and the Yoruba city-states around Benin. Large-scale slavery continued to thrive in parts of Korea until 1810, making Korea the longest-surviving large-scale slave system in modern history (660–1810).

During the eighteenth century, the American plantation complex spread to almost every island and colony in the New World, and the transatlantic slave trade exploded from 20,000 to 120,000 captives per year. In Africa, we see the emergence of the proto-typical slave state – militarized and centralized slave states born in the slave trade era – like Asante, Dahomey, Segou, the Sokoto Caliphate, and the trade "Houses" of the Niger Delta. Under pressure from the Portuguese slave trade, the Kongo Kingdom destabilizes. The Dutch establish large-scale slave systems in South Africa. Large-scale slavery expands to the Mascarene Islands off the coast of East Africa, producing commodities for the rapidly growing economies of Europe and America.

In the nineteenth century, slave exports to the New World remained at record levels, even after Britain abolished its trade in 1807. New coastal and interior areas of Africa are brought into the orbit of the transatlantic, trans-Saharan, and Indian Ocean slave trades, places like Cameroon, Gabon, Waidai, Zimbabwe, and Lozi. The Arab-Swahili slave trade, being less hindered by European abolitions, expanded on the east coast of Africa, establishing large-scale slave plantations on the nearby islands of Zanzibar, Pemba, and Madagascar.

What stands out in this long view of large-scale slavery in world history is what Sir Moses Finley calls the two great slave systems in world history: the ancient slave systems of the Greco-Roman world and the modern slave system of the New World, both occupying important places in the history of Western economic development and, according to Patterson, in the development of Western notions of freedom. There is a third case – Korea – that deserves more attention. Perhaps a closer look at the history of slavery and freedom on the Korean Peninsula can help explain the economic success of South Korea and the continuation of slavery in North Korea. In any case, the messages of Nieboer and Patterson could not be more different.

WARS PRODUCE SLAVE WEALTH

As natal aliens, enslaved people most often originate in war or kidnapping. Not all enslaved people originate this way, but most newly enslaved people do, if not by capture, then by trade for others' captives. We have already seen how distance from native land or point of capture increases the value of enslaved people. Distance also increases supply price.

Slave merchants were always intermediaries that facilitated the long-distance movement of enslaved people, which is why history is replete with examples of slave merchants solving the kinds of principal–agent problems associated with long-distance trade. We typically think of Genoa and Venice as incubators of individualistic norms and free trade, and they were, but they also dominated the slave trade of their time. The Maghribi traders made famous by Greif (1994, 1989) were likely involved in the trade of slaves and gold across the Sahara, connecting with a similar trade coalition called Wangara that operated south of the desert (Wilks 1962). The same applies to Muslim traders of enslaved Africans in the Indian Ocean and Christian traders of enslaved Africans across the Atlantic. Inikori (2002) has done more than perhaps anyone to highlight and document the impact of the transatlantic slave trade on the development of modern shipping practices, shipping technology, financial instruments, and maritime insurance.[1]

From this perspective, it is understandable why wars of empire-building are most conducive to slave trading and slavery. Burbank and Cooper, in their book *Empires in World History: Power and the Politics of Difference* (2010), define empires as "expansionist or with a memory of power extended over space, polities that maintain distinctions in the hierarchies as they incorporate new people" (p. 8). As the Roman Empire expanded over vast stretches of territory bordering the Mediterranean, so did slavery and slave trading. During Pax Romana, at the height of the Empire, the supply of captives from war became more difficult. The same applies to Charlemagne's Catholic Empire, the Carolingian empire, formed in the year 800 AD when Leo III was crowned King Charles of the Franks, Emperor of the Holy Roman Empire – a marriage of church and state that the French historian Jacques Le Goff calls the aborted *Birth of Europe* (2005). As the Carolingian empire expanded out of the Rhineland, defeating the Bavarians, Lombards, Saxons, and others, "not least of the empire's resources was a trade in people of the region – captives taken in Charlemagne's wars of expansion – who entered well-established slave trade routes through Venice and other southern ports to the Muslim world" (Burbank and Cooper 2010, p. 85).

Similarly, as the Muslim empire expanded in all directions following Mohammad's capture of Mecca in 629, the Muslim slave trade also expanded. The prohibition against Muslims enslaving Muslims (like in Christendom) pushed catchment zones to the empire's frontiers – into India, Russia, Africa, and Europe, the difference being Muslim Eurasia continued to enforce slavery at home, while Christendom Europe shipped it offshore. And, of course, when European empires expanded into the Americas after 1492, so did the trade in African captives across the Atlantic. A final example comes from Africa. As the Empire of Benin expanded in the Bights of the Niger Delta in the fifteenth and sixteenth centuries, captives were traded westward through the lagoons along the Lower Guinea coast of Africa, supplying the Akan of the Gold Coast with labor to clear what Ivor Wilks calls their *Forest of Gold* (1993).

THE SOCIAL REPRODUCTION OF SLAVE WEALTH

As part of the booty of war, captured slaves are captured wealth. Captives lose their freedom over life and labor and become the possession of another. The discounted surplus value of the enslaved person's future life and labor is now the present value of captured wealth.[2] This aspect of slavery amends our working definition of slavery to "natal aliens as wealth possessed by another."

Economists have modeled the optimal management of enslaved labor and have compared the relative efficiency and profitability of slave versus free labor systems. These are the kinds of issues any slave economy must address, especially concerning newly enslaved people who are almost always subject to trade, internally and externally. The market value of tradable slaves focuses economy-wide attention on choosing the optimal mix of supervision (carrot versus stick) to grow the wealth's value.

From the perspective of social reproduction, the norms and institutions we seek to trace are the ones that reproduce slave *status* over the generations – that is, the rules that govern the inheritance of social status, or cultures as defined by Henrich (2016), or social stratification as defined by Darity, Mason, and Stewart (2006), or caste as defined by Wilkerson (2020). Maintaining slave status by birth preserves slave wealth and supplements external supplies from war, kidnapping, and trade. Inheritance rules influence the preservation of slave status and the rates of preservation and growth of slave wealth.

We are back at the first problem of slavery – deciding who is free and who is slave – except now for the next generation. Table 3.2 summarizes five slave cultures found in world history, as described by Patterson, classified by how the rules governing the inheritance of social status influence the inheritance of slave wealth. Patterson (1982, Chapter 5) does not discuss these patterns as mechanisms for preserving slave wealth, or as different slave cultures. In fact, he might object to an economic interpretation of slaves as wealth. He discusses the different patterns of inherited slave status

Table 3.2 Five slave cultures in world history

	Status, by rule			
Inheritance rule	Father	Mother	Offspring	Wealth outcomes
Matrilineal	F	S	S	Preserves slave wealth
	S	F	F	Frees slaves (allowed)
	S	S	S	Preserves slave wealth for the mother's master
Patrilineal	F	S	F	Frees slaves
	S	F	S	Taboo or harsh penalty or "unthinkable"
	S	S	S	Preserves slave wealth for the father's master
Western	F	S	S	Preserves slave wealth
	S	F	S	Taboo or harsh penalty
	S	S	S	Preserves slave wealth for the father's master
Chinese	F	S	S	Free person and offspring reduced to slavery
	S	F	S	Free person and offspring reduced to slavery
	S	S	S	Preserves slave wealth
Muslim	F	S	F	Free if the father acknowledges parentage
	S	F	F	Free if the father acknowledges parentage
	S	S	S	Preserves slave wealth

Source: Orlando Patterson (1982), pp. 133–47.

to show that not all slaves originate in war and kidnapping, but also by birth. By treating the abrogation of freedom as the origins of slave wealth, I am able to appropriate Patterson's illuminating insights on inheritance rules to show how they influence the preservation and growth of wealth in slaves.

The slave cultures are listed in column one as Matrilineal, Patrilineal, Western, Chinese, and Muslim. Columns two and three denote the father's and mother's status. "F" indicates free, and "S" indicates slave. Column four derives the status of the offspring, given the status of each parent and the societal rules governing the inheritance of social status. In all five cases, if the father and the mother are "free," the offspring are free. That case is not problematic and is excluded from the table. When both the father and the mother are enslaved, the offspring are always enslaved, unless manumitted by the master, the only remaining issue being who owns the slave offspring, the master of the father or the master of the mother.

The problematic cases are where the father and the mother are of mixed social status. Initial conditions matter, like the inheritance rules before enslaved people were introduced, which are often difficult to change because they coordinate more than the preservation of slave wealth. Patrilineal descent systems struggled to preserve slave wealth, and often resorted to taboos and severe punishments to maintain patrilineal inheritance of status in the presence of slave wealth. Think of Table 3.2 as a list of five slave cultures that have influenced world history, around which there have been adaptations and changes across time and place.

MATRILINEAL SLAVE CULTURES. It is easiest to start with the matrilineal case, the first case in Table 3.2. Social status passes through the mother's lineage, where the mother's brothers (the offspring's uncles) share rights and obligations (*potestas*) in raising the children. The mother's maternal brothers have a say in property inheritance too. Patterson calls this the Asante pattern because matrilineal descent governed Asante, a Federation of Akan clans that emerged behind the Gold Coast of West Africa in the early eighteenth century (in current day Ghana). Matrilineal descent of social status preserves female slave wealth without contradicting the societal norms governing the inheritance of social status. According to the matrilineal inheritance rule, "the children of the union of a free man and a female slave were always slaves and were known as *Kanifa* or half-Akan" (Patterson 1982, p. 135). The offspring's status passes from the mother, who is enslaved, as in the first row of Table 3.2.

There is an additional incentive to incorporate enslaved women into matrilineal systems, other than the fact that matrilineal systems effectively preserve female slave wealth. In matrilineal systems, female slaves also increase the authority of fathers and patriarchy. As Patterson (1982) puts it, "the child whose father was the master of his mother was of special importance to the matrilineal Ashanti, for only over such children did the biological father have complete authority." R. S. Rattray in *Asanti Law and Constitution* (1929) also comments on this additional demand for enslaved women in matrilineal systems: "The possession of slaves was one of the surest and most satisfactory means of augmenting the members of the family who would come directly under the *potestas* of its head" (p. 45). According to Rattray, "the children of these children in the female line were considered slaves forever" (p. 136).

The most interesting outcome of the matrilineal case is what happens when the father is enslaved and the mother is free. In most slave cultures, this pairing is highly problematic, often considered taboo, and enforced by extreme penalties for the free women who violate the male-imposed taboo. This pairing does not pose a problem in matrilineal societies, as if to confirm the universality of the matrilineal rule in determining social status. According to Patterson, "the children of the union of a male slave and a free woman were always free and were in no way under the *potestas* of their slave father or his master" (Patterson 1982, p. 135). Furthermore, "the Ashanti pattern was the direct consequence of structural principles typical of matrilineal societies. Hence, it was found not only amongst all other Akan-speaking groups but, with the notable exception of the Tuareg of the Sahara and the Merina of Madagascar, in all matrilineal slaveholding societies" (p. 136).

The next row completes the matrilineal case. When the father and the mother are both enslaved, the offspring are also slaves, owned by the mother's master.

PATRILINEAL SLAVE CULTURES. The second case is patrilineal inheritance of status, which poses serious problems for preserving slave wealth. Patterson calls this the Somali Pattern, "a relatively unusual pattern," where "status was determined by the father" and where the "children of the union of a slave woman and a free man were free if the father acknowledged paternity." Alternatively, "unions between slave males and 'free' women were so strongly prohibited that they were nearly unthinkable" (Patterson 1982, p. 137). To encourage the preservation and growth of slave wealth while maintaining patrilineal rules for the inheritance of social status, there evolved "a low-caste, non-slave group among the Somali, the *Sab,* with whom male slaves were allowed to intermarry, and where the same (patrilineal) rules applied: the children of a female Sab and a male slave were slaves, while those of a male Sab and a female slaves became Sab" (p. 137).

To round out this relatively unusual case, "the child of the union of two enslaved people remained a slave but, unlike the Ashanti, the child always belonged to the master of the father. The master of the slave husband paid a nuptial gift to the master of the slave bride, and this legally compensated for the ownership of the children of the slave woman" (Patterson 1982, p. 137). "In Homeric Greece, it was the father status that was determinative for both free and slave. In certain Greek states, this pattern was held throughout the Age of Antiquity" (p. 138).

WESTERN SLAVE CULTURES. "This was the classic pattern found in many highly developed slaveholding systems and in most of the Western slave societies" (Patterson 1982, p. 139). The basic pattern is patrilineal for the free and matrilineal for the enslaved. The children of enslaved women are slaves regardless of the father's status. Like the taboo of the patrilineal Somali, "cohabitating free women became slaves, and the law grew progressively harsh over the issue" (p. 140). The Western pattern was widespread in the Greco-Roman world, Europe, and the Americas, presumably evolving out of the difficulty of preserving slave wealth using strict patrilineal descent rules. The Western pattern prevailed in ancient India before Buddha but changed drastically in Mauryan times. It "held among central and northern Germanic people, who applied it with extreme rigidity" (pp. 140–41). The primary difference between ancient Roman and modern American slavery was manumission and self-purchase in the Roman case and the socially constructed barriers of race in the Americas.

CHINESE SLAVE CULTURES. From the Han dynasty on, the primary Chinese rule for mixed parentage was *deterior condicio* – the offspring took the lowest parent's status – an effective deterrent to mixing. While this was the basic Chinese pattern, Patterson believes it was "humanized" over time:

> Between the eighth and 12th centuries A.D., if a free woman had a child by a slave, the child became a state slave and the woman was severely punished ... During the Yuan period (roughly the 13th to 14th centuries A.D.) slaves and "good" persons were allowed to intermarry, but the wives always assumed the status of the husband – that is, slave women married to "free" men became free, while "free" women married to slaves became slaves. (Patterson 1982, pp. 141–42)

Patterson believes the severe penalty for mixing followed by humanization over time explains why slavery in China never became a widespread institution.

That was not the case in Korea, where *deterior condicio* was strictly enforced. "In Korea where the rule applied prior to the Yi Dynasty (though only partially during the Koryo period) we find the most advanced slave system in the Orient and one of the most developed anywhere in the premodern world" (Patterson 1982, p. 143). "From very early, birth became the major source of slaves in the Koryo period. Considerable attention was therefore paid to slave-free unions with a view to restricting any generational 'leakage' from the slave population. The rules of status inheritance were frequently debated and repeatedly changed, rarely in favor of slaves" (p. 143). The basic Chinese pattern was also rigidly applied in Visigothic Spain and Lombardi until the early modern period. "In medieval Tuscany, the legal situation was a strange mixture of Roman and Lombardic law as well as local customs" (p. 144).

NEAR EAST/MUSLIM SLAVE CULTURES. Patterson considers the Near East/Muslim pattern to be the earliest and most liberal of the slave cultures. "Where one of the parents was free and the other a slave, the child inherited the status of the free parent whatever the sex, as long as the father acknowledged paternity" (Patterson 1982,

p. 144). The essentials of the system were incorporated into Islamic law and spread with Islam. "The key factor in the operation of this pattern amongst Muslims is the Islamic law of concubinage, which holds that a slave woman becomes free along with her children as soon as she bears a son for her master … Mamluks could also marry free women" (p. 145).

SUMMARY OF LESSONS

To summarize some of the lessons from the history of world slavery, an enslaved person is a natal alien who is possessed by another as wealth to be preserved and worked. The origin of slave wealth is found in the looting and booty of war and violence. It is the immediate creation of wealth in that it converts the freedom of life and labor into the possession of another. Being without kin or other social embeddedness, the enslaved person is potentially alienable, which focuses attention on their economic value as someone's wealth. Inheritance rules influence how slave wealth is preserved and grown over the generations, which can evolve into various cultural taboos and laws of social stratification.

Research since 1982 might alter some of the details, but the slave systems Patterson describes are discernible, primarily because the differences are related to the inheritance of slave status. Matrilineal lineage is most conducive to preserving slave wealth, except in cases where free women cohabitated with slave men, which was socially acceptable. No male-imposed taboo or penalty, and free women had the right and the power to free their children conceived with enslaved men. Patrilineal systems have difficulty preserving slave wealth because the inheritance rules constrain free men in their relationships with slave women. Mixed parentage would either free the offspring (when the man was free) or was taboo (when the woman was free). Western slave culture solved this problem by establishing matrilineal rules for enslaved people and patrilineal rules for free, with strict taboos against mixing between free females and enslaved males. The Chinese system of *deterior condicio* was the most draconian, reducing the partners and the offspring of mixed parentages to the status of the lowest parent, and served as a strong deterrent to mixing. This system may have been ignored or humanized in China, but strictly enforced in Korea. Finally, the Near East/Muslim pattern was the most liberal. While recognizing slavery, Muslim masters of concubines could free the offspring of mixed parents if the father acknowledged paternity.

CHAPTER 4

On the Origins of Western Freedom and Development

WHAT DO ECONOMIC HISTORIANS HAVE TO SAY?

We have before us two related but distinct questions about the impact of slavery and freedom on economic development: the comparative and the historical. The second part of this book will focus on the comparative: Can freedom and slavery order the mirror image? The present chapter focuses on the historical: What is the historical relationship between slavery, freedom, and development in the rise of the West? Does the abolition of slavery matter in the economic rise of Western Europe?

Modern economic history of Western Europe seldom, if ever, mentions the abolition of slavery or its impact on the spread of freedom and development. Scholars have proposed many factors, but the abolition of slavery is not one of them. A brief listing of some of the modern literature, in loose chronological order, shows both the important factors that have been emphasized and the general drift from materialist to idealist explanations.

Angus Maddison, for example, in *The World Economy: A Millennial Perspective* (2003) argues that data matter and collects available economic and demographic data on world economies that show the historic rise of Western Europe and its offshoots. Douglas North in *Structure and Change in Economic History* (1982) argues that institutions mattered, meaning property rights, transaction costs, and politics. Jared Diamond in *Guns, Germs, and Steel* (1997) argues that ecology mattered – that the primary axis of the continents and the availability of domesticable plants and animals favored Eurasia. Acemoglu, Johnson, and Robinson (2005) argue that constraints on executive authority mattered in explaining which European economies benefited most from the growing Atlantic trade after 1500. Findlay and O'Rourke (2007) in *Power and Plenty* argue that empire, trade, and war mattered in shaping the world economy of the second millennium. Joseph Inikori in *Africans and the Industrial Revolution in England* (2002) argues that Africans, slavery, and export-led growth mattered in explaining the Industrial Revolution in England. Robert Allen in *The British Industrial Revolution* (2009) argues that high wages and resource availability in Britain mattered. J. L. van Zanden in *The Long Road to the Industrial Revolution* (2009) argues that taking a longer view matters, back to at least the twelfth century. Yuval Noah Harari in *Sapiens* (2015) argues that imagination mattered, as groups of mythmaking and gossipy homo sapiens scale up using shared identity, religion, money, authority, etc. Deirdre McCloskey, in *Bourgeois Equality* (2016) argues that ideas and rhetoric mattered, as in the triumph of liberalism that unleashes the Great Enrichment, first in the Netherlands and then in Britain. Joel Mokyr in *Culture of Growth* (2017) argues that open-sourced science mattered, as in diversity and competition within the Society of Letters. Joseph Henrich, in *WEIRD* (2020), argues that cultural evolution mattered in the form of Christendom's Marriage and Family Program, the Protestant Reformation, and reading. And recently, Oded Galor in *The Journey of Humanity* (2022) argues that Malthusian virtue mattered, through natural selection's impact on the propensity to innovate, echoing an argument found in Gregory Clark's *Farewell to Alms* (2007).

All of these explanations, and many others, assume freedom was a necessary condition for the rise of the West, but none ask the historical question of origin. McCloskey and Henrich come closest. McCloskey (2010, 2016, 2020) has written extensively on the emergence of bourgeois freedom as a widespread social norm in Dutch society around 1700, ideas that spread to Britain in the eighteenth century. However, McCloskey never mentions the demise of slavery in Europe or the role it may have played in the evolution of liberty and liberalism. When slavery is mentioned, it is the exploitation of African-American slavery, an institution she argues could not possibly explain the Great Enrichment of modern economic growth. Prak and van Zanden (2023) locate the origins of Dutch capitalism earlier than 1700, between 1350 and 1566, but the only mention of slavery in their analysis is that it no longer existed in eleventh-century Dutch society (p. 51) and that Dutch capitalism predated Dutch involvement in the transatlantic slave trade, and, as a consequence, predates the kinds of violence and oppression emphasized in the New History of Capitalism literature.

Henrich (2020) investigates the origins of individualistic psychology in Western Europe, and defends his silence on the role of slavery because "there are many books already written on the subject" (p. 486). But there are not many books written on the subject of slavery and the rise of freedom and individuality in Western Europe. Like the others, Henrich is referring to slavery outside of Europe and the Williams thesis – the idea that the profits of American slavery fueled the Industrial Revolution in Britain.

Three of the most influential modern scholars on freedom are the social historian Orlando Patterson, the Nobel Prize-winning economist and philosopher Amartya Sen, and the economic historian Deirdre McCloskey. Patterson's twin volumes *Slavery as Social Death* (1982) and *Freedom in the Making of Western Culture* (1991) remain standard references in the history of world slavery, where he argues that the idea of freedom as a human right has a history and, in current parlance, its corridor is narrow (Acemoglu and Robinson 2019; North, Wallis, and Weingast 2009). Amartya Sen's book *Development as Freedom* (1999) is a powerful statement about how *substantive* freedoms (education, healthcare, food security, and democracy) allow people to "live the life they have reason to value" and are the fundamental sources of economic growth and improvements in social welfare. Deirdre McCloskey (2010, 2016) has written extensively on the rise of Western liberalism, arguing it to be the ultimate cause of the Industrial Revolution and the fundamental source of the Great Enrichment that followed.

Patterson is the only one to consider a possible connection between the abolition of slavery and the rise of the kind of freedom envisioned by Sen and McCloskey. We need to consider his arguments. We are already halfway there in that the Western solution to Patterson's "first problem of slavery" predicts a high internal rate of growth and persistence of wealth in slaves in the West. The social tensions between freedom and slavery co-existed for long periods of time in Western slave cultures. Recently, economic historians and development economists have claimed an increasing role for norms, culture, and institutions in explaining modern economic growth, but Patterson's hypothesis has not been included in this literature (Koyama and Ruben 2022). It should be.

PATTERSON ON SLAVERY AND FREEDOM IN WESTERN CULTURE

Patterson (1991) begins by noting that the tripartite norms of Western freedom (personal, sovereign, and civic) reflect off slavery because enslaved people have none of them. Remembering that enslaved people are acutely aware of their enslavement, Patterson then asks:

> Who are the first persons to get the unusual idea that being free was not only a value to be cherished but the most important thing that someone could possess? The answer, in a word: slaves. Freedom began its career as a social value in the desperate yearnings of the slave to negate what, for him or her, was a peculiarly inhuman condition. (p. 9)

Patterson wants to move beyond the oppositional nature of slavery and freedom (as in the first problem of slavery) to empower the desire for freedom among enslaved people with a force for social change, the kind of social change that could transform freedom from a political state of affairs (where some have it and others do not) into a universal social norm or human right.

The historical question is this: If the social life of freedom begins in a dialectical relationship with slavery, as in the first problem of slavery, and if slavery is found throughout history and worldwide, then why does freedom as a universal human right first emerge in the West? Because, Patterson argues, Athens and Rome were the first societies in world history to rely on slavery as a fundamental structural feature, a fundamental social norm and institution. Freedom from slavery, first and foremost, was an aspiration of a large segment of Greco-Roman society. In slaveholding societies, like the ones Nieboer documents, freedom may show its face but it is often "stillborn" because slaves are not numerous enough to carry the program to completion.

It may or may not be true that Rome was the first large-scale slave society in human history,[1] but several features of the Greco-Roman world suggest it was large and long-lasting. First it was indeed a large-scale slave society in that a large portion of the population were slaves. Second, Rome was an empire on the Mediterranean, an ideal environment for sustaining a large-scale slave empire. Third, the Roman/Western slave culture was the most efficient among slave cultures at preserving slave wealth over the generations.

Why do enslaved people want freedom? Because, Patterson argues, it is evident to them that wealth is the source of freedom and that only free people can acquire it. Even the *peculium* was denied slaves until the moment of freedom. According to Patterson, the idea of freedom in the Greco-Roman world found support from all social ranks: enslaved people's aspirational value of freedom; the elite's value of freedom from enslavement to barbarian outsiders (a fate worse than death); and citizens' value of freedom as protection from falling into slavery. As Patterson reiterates (2021), Roman society valorized freedom and celebrated the achievements of freedmen's climb up from slavery, like the American rags-to-riches stories that billionaires and African-American conservatives love to tell. Enslaved people's success and the institutions that promoted their success permeated Roman culture, language, and the arts.

Of course, the story does not end here. The Greco-Roman world did not abolish slavery and usher in an era of freedom as a human right, and large-scale slavery would be reborn in the New World, and with far fewer opportunities for enslaved people to earn their freedom. Instead, Patterson argues, the Greco-Roman idea of freedom as a human right was preserved and advanced through the doctrine of Pauline Christianity, a doctrine that maintained a universal brotherhood between slave and free. Dimitris J. Kyrtatas (1993), in reviewing Patterson's ideas, describes the normality of slavery in Paul's world and how it influenced early Christian thought.

> The apostle's town of origin, Tarsus, had a large-scale slave system; Roman Corinth was re-founded entirely by freedmen; in Paul's days, Corinth's slave population had been estimated at 1/3 of the urban population, another third being freedmen; Corinth was one of the major centers of

> the slave trade; in addition to all this, the Pauline congregations themselves seem to have consisted mainly of freedmen. To these congregations, slavery and emancipation were not simply an aspect of life; they were the very foundation of their existence. (p. 93)

Pauline's redemption theology, therefore, is a product of Western slavery. Again, Kyrtatas (1993):

> To abolish slavery (if this idea could ever occur to an early Christian) would amount to the abolition of the world – and it was not for men to decide on such matters. Hence, Paul took slavery for granted and used it as an appropriate metaphor in his redemption theology ... In Christianity there is place for one master alone. Slaves and human masters will become members of the Lord's great household. (p. 94)

The suffering and submission of slavery then became an educational principle, a lesson of humility that masters had yet to learn.

Was this the end of the master–slave relationship in the West? Of course not. According to Kyrtatas (1993), and to Patterson, it is simply the beginning of the end because "now the great heavenly Master was claiming universal recognition. The Western way to freedom still had a long course to run" (p. 95).

This is as far from economic history as one can get, but it is hard to deny the role of Christianity or the idea of universal brotherhood in the abolition of slavery and the expansion of freedom in the West. It runs through the Quaker denunciation of slavery in seventeenth-century America, to Bishop Samuel Adjai Crowther's abolitionist movement in nineteenth-century West Africa, to Martin Luther King's twentieth-century civil rights movement in the United States of America.

It is equally hard to deny that Christianity has justified slavery, colonization, and White supremacy. That thread runs prominently from the Catholic Church's justification for the crusades against Islam, to sanctions of New World slavery and slave trading, to justifications for colonizing the world's peoples, to modern ideologies of White supremacy and Christian nationalism.

Slavery and freedom are grand themes of Western economic development. Yet economic and social historians largely overlook the possibility of a historical relationship between the abolition of slavery and the unleashing of freedom dividends in Western Europe. In this, Patterson appears to stand alone. But is he right?

FROM SLAVERY TO FREEDOM IN WESTERN EUROPE

Let's investigate the question from our economic-historic perspective. The theoretical framework is the inefficiencies of slavery, the abolition of which unleashes a freedom dividend that grows with further liberations from bondage (like serfdom). Since slavery originates in war and the taking of prisoners as slaves, abolition begins when belligerents cease taking prisoners of war as slaves. When did this happen in Western Europe? And does it coincide with accelerations in economic growth?

It certainly did not happen before 900 AD. In that year, Western Europe was actually a slave catchment zone of expanding Muslim empires from the East. Fenoaltea (1999), in a rather unusual article entitled "Africa in the European Mirror: The Slave Trade and the Rise of Feudalism," argues that Europe in 900 AD was a slave catchment zone and explains why the Dark Ages of Europe look like the African side of our mirror image, as in "Africa in the European Rear-View Mirror."

Fynn-Paul (2009) describes the Mediterranean regions of 900 AD as two monotheistic regions trying to enforce no-slaving zones – no Christians enslaving Christians and no Muslims enslaving Muslims. Since the Muslim empires were more advanced economically and politically, they were spreading into Europe, Asia, and Africa, capturing slaves along their expanding frontiers. The Catholic Church, on the other hand, was still decentralized and unable to protect Christians from advancing Muslim armies. Strong political kingdoms could help, and some did, like the Carolingian Empire, but defectors were many, like the Vikings and the Venetians, who essentially became agents of Muslim demands for slaves. European warfare among clans and kingdoms still produced slaves, and slave merchants exported some to Muslim territories.

So European slavery and slave trading did not die because it became unprofitable after the fall of the Roman Empire. Maybe the supply price increased in some places, and the sources became more local, as many have argued, but European slavery and slave trading survived the fall of the Roman Empire (Finley 1980, 1973; Bonnassie 1991; Fenoaltea 1999; Rio 2021; Pijper 1909; Berman 1983). Slavery and slave trading survived wherever the conditions for the creation of slave wealth survived – wherever war and the long-distance trading of captives as natal aliens survived. In 840, for example, when even the City of Venice pledged to neither buy nor sell enslaved Christians in the Carolingian Empire nor sell Christians to Muslims, Venetians simply switched to trading Slavs from the East. As late as the ninth century, Charlemagne proclaimed, "There are free men and slaves, and nothing beyond that."

Within the European catchment zone, the best protections were offered by Church or state. The state had an army to protect its people. The Church did not, but could offer salvation, sanctuary, and employment. Henrich (2020) argues that the Church's opposition to polygyny and marriage among cousins and relatives was an effort to weaken clans and consolidate Church power and influence in secular matters. Kings, on the other hand, relied on the nobility and their clan networks and alliances to govern. Church and state joined forces in the Carolingian Empire (751–935 AD), where the Church anointed the king, and the king supported the Church (or the other way around), with investiture (the power to appointment bishops) being a contested political issue throughout.

Henrich (2020) and van Zanden (2009) offer accounts of the institutional changes that followed, institutions, they argue, that laid the foundation for an economic "big boom" in Western Europe, that predates the discovery of the Americas. Both accounts emphasize the Catholic Church, but in different ways. Henrich argues that the Church's Marriage and Family Program (MFP) successfully weakened clan networks and encouraged the spread of "individualistic" psychology and markets. For van Zanden, the critical development was the "power vacuum," created by the collapse of the Carolingian Empire, and how the Gregorian Reform, or Papal Revolution, of 1075–1120 consolidated a European-wide top-down *normative* authority of the Catholic Church, known as Christendom.

Did Church policy weaken clans within the Carolingian Empire to the point where the Pope could eventually replace the king as sovereign? Table 4.1 offers some simple but revealing evidence. It combines data

Table 4.1 The marriage of church and state in the Carolingian Empire

Era	Approximate dates	Average marriage prohibitions per decade	Percentage of Frankish acts referencing mancipia	Type of marriage prohibitions
Pre-Carolingian	300–750	1.20		First cousins and in-laws; tries ex-communication (716, 743)
Carolingian Empire	751–935	0.73		Second and third cousins; secular enforcements; "illegitimates" cannot inherit
	814–877		42.1	
	877–935		41.5	
Power vacuum	935–1140	1.0		Up to sixth cousin in 1140; reduced to third cousin in 1215; banns on marriage
	935–987		20.7	
	987–1031		17.3	
	1031–1108		1.5	

Sources: Henrich (2020), Appendix A, pp. 491–498; Bonnassie (1991), p. 57

from Henrich (2020) on Church marriage prohibitions and Bonnassie (1991) on Frankish Acts that refer to *mancipia* (involuntary servitude due to *mancipation*). According to these data, before the consolidation of the Carolingian Empire (circa 300–750 AD), the Church frequently issued local synods and prohibitions against kin marriages, focusing on in-laws and first cousins. The Church, however, was not yet centralized and lacked much secular authority to enforce what Henrich calls its MFP. Twice it attempted to enforce it by threat of ex-communication (in 716 and 743), but never tried again.

The Carolingian Empire politically consolidates circa 751–935, covering much of modern France, Germany, Belgium, and northern Italy. As a political compromise between church and state, the Church secured secular enforcements of its MFP within the empire's borders. In 755, King Pepin commanded that all marriages be performed publicly. In 757, he threatened secular punishment for anyone who married a first or second cousin. In 802, Emperor Charlemagne put his secular authority behind a 796 synod that required a waiting period during which neighbors and elders verified the legality of a marriage. He later added priests and bishops to the list of enforcers. With the backing of the state, Church prohibitions expanded to second and third cousins, even as the frequency of announcements declined by 60 percent (from 1.2 to 0.73 per decade), suggesting that it was becoming easier to broadcast policy changes and monitor compliance.

According to Bonnassie's data, over 40 percent of the Frankish Acts passed during this period reference *mancipia.* While Bonnassie does not detail the nature of these concerns, Rio (2021) describes several developments within the Carolingian Empire that suggest the Church's marriage prohibitions were weakening kinship networks, at least among non-nobles. The nature of unfreedom began to change, where identities were less inherited, less salient, and more challenging to verify, where unfreedom appeared to be a social station one could sink into because of the vagaries of life. These included women in sweatshops (*gynecaea*) who were not enslaved but "young women drawn from unfree families living on tenancies who had not yet married or were at some other particularly vulnerable point in their life cycle." They included agricultural workers without landholdings who were probably unfree tenants of some kind pulled in but eventually returned to unfreedom. They included penal slaves and part-time self-sales into slavery, something Romans had outlawed but Carolingians turned into a charitable act.[2] They included "those unfortunates who were not crucial enough to family strategies or too difficult to get on with or who simply nobody cared about enough to bail out. Inability to pay compensation marked out the condemned party as someone who either had been rejected by their habitual social network of support or did not have one in the first place" (Rio 2021, p. 435).

Frankish rulers insisted that courts settle disputes, courts presided over by a public official at or above the rank of count. The status of parents and relatives determined legal status, something becoming increasingly difficult to know, presumably because kinship networks were weakening and individuals were becoming more mobile. Landowners and other elites could accuse tenants of being slaves, and if tenants could not prove otherwise, landlords could use their legal leverage to adjust labor contracts to suit their needs – "uncoordinated, pragmatic reinventions to suit ever more innovative purposes in a changing range of contexts." According to Rio (2021), this explains the large number of documented complaints from tenants about being unjustly classed as unfree, and, by implication, the frequent mention of *mancipia* in Frankish acts.

Following the fragmentation of the Carolingian Empire and during what van Zanden calls the secular "power vacuum," a successful Papal Revolution (the Gregorian Reform) had little opposition. The legal historian Harold Berman (1983) refers to the newly centralized Catholic Papacy as "state-like, exercising the legislative, administrative, and judicial powers of a modern state" (pp. 113–14). It lacked an army, but proved its ability to recruit armies for the first (1096–1099) and second (1147) crusades against Islam, the first foreign wars against the enemies of Christendom.[3] Ekelund et al. (1996) refer to the newly centralized Catholic Church as a multidimensional monopoly selling salvation and collecting rents from downstream franchisees (monasteries), collecting fees from preempted marriage markets, and hoarding the treasures of successful crusades. Berman (1983) argues that the Catholic Church differed from a state because it established its sovereign authority over all the secular states of Western Europe.

To consolidate its authority in times of peace, the Papacy encouraged the formation of universities and the first legal system (as distinct from legal order), consisting of scholars who debated jurisprudence, theology, and philosophy; a court system that adjudicated conflicts among litigants; and university curricula that trained lawyers to argue cases before judges.[4] At universities, the Justinian Codex was "discovered" and widely debated – that "long lost" codification of Roman Law ordered in the sixth century by Justinian I, the Eastern Roman emperor in Constantinople.

According to Table 4.1, after consolidation around the Papacy, the Church's MFP becomes much more aggressive, and the frequency of Church pronouncements increase again. By 1140, marriage prohibitions have extended to the sixth cousin! The Church also strengthens the marriage banns, where potential marriage partners had to submit to public scrutiny of possible relatedness, followed by a public ceremony where both parties affirmed "I do" voluntarily. Royal Frankish concerns about the status of unfreedom virtually disappear. In 1215, presumably after the Church's MFP had achieved its goal, Church prohibitions receded to third cousins. Secular feudal and manorial laws emerge to secure the legal rights and obligations of the new legally defined vassal–lord relationship known as feudalism (Berman 1983, pp. 293–328).

The Papal Revolution established the Papacy as the final arbiter of moral authority throughout Western Christendom. Kingdoms, communes, and cities could tailor their laws and customs to meet their needs, but they all shared a common Christendom identity. After the successful first crusades against Islam, the Holy Roman Empire began to legally condemn slavery in its realm as a violation of man's likeness to God, as in the *Sachsenspiegal* of 1220. Freedom from slavery became an established norm throughout Western Christendom. One could say Western Europe was no longer a slave society as we have defined it. This was also when the spread of European individuality, voluntary associations, and economic growth began what van Zanden calls the long march to the Industrial Revolution.

FREEDOM AND DEVELOPMENT INSIDE CHRISTENDOM

What van Zanden (2009) adds to Berman's story is an interaction between the papal consolidation of "top-down" authority over Christendom and what he calls the silent "bottom-up" revolution of the kind of self-enforcing voluntary associations that reduce transaction costs – merchant guilds that credibly commit to punishing far-off places if they threaten guild members; voluntary city charters and communes that establish their own rules and regulations, to which members swear an oath to uphold and defend; even monasteries with their strict codes of conduct, work ethics, and ascetic lifestyles, yet open to anyone who wished to join. The canon laws of Christendom (over marriage, inheritance, property, and contract laws), the secular legal systems (feudal, manorial, mercantile, and urban law), along with courts and trained lawyers, evolve to form a kind of "rule of law" over all of Western Christendom.

Both of these accounts, Henrich's and van Zanden's, and many others, emphasize the power and authority of the centralized Catholic Church. They also marshal the same evidence of accelerated economic growth and development: growth of monasteries, population, cities, guilds, and universities. The growth dynamics typically begin with early innovations in agriculture technology like the plow. Hypotheses often refer to Christendom as a cause due to its "better magic" that purged the natural environment of pagan spirits and demons, unleashing a new "natural" laboratory that the Church was the first to exploit using subsidized monasteries as downstream franchisees (White 1962, 1982; Ekelund et al. 1996).

The Cistercian Order, founded in 1098, was at the forefront, experimenting with field rotation practices, livestock grazing, fertilizers, and the overall management of capital-intensive plow agriculture. Anderson et al. (2016) refer to the Cistercians as a pre-reformation root of the Protestant Reformation, where agricultural innovations increased local productivity and population. For Henrich (2020), the growth of monasteries is the "when and why" of the origins of WEIRD "prosociality" (pp. 350–52). For van Zanden (2009), they are the origin of written property contracts (pp. 43–45). The growth of cities, guilds, and universities followed, spreading individualistic psychology (Henrich 2020) and human capital acquisition (van Zanden 2009), eventually culminating in the Industrial Revolution of the early nineteenth century as the "escape velocity" that birthed our modern world.

In general, the dominant view of long-term development within Christendom is still Malthus, where these types of agricultural innovations drive population growth, and after controlling population growth, per capita income growth (Galor 2022). Clark (2007) emphasizes the Malthusian "Iron Law" of subsistence wages and how European wages returned to subsistence levels after the Black Death. Voigtlander and Voth (2013) place Malthusian dynamics within the European context of interstate war, urban growth, and plague to explain the increase in per capita income between 1300 and 1700 as a steady state movement to wages above subsistence. And Allen (2009) explains the Industrial Revolution in Britain as a substitution of coal-intensive machinery for these high-wage workers.

What these and other treatments of the rise of the West fail to consider is the possibility that the abolition of slave-taking throughout Western Christendom had any bearing on the acceleration of economic growth. Both Henrich and van Zanden acknowledge that freedom of association and individualistic psychology were necessary preconditions for modern economic growth, but both assume the abolition of slavery played no part. In support of my choice of freedom and slavery as social norms that explain the divergent paths of development in Europe and Africa, I have proposed a historical connection between the two – the decline of slave-taking throughout Christendom and the unleashing of freedom dividends, the "dark matter" so to speak, of the economic rise of the West.[5]

One should not think of these dividends as one-shot deals, but as dividends that grow over time, if allowed. The first effect is the inability to take Christian captives as slaves, so the scientific question is, "What did Europeans do with all those captives in all those wars that followed?"

Take, for, example, The Hundred Years' War of 1337–1453, a long-lasting conflict between the kingdoms of England and France over dynastic rights to the French throne. These tensions went back centuries, to when William the Conqueror, the Norman Duke, became king of England in 1066. Since then, English monarchs held title and lands within France, which made them vassals of the Kings of France. In 1328, Charles IV of France died without an obvious heir to the throne, and in 1337, after a series of succession crises, King Edward II of England renewed his claim to the French throne, this time by force of arms. War lasted for more than 100 years.

What happened to the vanquished during the Hundred Years War? They could not be enslaved because that was a sin. Ambühl (2013) documents, instead, the "democratization" of ransoming. Initially reserved for nobility, ransoming spread to rank-and-file soldiers until it became normalized, institutionalized, and expected, on both sides of the battlefield: how to signal surrender; the distribution of prisoner ownership rights; the ransom price; even "safe conduct" rights to retrieve the payment. As with social death, "the need to compel a soldier to surrender presupposes a hand-to-hand combat in which the soldier was defeated and had no option other than to surrender if you wanted to live" (p. 109), except now the fate was not enslavement but imprisonment until ransomed.

Ransoming also reduced the cost of war. As a widespread norm of war, ransoming was like an insurance policy against death or slavery in the event of capture. According to Ambühl (2013), "it is hardly conceivable that increasing numbers of non-noble soldiers would enroll in the armies if their fate in the event of their capture was inevitably death." And if a soldier was on the winning side of the battle, "a non-nobleman's capture of the nobleman ... could potentially change his life" (p. 39). Captors enjoyed the status of "master" upon taking the oath of his prisoner and were held responsible for the prisoner's welfare while in captivity. "Although by no means equivalent to the bonds of serfdom, the prisoner was not free and owed obedience to his master" (p. 21).

In general, prisoners were responsible for raising their own ransom, which required both an agreed-upon price and the exchange of money for freedom. This was easier for nobility and higher-echelon soldiers, whose rank and ability to pay could be assessed more easily. Prices ranged from £2,000 to £8,000 for counts and bishops, £500 to £2,000 for barons, and £50 to £500 for knights and esquires (Ambühl 2013, p. 148). Prices and exchanges were more difficult for commoners. Sometimes prisoners were released on the promise of "safe conduct" to secure the ransom for the prisoners left behind. Sometimes, ransom prices were negotiated in advance of a battle or the siege of a city, where an officer would announce the ransom to be paid for captured soldiers. A per diem for lodging became standardized as *les marz*, a percentage of the ransom demand. Ransoming became so normalized that:

> commoners such as John More and Jean de Rousselet, two sergeants-at-arms, could claim, toward the end of the Hundred Years War, to have been ruined by no less than seven and 14 captures respectively during their long careers in the service of the English crown in France. It indicates not only that the ransom culture embraced the whole social spectrum but also that the process of ransoming could run smoothly and quickly enough to allow a succession of returns to service and further captures. (Ambühl 2013, p. 10)

By the end of the war, we see mostly ransoming at the top and prisoner exchanges at the bottom, indicating greater government involvement in normalizing the new freedom from captivity (Ambühl 2013, pp. 150–59).

> The systematization of the process developed further in the 16 century. Scales of ransom became based on the wages of the soldiers ... Since it was the state that set the wages, this practice may point to greater involvement of the state. What is more, a new generalized system of prisoner exchanges controlled by the state was introduced in the middle of the 16th century

> and evolved towards the Spanish cartel general of 17th century conflicts. These cartels stipulated that, "every captain should ransom all of his captured men within 25 days. First, prisoners of equal rank on each side were to be exchanged free of charge; thereafter a ransom appropriate to the soldier's rank (usually the equivalent of one month's pay) was due, plus an agreed per diem (entertainment) for time spent in captivity." (p. 262)

Freedom from slavery was now universally practiced, even at the source, so to speak. And the ramifications did not stop there. Ransoming and prisoner exchange also reduced the cost of war by acting as an insurance policy in the event of capture. According to Hoffman (2015), in *Why Europe Conquered the World*, reductions in the variable cost of war increased the probability of war in the European theater, and increased learning-by-doing innovations in gunpowder technology, a primary reason why Europe was able to conquer the world. While Hoffman measures variable cost as the ability to tax citizens without them revolting against the crown, the ransoming of captives, as insurance against death or the permanence of capture, reduced the variable cost recruiting soldiers for war.

It may be no accident, then, that a technology first mentioned in ninth-century China, was not mentioned in Europe until 1267 (Hoffman 2015, p. 80), following the abolition of slave-taking. According to Hoffman (2015), innovations began during the Hundred Years' War, when:

> the armies of French King Charles VII (1422–1461) developed a highly effective artillery service ... that help[s] drive the English out of the stronghold they had occupied in France ... Afterward, or at the very end, the French also adopted better gunpowder and began using cast iron cannon balls and gun carriages that could hold artillery when it was fired, so that it did not have to be removed and placed on the ground or on a separate mount. (p. 39)

WAS PATTERSON RIGHT?

What is left of Patterson's hypothesis that (1) the tripartite norm he calls Western freedom emerged in the Greco-Roman world, and (2) the norm was preserved in the Pauline doctrine of Christianity? John

Francis Maxwell (1975) in *Slavery and the Catholic Church: The History of Catholic Teachings Concerning the Moral Legitimacy of the Institution of Slavery*, discusses a number of Church documents that address this issue. Maxwell indicates that the early Catholic Church adopted, from the Old Testament, case laws (that were conditional statements of the truth), rather than statutory law from the Torah (that were absolute), in order to justify the morality of slavery in certain circumstances. The Catholic Church also supported the curse of Ham myth until at least 1873. The idea of Church infallibility and its need to dismiss the Enlightenment explains why the Catholic Church waited until 1965 to condemn slavery.

However, in support of Patterson's hypothesis, *jus gentium* (Latin for the law of nations) was a concept of international law within the Roman system, not statutes or codes, but customary law held in common by all *gentes* (peoples or nations). *Jus gentium* contains references that support Patterson's claim that the idea of freedom as a human right emerged in the Greco-Roman world, phrases like "freedom is an expression of the natural law, the civil law introduced ownership"; "slavery is an institution of the *jus gentium*, by which one human being is subjected to the ownership of another, contrary to nature"; and "under the civil law, slaves are reckoned as non-persons, but not so under the natural law, because as far as the natural law is concerned, all men are equal" (quoted in Maxwell 1975, p. 27).

In the university and Church debates that followed the Papal Revolution, the customary laws of Europe, often unwritten and long-standing normative practices of peoples (like *jus gentium*), carried less weight than written civil codes and statutes (Berman 1983). There is no evidence that *jus gentium* had much influence on Western canon or secular legal traditions, except during the sixteenth and seventeenth centuries when the ideas were used to justify "social death" and the enslavement of war captives as a just alternative to killing them (Maxwell 1975, p. 80; Yamauchi 1994). Still, the customary laws in *jus gentium* support Patterson's claim that freedom norms emerged in the Greco-Roman world.

Second, the Pauline metaphor transformed places of worship into social spaces where slaves and free people co-mingled and interacted. Slaves, along with free people and freed people, interacted socially and personally, received communion together, and were baptized and married together in churches throughout Europe. According to Bonnassie (1991):

> They knew each other; they learned to regard themselves as Christians, that is as men and women. It is hardly surprising, therefore, that mixed unions, however severely punished by the law, happened. There is evidence of them as early as the seventh century … encouraging a solidarity of the wretched … The consensus necessary to the maintenance of the slave system was thus undermined at two levels: the free poor ceased to see slaves as the chattel they were designated as by the rich and forbidden to frequent by the law; the slaves found in the sacraments which they received the justification for their aspiration to the human condition and, in consequence, to liberty. (pp. 31–32)

Third, while the ideas in *jus gentium* were not incorporated into Western legal traditions, the Catholic Church did change its attitude toward slavery and placed its moral weight behind its abolition, but only among European Christians. According to Berman (1983, p. 320):

> As a result of the Papal Revolution the church for the first time gave a systematic legal formulation of its views on slavery. It took the position that slavery itself was not illegal but that it was a sin for a Christian to hold a Christian as a slave … Canon lawyers unanimously agreed that slavery was contrary to natural law, although there was also general agreement that it was lawful under positive law. (Footnote 6, p. 320)

This is the effective, normative abolition of slavery within European Christendom and coincides with (1) the Papal Revolution and the rising secular effectiveness of the medieval Catholic Church; (2) the application of *jus gentium* to Christians, and the emergence of "freedom from slavery" as a universal social norm in Western Christendom; and (3) the formulation of a Western legal tradition, rule of law, and the spread of voluntary corporate organizations that reduced transaction costs. In other words, the European side of the mirror image.

Berman (1983) explains why *jus gentium* did not inform the new mercantile contract laws of Europe, including contract laws concerning the trading of enslaved people:

> Indeed, it was the *jus gentium*, the (customary) "law of nations," applicable to those who were not Roman citizens, that governed most types of commercial transactions within the Roman Empire, especially those involving carriage of goods over long distances ... It is characteristic of the time, however, that the initial developments of mercantile law were left largely, though not entirely, to the merchants themselves, who organized international fairs and markets, formed mercantile courts, and established mercantile offices in the new urban communities that were springing up throughout western Europe. (pp. 339–40)

Individualistic merchants would self-order the new laws and institutions of trade, along the lines emphasized by Greif (2006), van Zanden (2009), Henrich (2020), and others. In a sense, Patterson is right. The idea of freedom as a natural right was born in the Greco-Roman world (*jus gentium*), and the Catholic Church normalized freedom from slavery in Christendom.

THE SLAVE TRADE AS CRITIQUE OF EUROCENTRISM

Does this mean the explanation I propose is Eurocentric? Are the mirror images of Africa and Europe driven primarily by Christendom and how it unleashed freedom dividends in Western Europe? Previous efforts along these lines often resort to what J. M. Blaut calls Eurocentric explanations of a "European miracle" of one sort or another, and this sure sounds like one.[6] But it is not.

In his 1993 book *The Colonizer's Model of the World: Geographical Diffusionism and Eurocentric History*, Blaut begins, in his combative, critical, and straightforward manner:

> The most important tenet of diffusionism is the theory of the "autonomous rise of Europe," sometimes (rather more grandly) called the idea of the "European miracle." It is the idea that Europe was more advanced and more progressive than all other regions prior to 1492, prior, that is to the beginning of the period of colonialism, the period in which Europe and non-Europe came into intense interaction. If one believes this to be the case – and most modern scholars seem to

> believe it to be the case – then it must follow that the economic and social modernization of Europe is fundamentally the result of Europe's internal qualities, not of interactions with the societies of Africa, Asia, and America after 1492 ... Therefore, colonialism must mean, for the Africans, Asians, and Americans, not spoliation and cultural destruction but, rather, the receipt – by diffusion – of European civilization: modernization. (p. 1)

According to Blaut, there are two tenets to a Eurocentric argument. First, the European miracle – the view that the origins of the European side of the mirror image are found in Europe alone, especially its freedoms and economic development. On this, no one escaped Blaut's sharp pen. In *Eight Eurocentric Historians*, Blaut (2000) dissects the arguments of eight of the most influential historians of Europe – Max Weber, Lynn White, Robert Brenner, Eric Jones, Michael Mann, John Hall, Jared Diamond, and David Landes – finding them all to be Eurocentric because they all locate the origins of the European side of the ledger in Europe's isolation from the rest of the world.

One need not agree with all of Blaut's criticism (and I do not) to accept that Eurocentrism is still the dominant view of world history, notwithstanding the research that followed the seminal article by Acemoglu, Johnson, and Robinson, "The Colonial Origins of Comparative Development: An Empirical Investigation" (2001). I am surprised Blaut does not include Orlando Patterson in his list. Patterson's argument is more Eurocentric than most. I could add to the list most modern economic historians, including Douglas North (1971, 2009), Greg Clark (2007), Oded Galor (2022), Joseph Henrich (2020), Dierdre McCloskey (2010), and Joel Mokyr (2017), among others. Some of these authors pay lip service to the contributions of colonial trade, plunder, and slavery, but none attach much weight to it.

The most recent work critiqued by Blaut, and the most influential today, is the ecological argument of Jared Diamond (1997). Diamond argues that the continent of Eurasia, the largest landmass on earth, was ecologically blessed with abundant domesticable species of plants and animals. In addition, the continent happened to run along a dominant east–west axis that facilitated the diffusion of knowledge, technology, and culture along ecologically similar latitudes. Diamond's fundamentals of world economic development up to 1492 explain why Eurasia conquered the world and was not itself conquered.

Today, no credible history of the world can ignore Diamond's perspective. One of the reasons for the immense and enduring popularity of *Guns, Germs, and Steel* is the relief readers get when Diamond locates the European miracle in the blessing of geography. There is no appeal to cultural explanations, like the structure of the European family or Western notions of freedom. There is no appeal to the Protestant ethic as a source of personal discipline, literacy, or work's redeeming value. There was no appeal to Malthusian population dynamics, where Europeans escaped the Malthusian poverty trap by controlling population growth while others did not. And no appeal to racial superiority or inferiority. In Diamond's view, the European miracle is a fate dealt by geography and ecology.

Much of Diamond's argument has survived empirical scrutiny, but it only applies to long-term development measured as "time since agriculture," as if we know where and when that happened. The race is from there to 1492. In *The Dawn of Everything* (2021), Graeber and Wengrow argue that no such agricultural "revolution" took place. Instead, societies bumped along through trial and error, yes and no, until some, but not all, chose, or were forced, to commit to a sedentary way of life. Domestication is undoubtedly an essential step in the growth of human population. Stationary bandits have better chances of survival and providing public goods to ensure the elites' survival (Olson 1993), but adopting a sedentary position against roving bandits increases the risks of predation, war, disease, and famine. In settling down to domesticate plants and animals, humans also domesticated themselves, for better or for worse.

There is still much debate about why humans domesticated themselves, where and when. A tension exists in this literature between the "choice" to settle down (Weisdorf 2005) and being forced to settle down by occupying kings and elites (Graeber and Sahlins 2017; Mayshar, Moav, and Pascali 2022). That debate need not detain us. An agricultural way of life that produces a surplus to support urban centers and trade is, at most, a *necessary* condition for modern economic growth. It is not a *sufficient* condition. Even the most cursory view of world history finds farmers and cities all over the map. Recent efforts to identify and document the sufficient conditions for the European side of the ledger are still Eurocentric at their core.[7]

The second tenet of the *Colonizers' Model of the World* is that the rest of the world modernizes as the European miracle diffuses worldwide after 1492. This tenet applies directly to the African side of our ledger, typically referred to as precolonial Africa – before the twentieth-century diffusion of Western norms and institutions via colonial occupation. According to Blaut, Eurocentric explanations for the underdevelopment of precolonial Africa appeal to African norms and "traditions" that predate European contact. The dominant view is still the Nieboer–Domar view of land abundance.

Enter the transatlantic slave trade as a critique of both tenets of the Eurocentric view – the European miracle and the colonizer's model. Blaut notes that the critique of Eurocentrism originated with colonial subjects, mainly African-American critics of both tenets of the Eurocentric argument:

> One can trace the origins of this critique to early writings by a small number of historians, most of them colonial subjects, often writing in exile … among them W. E. B. Du Bois, C. L. R. James, George Padmore, and Eric Williams … Williams' works ultimately had the strongest impact on Eurocentric history. It showed that the wealth from slavery and the slave plantation had been the crucial factor in the amassing of capital for the Industrial Revolution in England … and a sizable literature has grown up amongst European historians arguing about, and generally trying to counter, what is now generally called "the Williams thesis."

Much has been written for and against the Williams thesis, and the outpouring continues to grow. The arguments and the evidence, with Great Britain being the modal example, range from slavery playing no role,[8] to it playing a negligible role,[9] to it playing a significant role.[10] Recently, the debate has been rejuvenated by what Gavin Wright (2020, p. 2) calls "insurgent scholars known as New Historians of Capitalism," who argue that slavery and slave trading were critical for the Industrial Revolution in England and nineteenth-century economic expansion in the

United States.[11] The renewed interest is a welcome departure from the focus on static ratios like labor productivity, investment rates, and sectoral compositions (Darity 1992). Historians take a broader view than economic historians because the transatlantic slave trade and American slavery were felt everywhere in the eighteenth century. Their contributions have generated a number of responses, primarily from economic historians of the Cotton South, and for a variety of reasons.[12]

Spoiler alert: It is no longer possible to argue that slavery and the slave trade were not "critical factors in amassing the capital for the Industrial Revolution." Wright (2006, 2020) documents how the eighteenth-century Anglo-American trade and American slavery drove British mercantile growth and how British mercantile growth drove growth in British national income. Even early innovations in the British textile industry were driven by international competition with Indian textiles for the growing African slave trade (Broadberry and Bishnupriya 2009). Berg and Hudson (2023) marshal an enormous amount of evidence showing how American slavery contributed to everything from the revolution in European consumption patterns, textile production, financial capitalism, Atlantic science, the development of ports and their hinterlands, and the British Industrial Revolution.

A recent paper by Heblich, Redding, and Voth (2022) presents econometric evidence showing how, by 1830, the wealth of British slaveholders had influenced the location of British industrial activity – every thing from the percentage of local labor in the industrial sector, the adoption of steam power, and the location of cotton mills – all hallmarks of the Industrial Revolution. Even the Dutch, who pioneered capitalism as early as 1300, had to feed it with the products of slaves. According to Prak and van Zanden (2023), in 1650 slavery accounted for approximately 6.8 percent of the labor force of "greater Holland," meaning Holland, Surinam, the Cape Colony and the remaining Dutch East India Company domains. By 1770, the percentage was 24 percent (p. 181). If the freedom dividends of Western Europe had not been fed by slavery they could very well have died out.

A different but related critique of the European miracle is what economists and historians now call the Great Divergence between Western and Eastern Eurasia. Andre Gunder Frank's *ReOrient: Global Economy in the*

Asian Age (1998) is a self-conscious critique of the Eurocentric argument, where he notes that before 1492 Europe ran a chronic trade deficit with Asian economies, primarily China and India, because Asian economies were more advanced. Silver flowed from Europe to Asia, the "silver sink," to cover the trade deficit. According to Ward Barrett, even as late as "the 17th and 18th centuries, about 70 percent of the American production of silver arrived in Europe, and 40 percent of that was shipped to Asia" (p. 143).

In 2000, Kenneth Pomerantz published *The Great Divergence: China, Europe, and the Making of the Modern World Economy,* arguing that as late as 1750, East Asian development was comparable to, if not better than, Europe's in terms of life expectancy, consumption, and the extent of markets. The "Great Divergence" came after 1750 (some now date the divergence earlier) because European economies had vastly superior reserves of coal to power an industrial revolution, and because they had access to a growing transatlantic trade with the Americas, where they secured raw materials like cotton in return for manufactured exports like textiles. There is now a literature on divergences everywhere, even studies documenting "little divergences" among European economies. One gets the impression that studies today think they escape the charge of being Eurocentric if they can explain why Western Europe differed from China, and often without explaining why they think that.

Again, consider the contributions of the transatlantic slave trade and American slavery. Could the Triangular Trade of the seventeenth and eighteenth centuries explain why the economies of Western Eurasia leaped ahead of those in Eastern Eurasia for several centuries, a lead that is rapidly diminishing today? And could the enduring legacies of racial divisions that plague Western democracies be a price paid for this lead? Slavery and slave wealth impacted every aspect of the seventeenth and eighteenth-century Atlantic world. As such, it is impossible to explain the Great Divergence without considering the transatlantic slave trade.

As for the second tenet of Eurocentrism – that the African side of the ledger consists of African traditions that predate colonial diffusion – our attention shifts to demonstrating the impact of the transatlantic slave trade on Africa.

FROM FREEDOM TO SLAVERY OUTSIDE CHRISTENDOM

By 1300, freedom from slavery was a firmly established social norm in Christendom – by custom, not by law. By law, slavery was still legal and a protected property right, just sinful among European Christians. Nations could establish slave colonies offshore and feed the freedom dividends at home through trade. This is how one should read the discussion in Eltis (2000) where he argues that it was cheaper to transport slaves from Europe than from Africa (pp. 59–84). Once "Christendom" replaces "Europe" the barriers become obvious.

Almost laughable is an encounter in 1640 Barbados, where an enslaved African-American guide assigned to an English traveler believes the magic of the traveler's compass was because he was Christian. Having asked the traveler to request his master make him a Christian, the master replies (and I paraphrase), "Oh, no, no, no. By the laws of England, we cannot make a Christian a slave," to which the traveler replies, "But I am asking you to make a slave a Christian, not a Christian a slave," to which the master replies, "Oh, no, no, no. I would then have to free him, and all the other planters would curse me" (Ligon 2011, pp. 100–1).

Now that is a slave culture! How the transition from sin enforcing freedom among Christians to planters enforcing slavery among African Americans? According to Maxwell, "By the 12th century, it had become a custom of war in Christendom that the right to enslave only applied to unbaptized prisoners – in practice only to Moslems" (Maxwell 1975: 45). The custom continued to guide policy during the fifteenth-century expansion into the Atlantic. The Papacy threatened to excommunicate Christians who enslaved the inhabitants of the Canary Islands (in 1433, 1435, and 1476) because the prisoners were not Saracens, and Christians were only at war with Muslim Saracens (Maxwell 1975, p. 52). In the Americas, the justification for the enslavement of Indigenous peoples was cannibalism or resistance to conversion, but missionaries complained that enslaving Native Americans created hostilities that reduced the probability of converting them, so protections against enslavement improved.

At the very same time, Christendom explorers were moving down the west coast of Africa. Between 1452 and 1514, the Pope gave the kings of Portugal authority to enslave Saracens and other non-Christians at war with Christendom. During the first generation of exploration, this policy was probably applied without much discussion. Christendom had encountered Muslims all along the coast of Africa while searching for a sea route around the enemy (Thomas 1997, pp. 48–67). When innovations in the lateen sail allowed Portuguese sailors to tack into the wind and explore beyond Cape Blanc into regions south of the Sahara Desert, they continued to encountered Muslims as far south as the Senegal and Gambia river systems. The Muslim Empire of Mali in the western Sudan of Africa was well known in Christian and Muslim worlds. Emperor Mansa Musa established as much during his lavish pilgrimage to Mecca in 1324 (Gomez 2008, pp. 92–143).

By 1550, however, Portuguese explorers were enslaving Africans along the Lower Guinea Coast, and these were clearly not Muslims. Between 1550 and 1571, the issue was debated within the Papacy. Why are African captives enslaved and not Native Americans? Africans do not wage war against Christians, and their conversion to Christianity is easier (Maxwell 1975, pp. 66–68). The difference in policy could have been racism – that African pagans were considered a different category of humans to be denied admission to Christendom. Alternatively, the difference could have stemmed from the scarcity of Christian missionaries in Africa agitating against enslavement. Probably both. It was not until the nineteenth century that the Catholic Church condemned the African slave trade, and because of the suffering of enslaved people in Africa, not the Americas.

In the sixteenth and seventeenth centuries, legal scholars debated justifications for enslavement in hypothetical cases, where both parties were non-Christian, and both sides enslaved their captives. In theory, both sides could not be just. Legal scholars began to argue that in this case, *jus gentium* permitted enslavement as a means of saving prisoners from massacre – that enslavement was a just act even when the wars were not. Legal title to slave wealth was thereby secured (Maxwell 1975, p. 80; Yamauchi 1994). Christendom would have the best of both worlds – freedom dividends at home fed by commodities produced offshore by African-American slaves.

CHAPTER 5

African Development before the Transatlantic Slave Trade

THE POPULATION QUESTION

By now, you must be asking, "Why Africa?" Why did sub-Saharan Africa become the hunting ground for the enslaved people of Eurasian empires? In the medieval world, sub-Saharan Africa was the southern catchment frontier of the two monotheistic no-slave zones, down its east coast by sea and across the Sahara Desert by camel. By the middle of the fifteenth century, lateen sails enabled Portuguese caravels to sail down the west coast as well. The real question is why were sub-Saharan Africans vulnerable? Jared Diamond's influential book *Guns, Germs, and Steel: The Fates of Human Society* (1997) emphasizes ecological and environmental factors. Alternative explanations emphasize a tradition of slavery in Africa, and how it encouraged slave capture and export. The two are not mutually exclusive. Ecology can impact the evolution and spread of norms and institutions. But did it in this case?

The question typically brings us back to the question of population scarcity in Africa (or land abundance). Did it encourage the spread of slavery in Africa? By the late nineteenth century Africa was a low-population place compared to Western Europe (Kuczynski 1948, 1949), but we really do not know the population of Africa in 1500, or even 1800 (Guinnane 2023). Development economists have relied on a little book by McEvedy and Jones entitled *The Atlas of Population* (1978), which pretty much says, and I paraphrase, "We know something about the recent population histories of Western Europe and its offshoots, but we know very little about any other place, and least of all Africa." These "data" have been foundational in empirical tests of Malthusian-inspired endogenous growth models.[1] When they are run against estimates of exposure to international slave trades, the slave trades are found to have reduced the growth rate of the African population by three-quarters of a percentage point (Price and Whatley 2023) and predict populations in 1900 that are almost identical to those back-casted from more reliable 1950 and 1960 census counts.[2] Manning (1990) concludes, from simulations, that the counterfactual African population would have been "double that which actually lived in 1850" (p. 85).

Also inconclusive is one of the few efforts to estimate early African population from actual historical documents – Thornton's counts for seventeenth-century Kongo (1977). Between circa 1650 to 1700, Catholic priests recorded the number of unbaptized newborns between their visits to missions and villages. Thornton uses linear interpolations of life table models (Cole and Demeny 1966) that estimate a total Kongo population of 530,000 people and densities as high as forty-nine people per square kilometer in the capital and its environs, declining as one moves away from the capital (pp. 520–21). But even these population estimates include the effects of the slave trades. The Kongo kingdom was among the first to be destabilized by the transatlantic slave trade, disrupting the kingdom to the point where the king requested Portugal stop buying slaves in the area (Thornton 1983; Heywood 2009). In addition, Thornton's 530,000 population figure for 1700 (the Catholics estimated two million) implies a remarkable population growth rate of 2 percent per decade to reach the 1.4 million census count for 1948, suggesting that the Kongo kingdom, the largest exporter of slaves in all of Africa, did not suffer a population decline or even a slowing of population growth after 1700.[3] The Catholic missions' estimate of two million people was probably closer to the truth.

This is not much evidence for or against land abundance (or low-population density) as a long-term feature of Africa's past. Nonetheless, the assumption has played an outsized role in conceptualizing precolonial Africa. In addition to the theoretical arguments of Nieboer (1900), Domar (1970), and Hopkins (1973) about African slavery, Iliffe (2007) argues that African polygyny can be understood as a population growth strategy that matches females with wealthy men in order to increase the survival of offspring and grow a kinship-based population bound to location (pp. 96–103). Herbst (2000) argues that land abundance weakened state capacity because it increased the cost of broadcasting political authority over geographically dispersed people. More recently, Austin (2008) has amended the idea to include the cost of clearing land, and Fenske (2012) presents evidence that tighter land markets among the Egba of Nigeria reduced the frequency of overlapping property rights.

Africa, is a big continent. Variations in population density across time and place could be enormous, as could be the social and economic causes and consequences. Reducing the continent to a few noisy measures of population density could do more harm than good, especially if we are trying to understand how the environment of such a large land mass influenced uneven development and institutional choice.

THE FLY IN THE OINTMENT

On the other hand, the migration of human populations "out of Africa" is now a generally accepted fact of human history. While the details are by no means settled, genetics, archeology, and climatology tell a compelling story about how homo sapiens migrated out of Africa some 50–75,000 years ago and populated the world. Our concern here is not with the details of this story but with its implication for African population history. If sub-Saharan Africans could populate the world, why not Africa?

The likely answer, if not the whole answer, is that the sub-Saharan environment was a challenging place to grow people. Ecological and environmental factors seem to predict a widening economic gap between Africa and Eurasia, as well as regional inequality within Africa. I am referring to the ecological and environmental factors suggested by Diamond (1997) and Alsan (2015). Eurasian ecology was conducive to the adoption and spread of plow-based agriculture, Africa's was not. The main culprit is the tsetse fly, an insect that imposed severe constraints on the size of domesticated animal herds.

Map 5.1 shows the location of plow cultivation in Africa, taken from the *Ethnographic Atlas*, circa 1900. Unless Africa lost knowledge of plow technology, and there is no evidence that it did, then the plow never diffused widely in Africa before the twentieth century, confined primarily

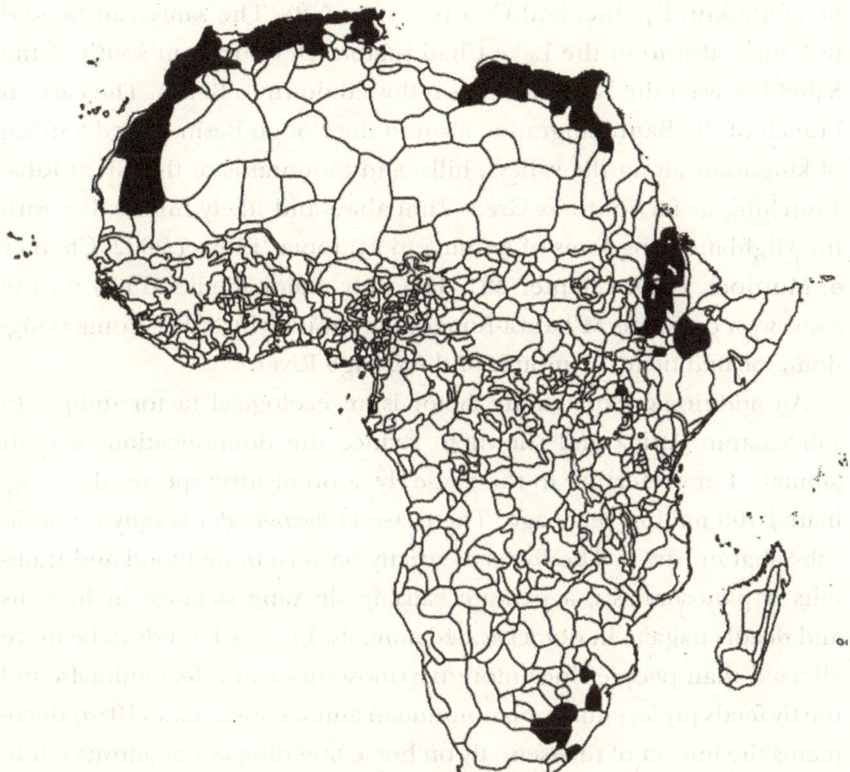

Map 5.1 The plow in Africa. Data source: The *Ethnographic Atlas*.

to the North African littoral, the Ethiopian Highlands, and the Southeast Plateau. The question is, why?

Diamond (1997) emphasizes three global ecological factors: the size of the continents, the dominant continental axis, and the endowments of indigenous plants and animals. Eurasia tops all three lists. Subsequent empirical tests tend to confirm the broad outlines of Diamond's thesis.[4] By contrast, Africa's dominant axis runs north–south, not east–west, with a slight counterclockwise rotation, running across the latitudes not with them. The broadest and longest east–west ecological band is the Sahara Desert, not a likely environment for agricultural innovations (see map 8.1). The medieval Sudanese empires of Ghana and Mali were located in the thin east–west latitude of the savannah between the desert and the rainforest, as were the medieval cities of Timbuktu, Djenne, and Gao (see map 5.2). The same can be said of Kamen-Borno in the Lake Chad region. Development south of the Sahel followed the Niger River as it flowed down to Benin. The eastern branch of the Bantu migration around the Congo Basin carved a string of kingdoms along the valleys, hills, and mountains of the Great Rifts, stretching as far south as Great Zimbabwe and likely interacting with the Highland Kingdoms of Axum and Ethiopia (Ehhret 2002, Chapter 4; Murdock 1959, Chapter 38). The only major medieval city on the southwest coast was M'banza-Kongo, the capital city of the Kongo kingdom, located near the mouth of the Congo River.

An additional explanatory factor is an ecological factor unique to sub-Saharan Africa and shown to reduce the domestication of draft animals. I am referring to the tsetse fly, a prehistoric species that originated 100 million years ago. The tsetse (*Glossina ssp.*) is only found in sub-Saharan Africa. The fly feeds strictly on vertebrate blood and transmits trypanosomiasis, a parasite causing sleeping sickness in humans and deadly nagana in domesticated animals. Livestock tends to be more affected than people since more trypanosomes can infect animals, and the fly feeds preferentially on nonhuman animal hosts. Law (1980) documents the impact of the tsetse fly on horse breeding as one moves southward from the savannah into the forest. The annual migrations of cattle herders in the savannah were influenced by the seasonality of tsetse fly proliferation, as was the timing of eighteenth-century annual incursions of Oyo cavalry down the Benin Gap to attack Dahomey.

Blaut (1993, pp. 80–81), while not denying the devastating effects of the tsetse fly, attributes its spread to ecological disruptions caused by land clearing and settlement, suggesting that the spread of the fly followed colonial occupation after 1890. There is some truth to this, but not the whole truth. Giblin (1990), whom Blaut cites, believes the tsetse fly always had devastating effects on bovine and human populations but that indigenous populations found ways to reduce the impact by managing low levels of mammal hosts and fly vectors. According to Giblin (1990, pp. 70–73), "Given the prevalence of tsetse, avoidance of vector would have been impossible. Cattle were kept in areas where intensive trypanosomal challenge could be prevented, but these locations were not extensive, and the precolonial cattle population was small ... Between the pockets of the concentrated population was uninhabited woodlands where *Glossina* and wild mammalian hosts throve."

The type of landcover Giblin is describing is called mosaic, agricultural land carved out of forest, a widespread type of landcover in Africa (see chapter 8). The key to adapting to the fly was managing a low level of exposure as a way of maintaining a low level of resistance – like "maintaining isolated thickets and woods where bushpigs rested during the daytime and whose nocturnal foraging exposed people"; or from people who entered the woods during the dry season as "travelers, hunters, gatherers of honey, and collectors of firewood and construction materials" (Giblin 1990, p. 73). Livingstone (1858) mentions losing many of the cattle he brought with him from the Southern Cape because they "rushed along to the water ... probably crossed a small patch of trees containing tsetse, an insect which was shortly to become a perfect pest to us" (p. 93). Locals managed to keep small herds of goats and mules, but Livingstone lost forty-three fine oxen he brought into the fly zone "from the slightest bite" (Livingstone 1858, p. 95).

The low-infection/small-herd equilibrium was also an unstable one. The "capacity for resistance in cattle can be defeated by heavy infection, and the resistance depends upon regular exposure (Giblin 1990, p. 65)." Livingstone (1858, pp. 92–97) observed that inoculation did not ensure immunity. Animals lightly bitten one year could perish by a more significant number of bites the next. Even King Sebituane lost much of his herd during a stormy year. As Blaut argues, the unstable equilibrium was indeed disturbed by colonial policies and population migrations after the 1890s, but the fly was always a severe constraint on animal draft power, agricultural productivity, and population growth.

Think of the fly as an exogenous ecological factor unique to sub-Saharan Africa with variation across space. The tsetse fly predates any conceivable agricultural revolution and existed long before the arrival of the first Bantu farmers. Documenting adaptations to the tsetse fly tell us a great deal about the long-term evolution of norms and institutions in fly-infested regions. Poverty is a given compared to fly-free zones. It is the fly in the ointment of any other telling of long-term sub-Saharan African development.

It was not until Alsan (2015) developed the tsetse fly suitability index (TSI) that researchers had a measure of potential fly infestation that was independent of seasonality, human interaction, or field experiment. "Using insect population growth models, gridded climate data, and geospatial software, the *potential* steady-state tsetse population can be calculated" (Alsan 2015, pp. 383–84, emphasis added). Alsan finds that "a one standard deviation increase in the TSI is associated with a 23-percentage point decrease in the likelihood an African ethnic group had large domesticated animals" (p. 384).

This does not explain everything, but it is the beginning. Plow-based agriculture helps explain why European populations grew more rapidly between 1200 and 1500. The classic analysis is White (1962), where the adoption of the heavy plow, three-field rotation, and the modern harness combined to create an era of peasant prosperity stretching across northern Europe. According to Maddison (2003, p. 33), Western Europe's population more than doubled, while Africa's grew by only 40 percent. In Malthusian-inspired endogenous growth models, population and technological innovation influence each other endogenously, feeding each other to increase both (Galor 2022; Kremer 1993).

THE PLOW IN AFRICA

The tsetse fly is an important factor in that it reduced the availability of animal power, but the fly was not universal. According to Gebregziabher et al. (2006), Ethiopia used a local lightweight plow called the *ard* for thousands of year. The Dutch introduced the ox-driven plow into temperate South Africa in the 1600, and European missionaries began introducing the plow in the 1920s. What was nearly universal was the serious risk of soil erosion. According to El-Swaify, Dangler, and Armstrong (1982), "the vast majority of tropical Africa lies within the high-risk class of sediment removal rates" (p. 14), not because of soil type but because of the weathering effects of tropical downpour and soil runoff, what they call the "erosivity of rainstorms" (p. 13).

South Africa, on the other hand, is in a temperate zone, void of the fly and tropical downpour. Phylogenetic analyses of more than 500 related Bantu languages have been able to trace Bantu migration paths across Africa, and find that the rainforest slowed migration toward the Southern Cape by more than 300 years (Currie et al. 2013;

Grollemund et al. 2015). Not that earlier arrival would have repelled the Dutch, but it is not inconceivable that it would have generated innovations in an indigenous Bantu plow.

The Ethiopian case is instructive too. Being in the highland, it is relatively free of the tsetse fly, but extremely susceptible to soil erosion. According to El-Swaify, Dangler, and Armstrong (1982):

> The Amhara Plateau – the part of East Africa in the Highlands that constitutes most of Ethiopia – may be mistakenly called a plateau. Although it rises abruptly to nearly 2000 m above the surrounding arid plains, included within this plateau are mountains that rise above 4500 m, as well as steep gorges and valleys that constitute one of the most erosive prone areas on earth. From here, the legendary, reliable removal of silt by the Blue Nile and other major tributaries occurs annually, for ultimate deposition on the floodplain of the Nile (pp. 23–24) ... Erosion has always provided massive quantities of sediment, even under ancient (undisturbed) conditions when the vast majority of the plateau was in forest. (p. 25)

Yet Ethiopians developed a plow-based agriculture suitable to its environment – the lightweight *ard* that carefully turned the topsoil, often requiring several passes. According to Gebregziabher et al. (2006), in typical colonizer fashion, "in 1939, Italians introduced a steel moldboard plow at the smallholder level, which was unsuccessful because of its heavy weight ... and the higher power requirements than that of the Ethiopia *ard*" (p. 134). The 1980s brought renewed interest in animal traction, after a series of failed attempts to diffuse tractors, but researchers again discovered that the "modern plow draft requirements did not correspond to the draft capacity of the domestic animals" (p. 131). Trials then began to study ways to improve the indigenous Ethiopian technology.

POPULATION DENSITY AND AFRICAN SLAVERY

Does low agricultural productivity imply that African slavery was widespread before the coming of Eurasian empires, facilitating a supply response that attracted further incursions from Eurasia? Did enslaved human power replace animal power? Again, this is a difficult question to answer because the historical record is so thin. Pre-existing Arabic documents contain observations of slavery in the medieval Muslim empires along the Sahel but very little evidence of African slavery before Muslim incursions. Rare discoveries, like the Coptic papyrus rolls excavated in Egypt ahead of the rising waters of the Aswan Dam, offer a glimpse into the Nile Valley of 758 AD (Fauvelle 2013). The Christian Nubian Kingdom of Nobadia, whose capital city of Dongola lay between the third and fourth cataracts of the River Nile (see Map 5.2), had trouble supplying the annual tribute of 360 slaves to Islamic Egypt. The tribute was a condition of its *baqt* treaty with Egypt. In 827 AD, Nobadia sent a prince to the caliph in Baghdad seeking to renegotiate the pact, to reduce the tribute, and to eliminate the arrears (Fauvelle 2013, pp. 28–35).

We also know that Portuguese traders in the fifteenth century had difficulty exchanging European goods for African gold and eventually intercepted a trade in war captives between Benin and the Gold Coast. Ryder (1969) does not describe Benin as a slave economy or that slavery was widespread in the region (pp. 1–65). The year 1440 began the era of Ewuare the Great and Benin's geopolitical expansion (Egharevba 1968, pp. 13–17). The war captives were apparently sold down the coast. By 1516, Benin placed a total embargo on the sale of male slaves to the Portuguese, an embargo that lasted until the close of the seventeenth century. The Kingdoms of Benin and Kongo collapsed under the weight of the transatlantic slave trade, and long before the eighteenth-century explosion, so we can assume, like Nobadia, they lacked the capacity, means, or desire to meet early demands. There is no documented evidence of slavery in the region of Great Zimbabwe. The Zulu were able to centralize their political system without slavery.

That is not to say there was no indigenous slavery in Africa before the coming of Muslim and Christian slave trades, just that there is not much evidence for or against slavery in Africa's distant past (Nwokeji 2011). Can the TSI help? Alsan (2015) finds that by the dawn of the twentieth century, "a one standard deviation increase in the TSI is associated with a 10-percentage point increase in the likelihood that an ethnic group used slaves" (p. 84). However, when placed within the context of the international slave trades, it only appears that the tsetse fly increased African slavery.

Table 5.1 The effects of the tsetse fly on the mirror image

	(1)	(2)	(3)
VARIABLES	Polygyny	Centralization	Slavery
Tsetse fly exposure, circa 1900	0.334***	-0.289***	0.387***
	(0.092)	(0.080)	(0.109)
Tsetse fly exposure, before exposure to slave trades	0.591***	-0.092	0.250
	(0.201)	(0.176)	(0.238)
CONTROLS	YES	YES	YES
Observations	376	382	340

Notes: Coefficients are the estimated coefficients from the probit specification. Robust standard errors are in parentheses. *** $p < 0.01$, ** $p < 0.05$, * $p < 0.1$. The dependent variables are from the *Ethnographic Atlas*. Centralization is "Large Chiefdom" and above. Slavery is "Never Slavery." Tsetse fly exposure, circa 1900, is the tsetse fly suitability index from Alsan (2015). Tsetse fly exposure, before exposure to slave trades removes the correlation between the tsetse fly suitability index and travel time to the nearest slave post (in days). Controls are regional indicators and observation date, taken from the *Ethnographic Atlas*.

The first row of Table 5.1 reports the results of probit regressions of slavery, polygyny, and political centralization on Alsan's tsetse fly suitability index, along with simple controls for broad regions of Africa (see Appendix Table A5.1 for the full table of regression coefficients). Since the TSI is lab-based and captures the ecological probability of fly infestation, it is independent of human presence or institutional choice. According to the first row of Table 5.1, at the dawn of the twentieth century, tsetse fly suitability increased polygyny and slavery and reduced political centralization, similar to the findings in Alsan (2015).

The second row, however, removes the correlation between the TSI and travel time to the nearest slave port (see Chapter 8 for a discussion of how travel time is calculated). Think of this coefficient as the impact of the TSI on institutional choices before the region was exposed to international slave trades. The TSI still predicts polygyny, but not slavery or political decentralization. Since the tsetse fly is ancient in origin, and the TSI is independent of human activity, the implication is that the exposure of tsetse fly zones to international slave trades encouraged the spread of slavery. Polygyny may be an institutional response to an ancient environmental constraint (the tsetse fly), but not slavery or political decentralization. To explain these two institutions, we need to consider the impact of exposure to international slave trades.

THE GOLDEN ALTERNATIVE

Gold was another environmental feature of Africa. Africans exported large quantities of gold long before they exported large numbers of slaves. Figure 5.1 reports available estimates of annual additions to the world's stock of gold between 1000 and 1800. Table 5.2 reports Africa's shares of the additions. In the sixteenth century, Africa added as much as the Americas. As late as the seventeenth century, Africa still contributed 22 percent of new world supplies. American production ramps up in the eighteenth century following discoveries of large deposits in Brazil. The Brazilian discoveries (mined, incidentally, by enslaved Africans from the Gold Coast) effectively priced African gold miners out of the international bullion market.

Table 5.2 World gold production, in tonnes

Years	World	Americas	Africa	Europe
1493–1600	714	280	255	148
1601–1700	900	590	200	100
1701–1800	1900	1620	170	108
Totals	3514	2490	625	356

Data source: Ward Barrett (1990).

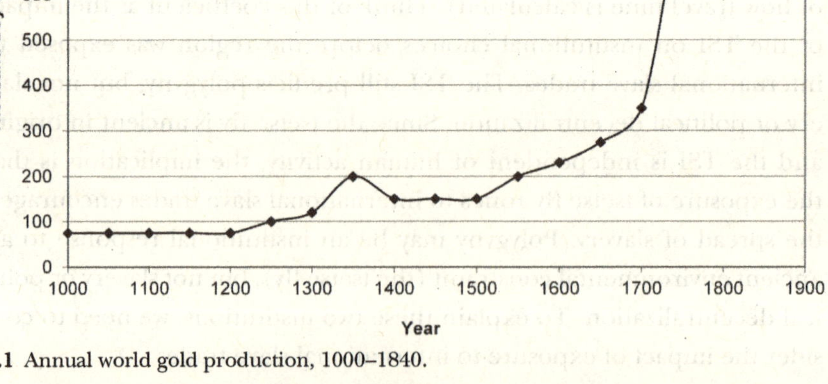

5.1 Annual world gold production, 1000–1840.

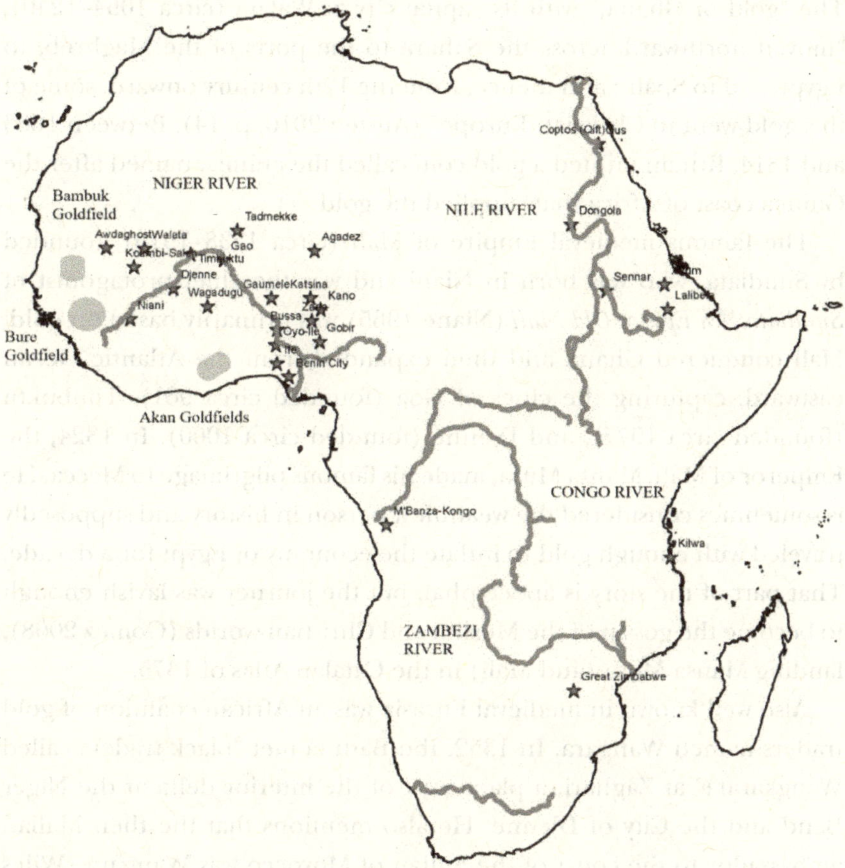

Map 5.2 The golden age of precolonial African economic development.

Changes in the value of gold had wide-ranging effects on African economies. It not only impacted the employment and earnings of miners, it also impacted money and financing. Gold as money circulated widely in medieval Africa. Map 5.2 marks the locations of major West African goldfields and major cities before 1500, cities taken primarily from Chandler and Fox (1974, pp. 196–216). The Bambuk and Bure gold fields were located northwest of the Niger River as it flowed northeastward toward the Sahara Desert. The Niger then turns southeastward toward the Niger Delta, a fact that alluded European explorers for centuries. These were the primary sources of European gold (Zimbabwe exported gold into the Indian Ocean). African empires jockeyed for control of this trade.

The "gold of Ghana," with its capital city at Walata (circa 1054–1240), "moved northward across the Sahara to the ports of the Maghreb, to Egypt, and to Spain; and thence, from the 12th century onward, some of this gold went to Christian Europe" (Austen 2010, p. 14). Between 1663 and 1814, Britain minted a gold coin called the guinea, named after the Guinea coast of Africa that supplied the gold.

The famous medieval Empire of Mali (circa 1238–1513), founded by Sundiata, who was born in Niani and was the chief protagonist of *Sundiata: An Epic of Old Mali* (Niane 1965) was primarily based on gold. Mali conquered Ghana and then expanded from the Atlantic Ocean eastward, capturing the cities of Goa (founded circa 961), Timbuktu (founded circa 1077), and Djenne (founded circa 1000). In 1324, the Emperor of Mali, Mansa Musa, made his famous pilgrimage to Mecca. He is sometimes considered the wealthiest person in history and supposedly traveled with enough gold to inflate the economy of Egypt for a decade. That part of the story is apocryphal, but the journey was lavish enough to become the gossip of the Muslim and Christian worlds (Gomez 2008), landing Mansa Musa (and Mali) in the Catalan Atlas of 1375.

Also well known in medieval Eurasia was an African coalition of gold traders named Wangara. In 1352, Ibn Battuta met "black traders called Wangkarata" at Zaghari, a place west of the interior delta at the Niger Bend and the City of Djenne. He also mentions that the then Malian ambassador to the court of the Sultan of Morocco was Wangara (Wilks 1982a, 1982b). Wangara were Malians who specialized in the management of long-distance commerce. The growth of the West African gold trade was closely tied to extensions in the range of their activities. They were the first link in the chain that reached from the producers of gold in West Africa to consumers in the Mediterranean Basin and beyond. Islamic maps sometimes depict the western Sudan north of the forest as Wangara.

Wangara collected and dispersed reliable information about far-off transactions. Honesty was a hallmark, strengthened by their religious faith and missionary zeal. Valentim Fernandes, a writer from Lisbon in the 1500s, states, "They trust each other, without receipts, without documents, without witnesses ... They are so honest that if one of them dies unexpectedly, his sons or his heirs rush at once to settle his debts very exactly" (quoted in Wilks 1982b). They functioned like the coalition of Maghribi traders (Greif 1989), and for similar reasons – asymmetric information, no formal court system, and the need for a mechanism to keep distant members honest. When entering a new area, they adopted pre-existing business practices and local trading patterns while maintaining their separate ethnic and religious identity. Once established as local merchants and missionaries, they introduced commercial innovations like credit, banking, and long-distance trade (Adekunle 1994; Lovejoy 1987). They were not averse to trading enslaved people or using slaves as porters in their caravans.

By the time the Portuguese arrived at the Gold Coast in 1471, Wangara traders were operating as far south as the Akan gold fields (Wilks 1982b). A major regional trading depot was the city of Begho on the northern outskirts of the forest, a city Wangara had colonized. Begho contained a large section for Wangara (the Kramo quarters), a section for artisans (Dwinfor), a section for the original inhabitants (Nyarko), and a section that served as the spiritual center of the town (Brong). Begho also integrated the Niger River and eastern Hausa trades. By 1350, Begho was a town of about 10,000 inhabitants. Iron slag mounds dating from 1100–1750 and other artifacts confirm Begho as a thriving center of manufacture and trade (Posnansky 1976).

Much of Begho's economic activity centered on the gold coming out of the Akan forest located just south of the city (Wilks 1961). Matrilineal Akan clans were expanding their agriculture enterprises into the forest areas, using the revenues from trans-Saharan gold exports to purchase the laborers they needed to clear the land, a vast undertaking that took 500 person-days to clear an acre of its 1,250 tons of vegetation (Wilks, 1993, pp. 51–66). Most of this labor power was slave labor imported by Wangara from the Muslim catchment zones in the north.

Portuguese gold traders then approached by sea, but initially had difficulty finding something to sell. In 1510, the governor of Elmina Castle complained about the quality of the cloth he was getting from Portugal, noting that the Akan preferred the Mandinka-supplied cloths from the north (Wilks 1982b). In 1513, they complained again, and maintained that a sufficient supply of slaves and other goods would seal "this Mandinga leak." Exploiting their new ocean-going technology, the

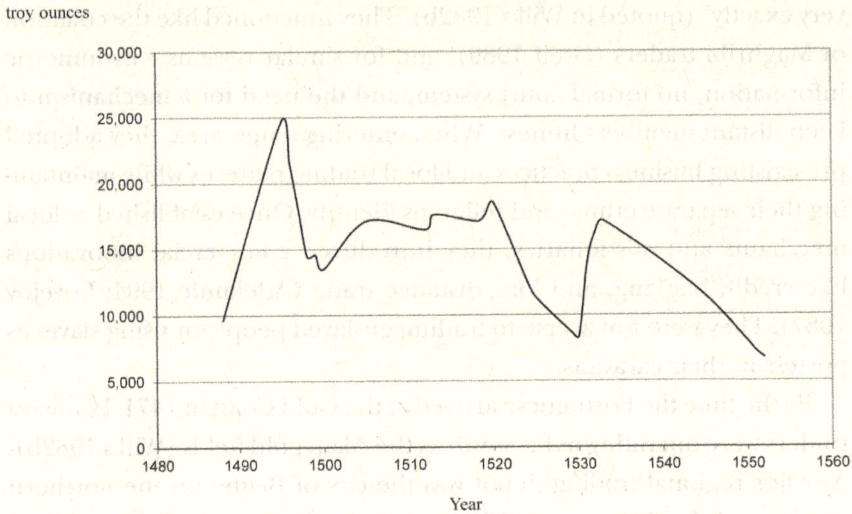

5.2 Early Portuguese gold exports from the Gold Coast, 1480–1560. Source: Ivor Wilks (1982b, pp. 463–72).

Portuguese were able to compete with the Mandinka trade by importing war captives from the expanding Benin Empire down the coast. After 1515 the new sailing technology allowed them to operate regional slave markets centered on the offshore islands of Sao Tome and Principe. Available figures on the Portuguese take are gross underestimates because they do not include smuggling, but they demonstrate the extent to which early Portuguese traders intercepted some of the trans-Saharan gold trade by trading in slaves (Figure 5.2). There is no evidence, however, that the Akan enslaved each other, an important distinction to make and a practice that would change dramatically in the eighteenth century.

Much of West Africa was integrated like this. Gold dust and nuggets circulated widely over much of the western Sudan. Gold circulated as the currency of long-distance trade, with cowrie shells used for smaller local transactions. Elaborately forged gold weights were used to settle accounts, and commodity prices were often quoted in well-known local denominations. Over time, and following increased contact with foreign traders, the weights came to reflect the denominations of foreign currencies as well (Garrard 1980).

In many ways, gold ruled trade and politics in the medieval western Sudan. Gold, not slaves, drove the trans-Saharan trade. Gold, not slaves, motivated the original Portuguese explorations down the west coast of Africa. Gold, not slaves, was the primary West African exchange earner. As an industry, gold mining influenced the demand for local labor and, as a consequence, the number of captives available to export. As a store of wealth, gold facilitated surplus extraction by elites and the centralization of political and military authority.

GOLD AS A WINDOW INTO AFRICA'S PAST

The opportunity cost of using gold as money is the forgone return on gold as an asset. The rate of return on the asset is the rate of appreciation in its value and the services it provides, such as jewelry, ceremonial pieces, and a store of wealth. If the rate of appreciation declines, more gold will be advanced out of existing stocks to serve as money, working capital, and loans. If holders anticipate a devaluation in the value of gold, they will convert some of their gold into other forms of value. They could extend loans, invest in projects, or make consumption purchases outright. Gold's devaluation increases the amount of gold circulating as money and working capital for trade and investments.

Data on the value of gold in medieval Africa do not exist, but abundant data exist for England. Over 3,000 miles separate England and the Gold Coast, but the high value-to-weight ratio of gold integrated the world bullion market like no other. A decline in the value of gold in London would eventually translate into declining values in West Africa, especially since West Africa was a major supplier of European gold. An Anglo-African gold-for-commodity exchange integrated the regions further.

Figure 5.3 graphs the purchasing power of an ounce of gold in the City of London, measured as the official British price of gold divided by the London retail price index. To smooth out fluctuations, I report ten-year moving averages. In 1717, Sir Isaac Newton, as Master of the Mint, set the official price of an ounce of gold at £4.25, where it stayed until Britain left the gold standard in 1931. I normalize London retail prices by the average price index for the period 1717–1740. As you can see, the average normalized value of an ounce of gold during these years was £4.25. On this timeline I place some of the event history discussed earlier. To facilitate discussion, I divide the timeline into three periods.

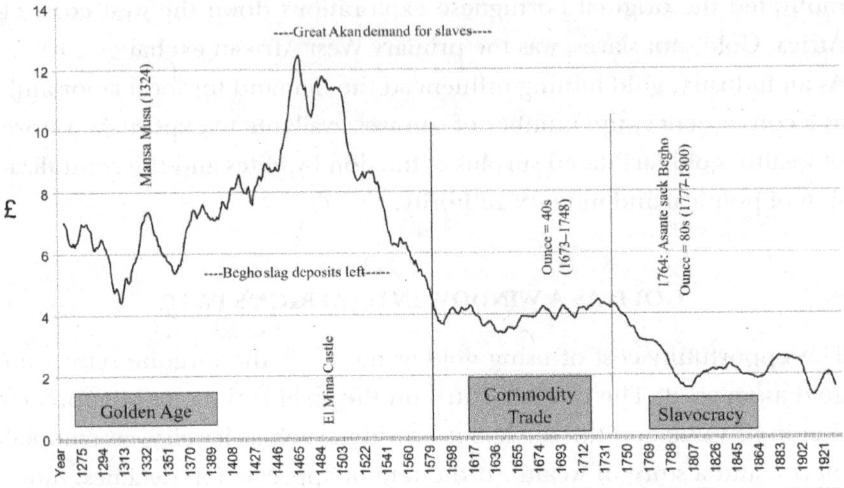

5.3 Real British official gold price per ounce. Data sources: Officer and Williamson (2025) and Clark (2013).

The first period I call a "golden age" because the value of gold was so high. One can understand why Portuguese sailors risked dangerous and uncharted waters to search for "the blacks who mine the gold." Note that the pilgrimage of Mansa Musa occurred before the peak in gold values. The height of Mali was yet to come. This was the classic age in Sudanese and Zimbabwean economic and political development.

The second period is an "age of trade" ("commodity trade" in the figure) that runs from approximately the beginning of the seventeenth century to the beginning of the eighteenth century. The real value of gold in England remained remarkably stable during this period. A unit of account called "the trade ounce" emerges out of repeat Anglo-African trade.[5] In England, the trade ounce was the cost of trade goods that a knowledgeable trader thought would fetch an ounce of gold on the coast of Africa. It was a bundle of goods valued at half an ounce of gold in England, otherwise the long-term commercial venture would not be profitable. This was an easy and straightforward calculation for a London African trader to make. Between 1673 and 1748, the account books of English traders record a fixed trade ounce of approximately 40 shillings worth of trade goods, or £2 (Johnson 1966). In Figure 5.3, £2 was approximately half the real value of an ounce of gold in London at this time.

The stable Anglo-African exchange rate reduced international exchange risk on both sides of this cross-cultural trade. If African traders were willing to exchange an ounce of gold for an assortment of British goods that cost no more than 40 shillings in England, then expectations on both sides of the transaction were realized, and repeat trade would proceed. Exchange-rate stability reduced transaction risk and facilitated the growth of supply networks on both sides of the market.

Figure 5.4 provides independent confirmation that the international value of gold offers a valuable window into West African economic history. It places a different event history on the timeline, this one taken from the classic study of the Gold Coast by Ray Kea (1982). Kea begins his middle period in the sixteenth century, not the seventeenth century. The sixteenth century was a century of declining gold values, so we expect increased circulation of gold as money and merchant capital. Kea confirms this, documenting the spread of cash rents among the Akan during this period, a new form of surplus extraction. Even tributes were paid in cash. Kea characterizes the period as one of increasing urbanization, specialization, and trade.

The well-known Akani trading group emerges during this period. Centered on Assin, in the country of Accania, this large-scale mercantile

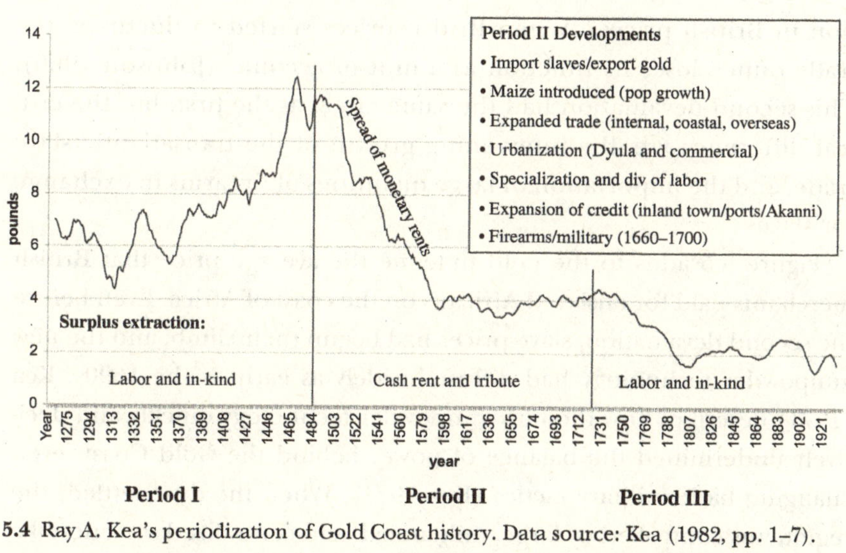

5.4 Ray A. Kea's periodization of Gold Coast history. Data source: Kea (1982, pp. 1–7).

trading group operated during the sixteenth and seventeenth centuries. A ruling council directed trade over an extensive area, often setting prices and directing the movement of goods, including large quantities of textiles and metal wares from Begho to the Gold Coast. The Akani trading organization descended from Akan elites who converted some of the gold they had accumulated during the fifteenth century appreciation into merchant capital during the sixteenth-century depreciation. When the international value of gold stabilized in the seventeenth century and the trade ounce reduced international trade risk, the Akani was in a position to dominate regional trade. According to Kea, "its history predates 1600, for the large-scale trade of the 17th century presupposes an earlier period of merchant capital accumulation and concentration. It is likely that the initial stages of merchant capital formation in Accania date from the 15th century ... By the 17th century, Akani trading capital was dominant throughout much of the region" (Kea 1982, p. 249). Kea's analysis is a kind of independent confirmation that the international value of gold is a good proxy for the cost and availability of trade capital in medieval and early modern West Africa.

The third period includes another devaluation due to the large discoveries of gold in Brazil. English trade books record the trade ounce increasing from 40 to 80 shillings, reflecting the general inflation in British prices.[6] When British prices started to fluctuate, the trade ounce loses its function as a unit of account (Johnson 1966). This second devaluation had the same effect as the first, but the critical difference was the intervening growth of the transatlantic slave trade, and the importation of large quantities of firearms in exchange for slaves.

Figure 5.5 adds to the gold timeline the average price that British merchants paid for enslaved Africans on the coast of Africa. Even before the second devaluation, slave prices had begun their climb, and the new gunpowder technology had diffused widely as early as the 1690s. Kea (1971) describes how the new gunpowder technology quickly and decisively undermined the balance of power behind the Gold Coast, even changing basic military tactics (Kea 1971). When the dust settled, the region was controlled by large, militarized, and centralized societies like

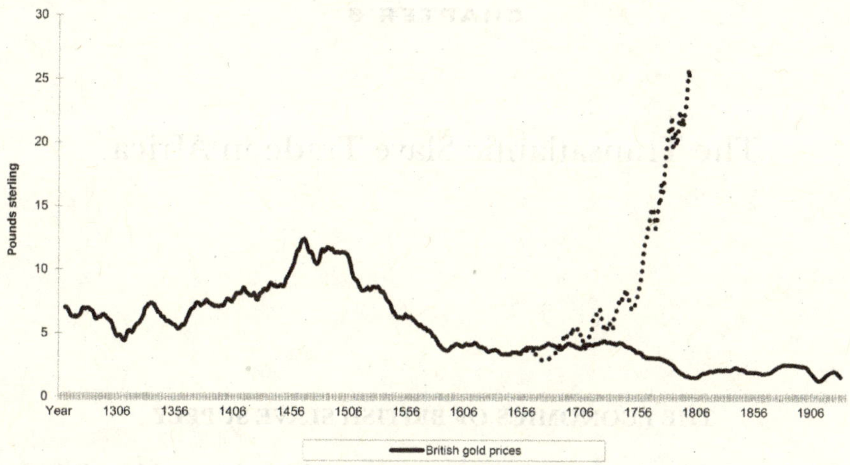

5.5 Real British gold prices and real British slave prices. Data sources: Figures 5.3 and 6.2.

Asanti, where all roads now led to the capital city of Kumasi, including roads that previously ran into and out of cities like Begho. When independent cities resisted, they were sacked, and fundamental alliances redrawn, like the sacking of Begho by the Asante in 1764. These were revolutionary times!

CHAPTER 6

The Transatlantic Slave Trade in Africa

THE ECONOMICS OF BRITISH SLAVE SUPPLY

The slave prices displayed in Figure 5.5 are the prices paid by British merchants on the coast of Africa. Figure 6.1 reports the corresponding number of British slave purchases and those of other European empires. Britain was a latecomer. The Portuguese and Spanish had been trading slaves since the middle of the fifteenth century, but the British Empire did not enter the trade until the middle of the seventeenth century. By the end of the eighteenth century, the British slave trade was one of the largest in the world. This section explains how Britain accomplished this.

The British demand for enslaved Africans arrived on the coast of Africa as ships laden with cargo looking for enslaved people to buy. The ultimate African destinations were largely determined before ships left Britain, with cargos carefully selected to meet the anticipated preferences of intended African consumers (Metcalf 1987b; Metcalf 1987a; Eltis 2000). The most popular items were textiles of various kinds, iron bars, firearms and other weapons, rum, cowrie shells, and a vast array of manufactured goods.[1]

On the coast of Africa, these commodities ($CARGO_t$) were traded for enslaved people ($SLAVES_t$) who were captured in wars and raids in the interior. The average exchange between $CARGO_t$ and $SLAVES_t$ is the average $PRICE_t$ that British merchants paid for enslaved people on the coast of Africa in year *t*.

$$PRICE_t \equiv \frac{CARGO_t}{SLAVES_t} \quad (1)$$

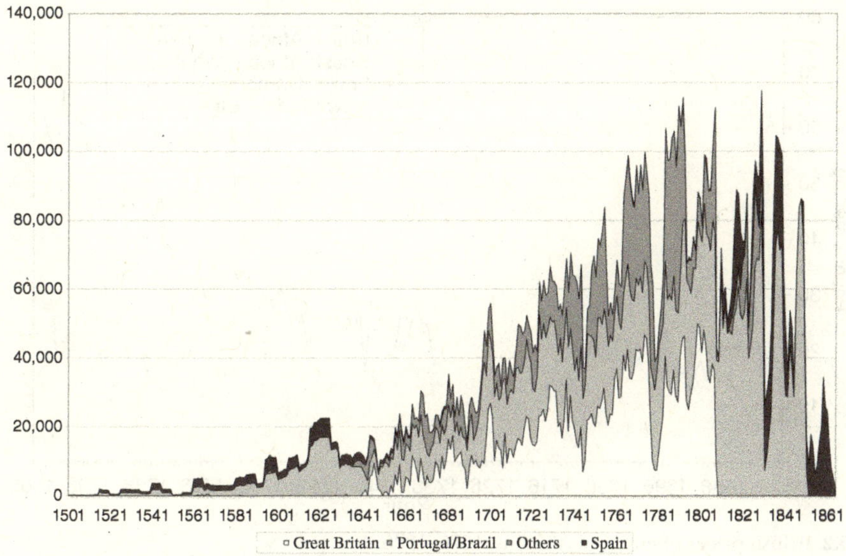

6.1 Transatlantic slave exports, 1500–1860. Data source: The Trans-Atlantic Slave Trade Database (2009).

Annual estimates of $CARGO_t$ are found in the Anglo-African Trade Statistics, recorded in the British Customs Office and digitized by Johnson, Lindblad, and Ross (1990). The Anglo-African Trade Statistics contain annual estimates of the real value of British $CARGO_t$.[2] The British Customs Office set the value of cargo items at "official prices," primarily 1699 prices that did not change over the eighteenth century. Hence, changes in $CARGO_t$ reflect changes in the quantities of items shipped to Africa, not their prices. It is the appropriate measure for our purposes because we want to document the responses of African slave exporters to changes in the number of $CARGO_t$ items they received. Estimates of $SLAVES_t$ come from the Trans-Atlantic Slave Trade Database and measure the number of enslaved Africans boarding the British ships that carried $CARGO_t$ to Africa.[3] If, for example, the ships carrying $CARGO_t$ left Britain in 1750, $SLAVES_t$ measures the number of enslaved Africans purchased by those ships and their $CARGO_t$.

The resulting $PRICE_t$ series (labeled "British – Whatley") is graphed in Figure 6.2, along with several other price series for comparison. $PRICE_t$ closely tracks the annual price series constructed by Richardson (1979), who uses a similar method and similar data.[4] $PRICE_t$ also tracks a price

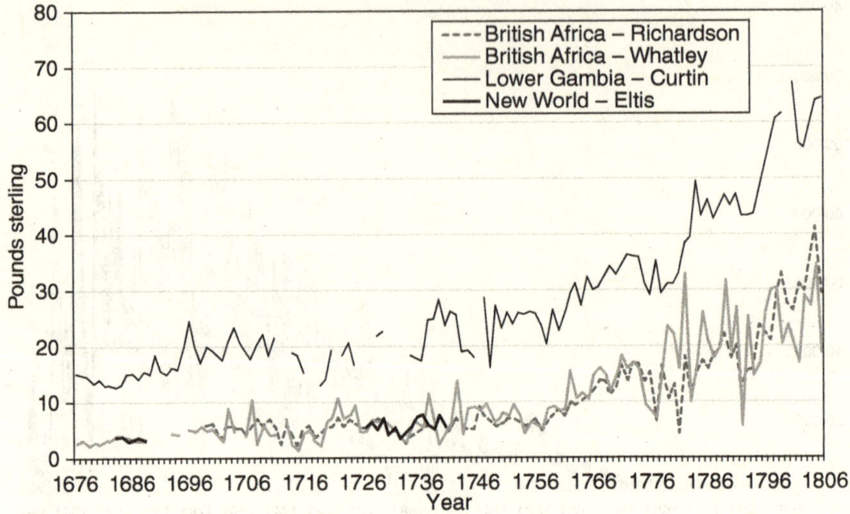

6.2 British prices of enslaved Africans, 1676–1806.

series for the lower Gambia compiled by Curtin (1975b), but only when he uses the records of account books similar to those used by the British Customs Office.[5] $PRICE_t$ tracks the price series compiled by Eltis and Richardson for enslaved Africans newly arrived in the Americas (Eltis and Richardson 2004).[6] The higher American prices reflect the additional cost of the Middle Passage, but the trends are similar.[7] $PRICE_t$ averaged around £5 until the middle of the eighteenth century, then it begins to rise sharply. By the end of the century, it stood somewhere between £25 and £30, a fivefold increase in fifty years.

An advantage of time series data like these is the ability to track trends and changes over time. Figure 6.3 places both $PRICE_t$ and $SLAVES_t$ on the same graph, with five-year moving averages to highlight trends. If there was a correlation between price and quantity before the middle of the century, it was a negative one. According to equation (1), $SLAVES_t$ exports (African supplies) were increasing faster than $CARGO_t$ (British demand) and driving down $PRICE_t$. The second thing to notice is how the pattern changes sometime around the middle of the century, when $PRICE_t$ and $SLAVES_t$ begin to move together. According to equation (1), $CARGO_t$ was increasing faster than $SLAVES_t$, driving up both $PRICE_t$ and $SLAVES_t$ together.

Statistical tests confirm a break in the $PRICE_t$ series at 1740. Easaw and Ghoshray (2023) apply a number of robust econometric tests to the

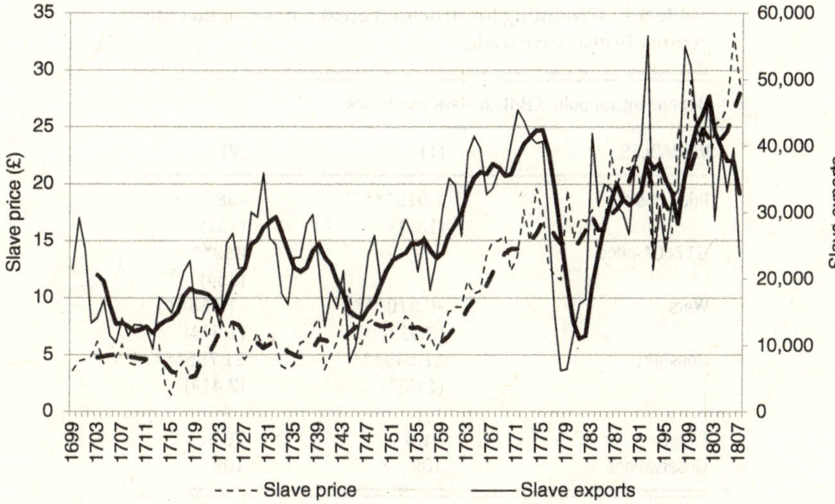

6.3 British prices and quantities of enslaved Africans. Data sources: Figures 6.1 and 6.2.

Whatley price series. They find no significant trend in the price series before 1740 but a positive increase of 2.4 percent per year thereafter. Table 6.1, therefore, reports a simple ordinary least squares accounting.[8] By construction, the correlation between $PRICE_t$ and $SLAVES_t$ should be *negative*, but we find no significant correlation before 1740 and a statistically significant *positive* one after 1740. These results do not confirm the dominance of African supply shifts before 1740 and British demand shifts after, but they are consistent with that interpretation.

We can do better. Changes in the relationship between the two variables can tell us something about the structures behind supply and demand, as well as the relative importance of supply and demand factors in the evolution of the system. Figure 6.4 depicts the internation market for slaves. The market is in equilibrium at P* and Q*, at which point there are no tendencies for price or quantity to change. If something happens on the supply side (inside Africa) that increases the number of slaves available for purchase at each and every price, then the supply curve will shifts out from (1) to (2), and equilibrium quantity increases while the equilibrium price decreases. Likewise, if something happens to increase the quantity demanded at each and every price, the demand curve will shift from (1) to (2), and equilibrium quantity will increase.

Table 6.1 Accounting for structural breaks in the eighteenth-century British slave trade

Dependent variable = British slave purchases		
VARIABLES	(1)	(2)
Price of slaves	1,015***	-38
	(137)	(451)
G1740* price		889**
		(354)
Wars	-6,570***	-7,818***
	(2,013)	(1,944)
Constant	17,549***	21,755***
	(1,663)	(2,414)
F-stat	31.5	26.8
Observations	109	109

Notes: Newey-West standard errors in parentheses, max lag (1) *** $p < 0.01$, ** $p < 0.05$, * $p < 0.1$. The dependent variable is the number of British slave purchases per year. Price is the slave price paid by British merchants on the coast of Africa. G1740 is a dummy variable = 1 for years greater than or equal to 1740, zero otherwise.

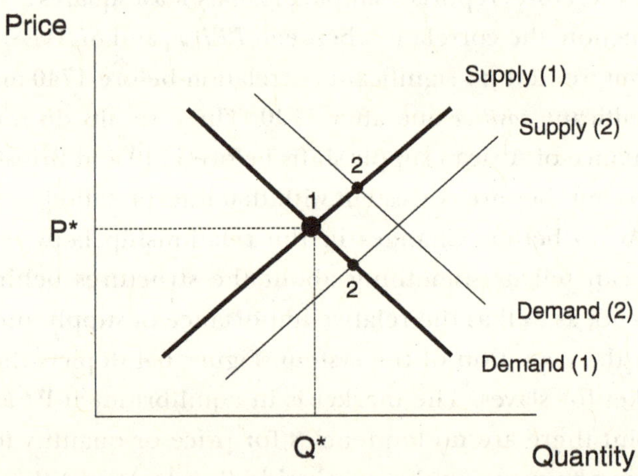

6.4 The eighteenth-century British slave market.

Suppose the supply curve looked like the one depicted in Figure 6.4. Curtin (1975a) calls this the "economic model" of African slave supply because increases in slave prices were required to cover the additional costs of capturing and exporting additional people. On the other hand, if African slave exports did not respond to changes in

British demand, then the supply curve in Figure 6.4 would be perfectly vertical (perfectly inelastic), and the number of $SLAVES_t$ exported would be independent of demand. Curtin calls this the "political model" of slave supply, where slave exports were byproducts of political wars and conflicts that had nothing to do with the demand for slaves. $PRICE_t$ simply clears the market of a politically generated supply of war captives.

On the African supply side, imported gunpowder technology might increase the productivity of African resources devoted to capturing people and marching them to the coast. According to Hoffman (2015), when measured as the rate of successful fire per infantry man per minute, productivity of the gunpowder technology in European wars increased precipitously between 1600 and 1750, from 0.2 to 2.0 successful fires per minute. The matchlock musket first appears between 1450 and 1500, and by the late 1600s the flintlock and bayonet had replaced it, a technology not found in China (p. 59), but one that proved effective in humid tropical environments like sub-Saharan Africa.

European shipments of firearms to Africa accelerated in the late seventeenth and early eighteenth centuries.[9] This is also when African slave exports began to increase. Before then, the older matchlock musket proved ineffective in tropical climates and the Catholic Church prohibited their sale to non-Christians. The sale of large numbers of guns and gunpowder to Africans began with Protestant slave traders not bound by Catholic prohibitions.[10] The Dutch were the first to sell large numbers, followed by the English as their participation in the slave trade grew. Fearful of losing their competitive position, the Portuguese quickly followed suit. By the 1680s, the more reliable flintlock technology was replacing the matchlock technology and firearms became a staple outbound cargo on most slave ships destined for Africa.

Thus began a period of sustained growth in both firearms shipments to Africa and slave exports out of Africa. Between 1680 and 1685, the British Royal African Company shipped only 2,615 firearms per year to Africa (Davies 1975, p. 356). By the end of the eighteenth century, Inikori (1977) estimates that the British were shipping 150,000 to 200,000 guns per year, and the total for all of Europe was between 300,000 and

400,000 per year. Eltis and Jennings (1988) estimate a tenfold increase in firearms between the 1680s and the 1780s, increasing from 20,000 to 200,000 per year.

We do not have a reliable time series on firearms shipments to Africa, but we do have a reliable series for gunpowder. For our purposes gunpowder is a better measure than guns. There were so many kinds of guns that it would prove difficult to construct a reliable annual index. Also, firearms are durable goods. Converting trade flows into annual stocks available for slave production would require estimates of depreciation rates, and ideally a different depreciation rate for each type of gun. Even if the stock of guns could be estimated, their capacity as weaponry was still largely determined by the amount of gunpowder available to activate them.

Gunpowder, on the other hand, is a more homogeneous product and easier to handle quantitatively. While there were different grades of gunpowder, a poor grade was always shipped to Africa to match the poor quality of the firearms shipped there.[11] Gunpowder is measured in standardized pounds or barrels, something we could not do for guns. And gunpowder does not last nearly as long as guns, especially in the humid tropics.[12] The analysis that follows assumes that the flow of gunpowder largely determines the productive capacity of the gunpowder technology. *GUNS* (gunpowder) should influence the number of enslaved people captured and marched to the coast.[13] Gunpowder imports should also be lagged because it may take time for additional gunpowder to produce additional slaves for export.

Results are reported in Table 6.2 (see the Appendix to Chapter 6 for the full specification). They confirm the implications of Figure 6.3. *CARGO* includes gunpowder, but an additional independent *GUN* effect was statistically significant before 1740. After 1740, the independent *GUN* effect fell to zero, and the *CARGO* effect, as a demand shifter, became more robust. It also took time for changes in gunpowder to produce more slave exports. There is no support for the political model of slave supply because the coefficient on *CARGO* is always positive, large, and significant. Changes in British gunpowder and changes in British demand for enslaved Africans reallocated African resources away from other pursuits and toward the production and export of enslaved people.

Table 6.2 The impacts of guns and cargo on British slave exports, before and after 1740

Dependent variable = Change in British slave purchases			
	1699-1807	1699-1739	1740-1807
VARIABLES	(1)	(2)	(3)
Δ(t) British gunpowder (lb.)	0.112*	0.178*	0.006
	(0.063)	(0.098)	(0.070)
Δ(t-1) British gunpowder (lb.)	0.089**	0.130*	0.051
	(0.044)	(0.070)	(0.058)
Δ(t) Cargo items	0.466***	0.277**	0.612***
	(0.073)	(0.102)	(0.082)
F-Stat	26.35	5.93	26.84
Observations	106	38	68

Sources: See the Appendix to Chapter 6, Table A6.1 columns (4)-(6).
Notes: Variables are in natural logs and are stationary (see Whatley (2018)). Newey-West standard errors in parentheses, with max lag(1). *** $p < 0.01$, ** $p < 0.05$, * $p < 0.1$.

THE GUN–SLAVE CYCLE

We can do better. Rather than treating *GUNS* and *CARGO* as exogenous shifters of endogenous *SLAVES*, we can treat the three variables as if they influence each other dynamically, contemporaneously, and intertemporally. This is the idea behind the gun–slave hypothesis, several versions of which are found throughout the literature on the transatlantic slave trade. One version of the hypothesis, guns-for-slaves-in-production, argues that imported gunpowder technology facilitated capturing people and marching them to the coast. In 1730, for example, the Dutch Director General at Elmina Castle described what he saw along the Gold Coast of Africa as guns-for-slaves-in-production: "The great quantity of guns and gunpowder which the Europeans have brought have *caused* terrible wars between the Kings and Princes and Caboceers of these lands, who made their prisoners of war slaves; these slaves were immediately bought up by Europeans" (quoted in Richards 1980, p. 46, emphasis added).

Running in the opposite direction is slaves-for-guns, which claims that it was increases in slave exports that attracted the European gunpowder technology to Africa. This version emphasizes how African elites sought the latest military technology to fight nation-building wars for reasons that had little to do with the international slave trade, like Curtin's political model of slave supply. The proclamation of King Ose Bonsu of Asante is often enlisted in support of this view: "I cannot make war to catch slaves in the Bush, like a thief. My ancestors never did so. But if I fight a king, and kill him when he is insolent, then certainly I must have his gold, and his slaves, and the people are mine too" (quoted in Dupuis 1824, p. 163).

In his study of the eighteenth-century Bambara Kingdom of Segu, located in the Middle Niger valley, Richard Roberts (1987) states: "Making war not only gave slave warriors their specialized occupation; it gave them the means to renew their tools of production. Warriors needed a constant supply of weapons, including lances, horses, and after the mid-eighteenth century, steady supplies of firearms, flints, lead shot, sulfur, and gunpowder" (p. 35).

A third version claims that the two processes reinforced each other and evolved into a self-perpetuating gun–slave cycle, where increases in $GUNS_t$ increased $SLAVES_{t+1}$, which attracted $GUNS_{t+2}$, which increased $SLAVES_{t+3}$ ... you get the picture. The gun–slave cycle essentially endogenizes the slaves-for-guns channel by recognizing how the external slave trade influenced the economic, political, and military motivations of Africans.[14] Gemery and Hogendorn (1974) referred to this dynamic as a prisoners' dilemma arms race of "raid or be raided" that few Africans could escape, even if they wanted to. Once a gun–slave cycle was established in a region:

> States playing no role in the slave trade, and therefore not receiving muskets in payment for slaves, found themselves on the losing side of an arms race. Their dilemma: without firearms defense was precarious. To get muskets, there must be something to export. The only item in great demand was slaves. Thus, it is not surprising that slave trading spread rapidly, especially in the eighteenth century when the flintlock replaced the cumbersome matchlock. (p. 242)[15]

In Whatley (2018), I specify a vector error-correction model that is flexible enough to estimate the dynamic contemporaneous and intertemporal relationships among these three variables (*SLAVES*, *GUNS*, and *CARGO*). Three results emerged from that analysis. First, the three endogenous variables were co-integrated in a long-run equilibrium relationship that spanned the eighteenth century. In other words, *GUNPOWDER* and slave prices (*CARGO/SLAVES*) were systematically related to each other, what Basil Davidson (1961) calls "the inner logic" of the transatlantic slave trade.

Second, departures of any of the three variables from their long-run equilibrium path (like shocks to the system from wars in Europe) set in motion adjustments among the variables that returned the system to its equilibrium path. When gunpowder imports were above their long-run equilibrium path, next year's slave exports increased, evidence of guns-for-slaves-in-production (which takes time) as opposed to guns-for-slaves-in-exchange (which is a contemporaneous transaction).[16] Third, slaves-for-guns show up in the coefficients on lagged slave exports. Increases in African slave exports attracted additional British gunpowder for two or three more years.

Together, these three dynamics formed a gun–slave cycle that magnified the impact of any piece studied in isolation.[17] Assuming that the flow of information from Africa to Britain followed shipping routes in the North Atlantic, impulse–response functions estimate large increases in African slave exports in response to exogenous increases in British gunpowder shipments. Figure 6.5, taken from Whatley (2018), shows the cumulative increase in slave exports that followed an exogenous increase in gunpowder. The left panel shows the path that followed an exogenous 1 percent increase in cargo that contains the average amount of gunpowder. The right panel shows the path that followed an exogenous 1 percent increase in gunpowder itself, typical of situations following

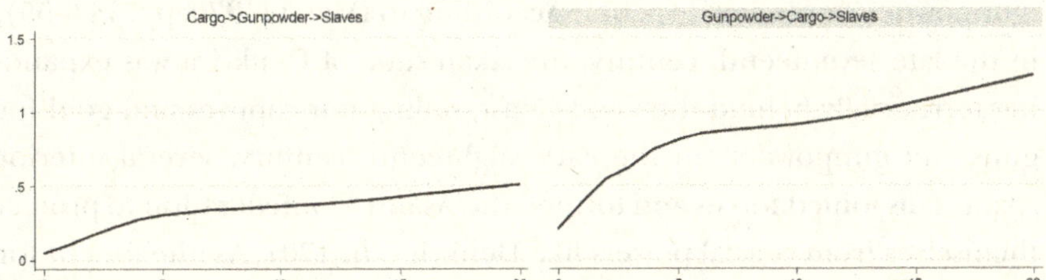

6.5 The cumulative effects of gunpowder shipments on slave exports. Source: Whatley (2018).

European wars when excess gunpowder was dumped on Africa, or like the Seven Years War, when British slave ships sat in London harbor waiting for government exemptions for the private export of gunpowder to Africa. The average response was somewhere between these two simulations. After a gun–slave cycle was established in a region, a 1 percent increase in gunpowder set in motion a five-year gun–slave cycle that increased slave exports by an average of 50 percent, and the impact continued to grow asymptotically over time.

This is Rodney's "gale-force wind," Harari's "trifecta of capitalism, empire, and science," and Acemoglu and Robinson's "critical juncture." Once a region was caught up in a gun–slave cycle, the previous balance of power among states, chieftaincies, and villages was undermined. The new normalized expectation of "raid-or-be-raided" produced an explosion of slave production, slave trading, and slave exports.

THE GUN–SLAVE CYCLE IN ACTION

This "raid-or-be-raided" equilibrium is, by definition, a regional equilibrium, not a continental one. Continental slave exports (Figure 6.1) follow a smooth, monotonically increasing path, but not regions. Figure 6.6 reports regional time paths of British (dashed lines) and total (solid lines) slave exports for broad regions of the Guinea Coast of Africa, the coast most affected by the British slave trade. The bold lines are six-degree polynomials that capture changes in trends.

The top two panels (the Gold Coast and the Bight of Benin) show explosive growth in slave exports before 1740. Most historians believe a gun–slave cycle operated here. Even Thornton (1999), not a proponent of the gun–slave cycle, states that "here it has been possible to speak of a 'gunpowder revolution'" (p. 61). According to Daaku (1970, pp. 144–55), in the late seventeenth century, the Akan state of Denkyira was expanding territorially behind the Gold Coast, selling war captives and gold for guns and gunpowder. In the early eighteenth century, several interior Akan clans joined forces and formed the Asante Confederation to protect themselves from coastal powers like Denkyira. In 1701, Asante fought for and won independence from Denkyira. The victory was closely tied to Asante controlling access to firearms and blocking Denkyira's access to

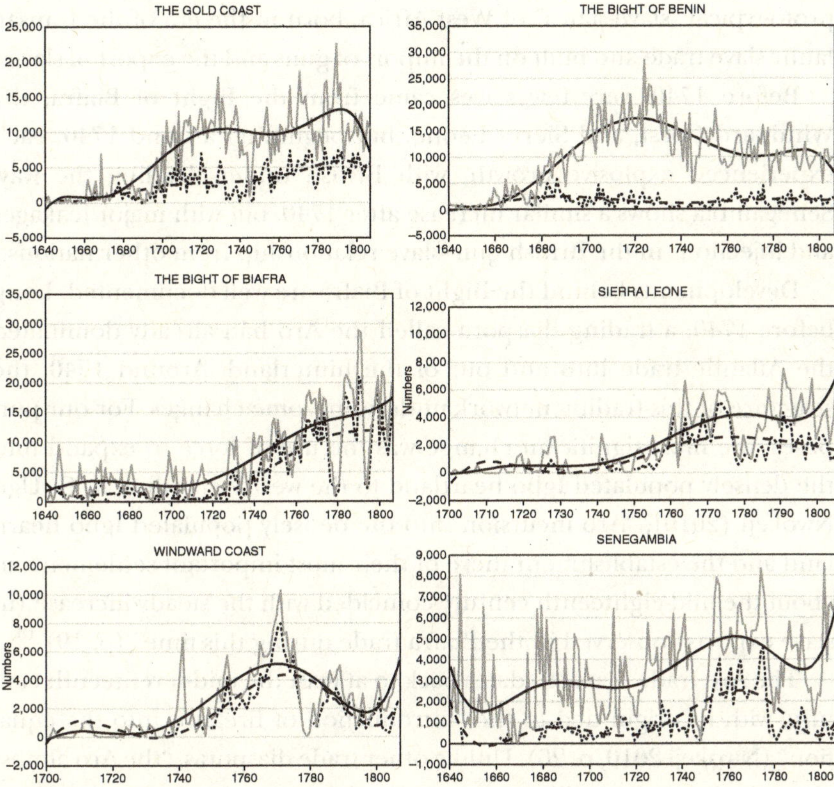

6.6 Gun–slave cycles and regional slave exports, 1640–1807. Data source: The Trans-Atlantic Slave Trade Database (2009).

firearms. Once secured, Asante embarked on an aggressive campaign of territorial expansion, such that by 1750, it claimed the majority of what is now the state of Ghana. Asante controlled its northern territories by prohibiting the flow of armaments northward (Wilks 1975, pp. 18–25). In 1730, the Dutch Director General at El Mina was describing the gun–slave cycle along the Gold Coast.

Behind the Bight of Benin, a similar dynamic unfolded in the geopolitical struggles between Alladah, Whydah, Dahomey, and Oyo. According to Law (1991), by 1730, these geopolitical struggles culminated in the regional dominance of Dahomey, a militarized state boasting a large standing army of riflemen. The details differ, but both nation-building efforts relied heavily on the importation of firearms, the exportation of slaves, and control of the flow of guns (Kea 1971, p. 201). These are the proto-typical "slave-states" of West Africa, born in the era of the transatlantic slave trade and built on the import of guns and the export of slaves.

Before 1740, very few slaves came from the Bight of Biafra, the Windward Coast, and Sierra Leone, but beginning around 1740, each experienced explosive growth, with British traders leading the way. Senegambia shows a similar increase after 1740, but with major leakages and injections in the British gun–slave relationship from other nations.

Developments behind the Bight of Biafra are well documented. Long before 1740, a trading diaspora called the Aro had already dominated the Atlantic trade into and out of the hinterland. Around 1740, the structure of this trading network underwent some changes. For our purposes, the most significant change was the use of force to expand into the densely populated Igbo heartland to the west. According to G. Ugo Nwokeji (2010), "Aro incursion into the densely populated Igbo heartland and the establishment there of their most important settlements in about the mid-eighteenth century coincided with the steady increase (in slave exports) observed in the Biafra trade during this time" (p. 19).[18]

The Aro trade diaspora dates back to at least the mid-seventeenth century, with its origin tied to the "introduction of firearms into the equation" (Nwokeji 2010, p. 26). Unlike other trade diasporas, "the Aro almost always had access to military resources, which was often a decisive factor in their dealings with hinterland groups" (p. 55). The push into the Igbo heartland resulted "by the mid-eighteenth century in Bonny's supersession of Old Calabar as the Biafra's principal port just as the Aro expanded westward" (p. 45). The firearms coming into Bonny in exchange for these slaves were British-made firearms known as Bonny rifles.

The export trends for Sierra Leone, Windward, and Senegambia are more difficult to interpret, primarily because a vast highland plateau complicates the inland geography behind the coast. Transportation waterways fan out from these highlands in all directions, making it challenging to assign coastal slave exports to any particular region or conflict.[19] In addition, on the northern slope and down into the Middle Niger valley, the transatlantic trade competed with the trans-Saharan trade. Still, increases in slave exports along the Atlantic coasts coincided with several interior conflicts that expanded trade toward the Atlantic to secure the latest weaponry.

Thornton (1999) discusses Senegambia and Sierra Leone. The significant political development of the eighteenth century was the 1726–27 formation of Futa Jallon in the highlands. Thornton reports that "firearms were desired everywhere, and it was probably inability to obtain them rather than a rejection of their military utility that caused them to be scarce in inland areas like Futa Jallon in the 18th century" (p. 46). However, the King of Futa Jallon "appreciated guns, for he sold slaves to obtain guns and gunpowder whenever possible" (p. 46). As late as 1794, "guns were still rare … but Susus, near neighbors who had better coastal access, were almost all equipped with guns. The leaders of Futa Jallon were anxious to obtain more supplies of Muskets and artillery, and prepared to sell slaves in large numbers to acquire them to protect themselves against their enemies" (p. 46).

Curtin et al. (1995, p. 197) claim that the slaves exported from the eighteenth-century Senegambia coast were largely Mande victims of the rise and expansion of Bambara states in the interior, one of which was Segu. Richard Roberts (1987, pp. 58–62) describes Segu as a warrior state based on a steady influx of firearms, especially after the mid-eighteenth century (p. 35). He also explains how Segu's trade shifted toward the Atlantic coast to obtain adequate supplies:

> The Middle Niger valley was surrounded by three export regions. Trade with the Maghrib, Senegambia and the southern forest zone followed different routes … At least some of the slaves produced by the warriors of Segu found their way into the Atlantic economies. Even more direct, however, was the dependence of the Segu political economy on firearms, gunpowder, and other European manufactures, which could best be supplied through the Atlantic coast trade. Demand for these commodities increased the importance of the westerly and southwesterly direction of trade. (Roberts 1987, pp. 59–60)

These are just a few examples, but they highlight the importance of imported gunpowder technology in growing the transatlantic slave trade. Many examples can also be found among the decentralized societies of West Africa. In fact, most enslaved Africans may have originated in skirmishes and kidnappings involving decentralized villages trying to defend against enslavement by more centralized societies, warlords, and bandits. They deployed a variety of defensive strategies (Diouf 2003) like building walls (Thornton 1999), moving to rugged terrain (Nunn and Puga 2012), paying tribute (Wilks 1975, pp. 19–23), and securing guns and other imported weapons (Hawthorne 1999; Klein 2001). The latter strategy, and paying tribute in slaves, pulled decentralized societies into the orbit of a gun–slave cycle.

THE INLAND PENETRATION OF CAPTURE

If we could trace exported slaves back to their place of origin, we could be more precise about the location and intensity of the kinds of conflict that produced slave exports. We could then begin to document how the associated conflict influenced norms, institutions, and development going forward. Nunn (2008), in what has become a seminal article, introduces an effort to do precisely that. His method is controversial, but his estimates of the inland origins of slave exports correlate with later measures of economic underdevelopment in catchment zones.[20] This section looks closely at his methods to see if his estimates of the origins of slave exports are representative of what actually happened inside Africa. It turns out that they are not representative of sixteenth and seventeenth-century origins, but representative enough for the eighteenth and nineteenth centuries to correlate with firsthand accounts of inland penetrations recorded by David Livingstone himself.

To estimate the inland origins of coastal slave exports Nunn matches the ethnicity of exports to the inland locations of their ethnic homeland. The inland homelands are those depicted in Murdock's map of ethnicities, found at the back of his book *Africa: Its Peoples and Their Culture History* (1959). But how does Nunn know the ethnicity of the people exported? The Trans-Atlantic Slave Trade Database does not record the ethnicity of slave exports. Here, Nunn (2008) uses counts of African ethnicities *in the Americas* to distribute African coastal exports to their homelands *inside Africa.* "Information on the ethnicities of slaves (in the Americas) ... come from 54 different samples, totaling 80,656 slaves, with 229 distinct ethnic designations reported" (Nunn 2008, p. 146).

Nunn wants to distribute coastal slave exports to geographic regions that eventually become post-colonial nation-states. If, for example,

Ghanaian ethnicities account for 32 percent of the ethnicities found behind the Gold Coast, then 32 percent of the exports from that Gold Coast are allocated to the state of Ghana. By necessity, this is done first by each ethnic homeland and then summed by state. Inland origins could change over time, so Nunn allocates exports by homeland for each century and then by state to get the overall totals. The resulting estimates of slave exports by ethnic homeland and by states have been used by development economists to study spatial correlations between slave catchment zones in the past and measures of underdevelopment later, some effects lasting well into the late twentieth century and beyond. These are the first indications that the effects of the slave trades were substantial and lasting.

However, we need to first establish the representativeness of the African-American samples that underly Nunn's estimates of the inland origins of African slave exports. Nunn (2008, pp. 147–48) lists the locations of his American samples, their dates, the number of African Americans in each sample, and the number of African ethnicities found in each African-American sample. Table 6.3 estimates how well these samples capture the inland origins of African slave exports. The first column uses data from the Trans-Atlantic Slave Trade Database to count, by century, the coastal origins of the enslaved Africans disembarked in America. For example, 53 percent of the enslaved Africans who disembarked in sixteenth-century America came from the Senegambia region of Africa (the area closest to Europe), and 11 percent came from West Central Africa (the region closest to Brazil).

Do Nunn's African-American samples come from the American regions that received these captives? If they do not, then the African-American samples give a distorted picture of the inland origins of the African slave exports. For example, an African-American sample from a region of America that received no African slaves can tell us nothing about what is happening inside Africa, while samples from regions that received many can tell us more than samples from regions that received only a few.

Columns two and three in Table 6.3 weight the African-American samples from American regions by the percentage of imports they received from African regions, and then sums the products across

Table 6.3 How reliable are Nunn's (2008) estimates of inland catchment zones?

	Sixteenth century			Seventeenth century			Eighteenth century			Nineteenth century		
	African	American		African	American		African	American		African	American	
Region of Africa	% of exports	# Observations	# Ethnicities	% of exports	# Observations	# Ethnicities	% of exports	# Observations.	# Ethnicities	% of exports	# Observations	# Ethnicities
Senegambia	53	2,109	40	10	302	24	4	4,991	77	2	834	39
Sierra Leone	1	40	1	0	0	0	3	582	10	2	2,400	41
Windward Coast	0	0	0	0	0	0	3	235	5	1	445	8
Gold Coast	0	0	0	5	0	0	11	911	20	2	1,622	44
Bight of Benin	0	0	0	17	58	9	19	5,297	74	8	7,821	141
Bight of Biafra	4	92	6	9	70	6	13	1,413	42	9	11,929	190
West Central Africa	11	7,849	145	39	1219	103	28	7,154	104	43	9,813	340
Southeast Africa	0	0	0	1	0	0	1	602	8	10	1,113	69
Other Africa	32	4,960	69	18	384	35	18	3,878	71	24	7,417	168
Totals	100	10,155	198	100	2,036	176	100	25,052	411	100	43,413	1041

Notes: African exports are the percentages of total African slave exports from the various regions of Africa. The sizes of the African-American samples used to assign African exports to African ethnicities are estimated as follows. First, I identify the locations of the African-American samples of African ethnicities found in Nunn (2008, Table 1). Using data from the Trans-Atlantic Slave Trade Database, I calculate the African origins of the slaves imported into these American locations. Applying the African origins of American imports (in percentages) to the American sample sizes allocates the American samples across the African regions. Applying the African origins of imports (in percentages) to the number of ethnic groups in the American samples allocates the ethnicities in the sample across the African regions.

American regions. This estimates the number of observations and ethnicities for African regions predicted by the locations and sizes of the African-American samples. For the sixteenth century, for example, the locations and sizes of Nunn's African-American samples predict only 2,109 observations from Senegambia, or 21 percent of the total number of observations (2,109/10,155), a gross under-estimate of the 53 percent of Africans who actually came from Senegambia in the sixteenth century. Oversampling comes from regions that received the 11 percent from West Central Africa.

Total numbers may be more important than percentages. 2,109 expected observations on Senegambian ethnicities may be enough to allocate the Senegambian coastal exports to the forty or so inland ethnic homelands in Senegambia. That is an average of fifty-three observations per ethnicity. For West Central Africa, there is an average of fifty-four observations per ethnicity. However, we get very little information from American regions that received enslaved Africans from Sierra Leone and the Bight of Biafra.

The quality of information gets worse in the seventeenth century. The sizes of the African-American samples get smaller (2,036 American observations on 176 African ethnicities), and the slave trade diffuses geographically in both the Americas and Africa. It is difficult to see how any of these numbers could be used to adequately allocate slave exports to inland origins in the seventeenth century.

The numbers for the eighteenth century, however, are much better. The African-American samples get larger, their spatial coverage improves, and the number of ethnicities they contain increases especially for Senegambia and the Bights of Benin and Biafra. Sample sizes get even larger and more representative in the nineteenth century. The best allocations of coastal exports to inland locations are for the eighteenth and nineteenth centuries. The overall totals are useful, but primarily because the eighteenth and nineteenth centuries dominated the totals.[21]

With these caveats in mind, Maps 6.1 and 6.2 depict Nunn's estimates for eighteenth and nineteenth-century penetrations of capture in South Central Africa (hashed places were politically centralized). In the eighteenth century, much of the interior was spared, but nineteenth-century

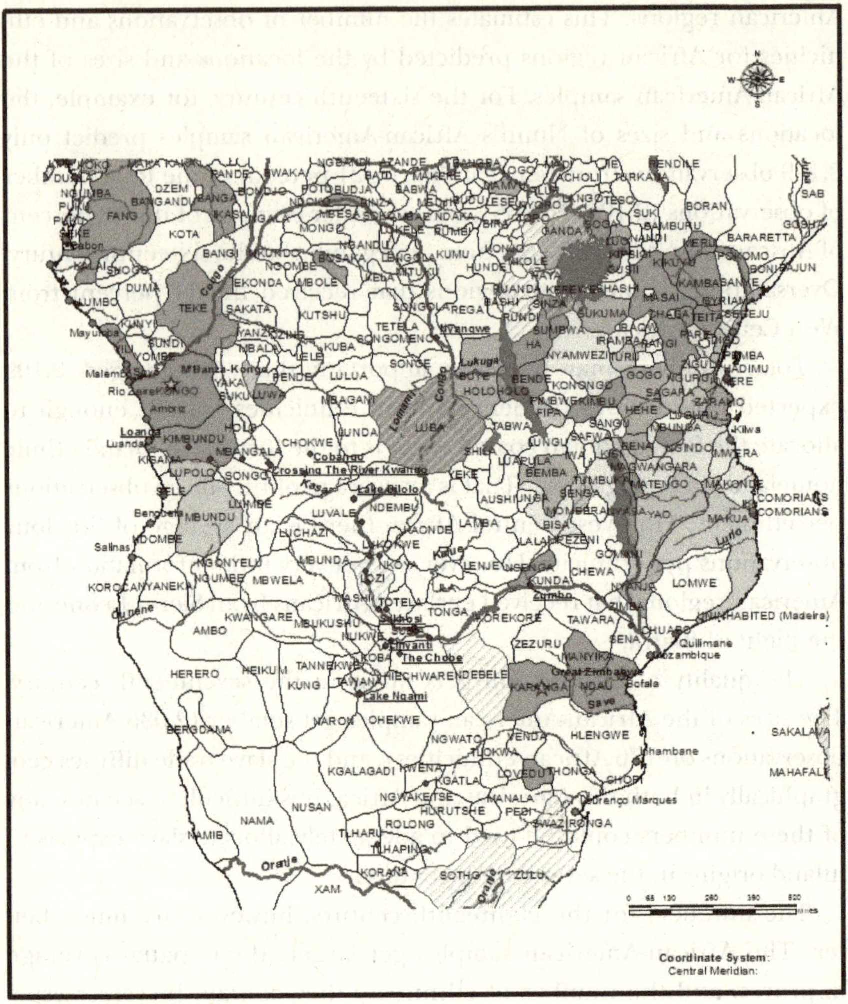

Map 6.1 The penetration of slave catchment zones, eighteenth century.

penetrations ran clear across the continent, from the Atlantic to the Indian Ocean.

The maps also mark the precise locations of David Livingstone's travels in the 1850s (names underlined and locations emphasized in map 6.2). Livingstone (1858) walked through territories that were becoming exposed to international slave trades. Below is his firsthand account of the dynamics of penetration as he saw them. Note the ever-present role of the gun–slave cycle and how it spearheaded the penetration.

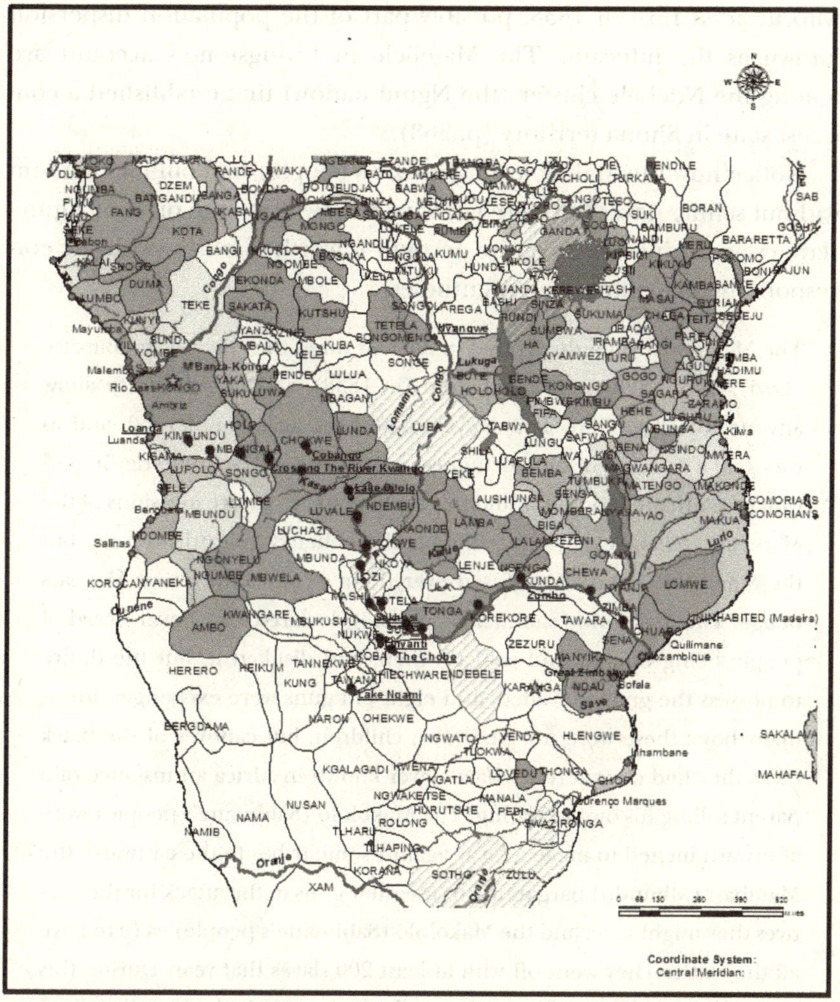

Map 6.2 The penetration of slave catchment zones, nineteenth century.

To set the stage for Livingstone's account, note that the Mambari slave traders are among the Mbundu on Murdock's map (Murdock 1959, p. 370), located near Portuguese slave ports on the west coast of Africa. Barotse is Lozi on the map, located in the interior, midway between the coasts (politically centralized, circa 1900). King Sebituane was chief of the Makololo, who ruled a kingdom that stretched from Twana to Naliele, twelve days travel north. Murdock (1959, p. 368) identifies Makololo (Kololo) as Sotho (politically centralized, circa 1900), who invaded Lozi in 1838, possibly part of the population dispersion known as the mfecane. The Matebele in Livingstone's account are among the Ndebele cluster (the Nguni nation) that established a conquest state in Shona territory (p. 368).

Notice how the Makololo (Sabituane's people) had built a kingdom without selling slaves but were eventually drawn into the orbit of a gun–slave cycle. Livingstone's entire account is worth quoting (with the corresponding map names in parentheses):

> The Mambari (Mbundu) visited in ancient times the chief of the Barotse (Lozi), whom Sebituane conquered (in 1838), and he refused to allow anyone to sell a child. They never came back again until 1850; and as they had a number of old Portuguese guns marked "Legitimo de Braga," which Sebituane thought would be excellent in any future invasions of the Matebele (Ndebele), he offered to purchase them with cattle or ivory, but the Mambari (Mbundu) refused everything except boys about 15 years of age. The Makololo (Sabituane's people) declared they never heard of people being bought and sold till then, and disliked it, but the desire to possess the guns prevailed, and eight old guns were exchanged for as many boys; these were not their own children, but captives of the black races they had conquered. I have never known in Africa an instance of a parent selling his own offspring. The Makololo (Sabituane's people) were afterward incited to make a foray against some tribes to the eastward; the Mambari (Mbundu) bargaining to use their guns in the attack for the captives they might take, and the Makololo (Sabituane's people) were to have all the cattle. They went off with at least 200 slaves that year. During this foray, the Makololo (Sabituane's people) met some Arabs from Zanzibar, who presented them with three English muskets, and in return received about 30 of their captives. (Livingstone 1858, pp. 105–6)

CHAPTER 7

How African-American Slavery Grew the Free Economies of Europe

THE ECONOMIC HISTORY OF THE NEW HISTORY OF CAPITALISM

In the 1960s and 1970s economists and historians vied for dominance in the field of economic history. Not surprisingly, economists won on their turf, and cliometrics, the careful testing of deductive hypotheses about the economic past, was born. The publication of *Time on the Cross* by Fogel and Engerman (1974) is often taken to be the final nail in the historians' coffin, but it is important to remember that *Time on the Cross* generated a flurry of criticism from both historians and economists (David et al. 1976).

There were many issues at stake, but the most important was the relative efficiency of the slave sector compared to the free sector. *Time on the Cross* argued that the slave sector was as "efficient" as the free sector, primarily because the slave sector was able to drive slaves in gangs of sixteen or more, exploiting economies of scale that the free sector could not achieve with its smaller family farms. The debate focused on the quality of the data and the economic models behind their interpretation.[1] No historians were involved in this debate, and how could they be? This was pure cliometrics debating the economic efficiency of slavery. One unanticipated consequence of the cliometrics victory was the "cultural turn" in history, a retreat from studying the institutions and markets that cliometricians claimed as their own.

Within this context, the "new history of capitalism" (NHC) marked a return among historians to investigating the institutional history of economies. Using documents that focus on aspects of capitalism that economists often overlook, like the dark side of slavery, the NHC paints a picture of the rise of the West that is often at odds with the one painted by economic historians. Ironically, while economic historians were focusing on a cultural explanation of the rise of the West (see Chapter 4), the NHC focused on the brutality of slavery, the violence of empire, and the exploitation of labor. While economic historians drifted toward studying the *Culture of Growth* (Mokyr 2017), *Bourgeois Dignity* (McCloskey 2010), and *How the West Became Psychologically Peculiar* (Henrich 2016), the NHC was studying *Slavery and Empire* (Johnson 2013), *Slavery and the Making of American Capitalism* (Baptist 2014), *Empire of Cotton* (Beckert 2014), and *Empire of Guns* (Satia 2018).

Economic historians have been critical of some of this literature, not because they disagree with the project, but because, like in the 1960s and 1970s, some of the economic history literature has been overlooked or misinterpreted, and some of the economic analysis has not been correctly applied.[2] I too have been guilty of this, critical of a chapter that claimed guns in Africa were simply prestige goods (Whatley 2022b). Unsubstantiated claims like these can raise suspicions about other claims. The real problem, however, is that historians and economic historians simply do not talk to each other. It feels like déjà vu all over again (Morris 2020), except this time the historians seem to be agreeing with *Time on the Cross*; that slavery was efficient enough to drive the expansion of capitalism, while economic historians are skeptical.

Take, for example, the debate about the contributions of slave labor to the US economy. Using very different empirical methods, the NHC (as in Stelzner and Beckert 2023) and economic historians (as in Rhode 2024) find that on the eve of the US Civil War, the contribution of enslaved African Americans to national product was approximately equal to their share of the population. As if to confirm that this is evidence of the inefficiency of slavery, not its efficiency, Rhode concludes:

> Although the enslaved were forced to work more than the free population … they were also forced to work in activities – agriculture and domestic service – where the value of output per worker was generally lower than the overall average in the economy. The economic surplus

> generated by the enslaved was due chiefly to the low value of the very basic consumption bundle provided to the enslaved rather than to exceptionally high labor productivity.

Notwithstanding the lack of exchange and the different methods, few scholars on either side of this debate would deny the brutality of slavery or the importance of innovation and technological change in the expansion of the free sectors. The issue is not the existence of slavery or freedom, but their interactions, how, when, and where. When does the expansion of American slavery drive the expansion of the free sector? When does the expansion of the free sector drive the expansion of slavery? Gavin Wright (2020), for example, has argued that the expansion of the slave sector drove the expansion of the free sector when eighteenth-century sugar dominated, but that the expansion of the free sector drove the expansion of the slave sector when nineteenth century cotton dominated.

THE TRIANGULAR TRADE

One way to address this issue is through the prism of the Triangular Trade, because the Triangular Trade is where the two sectors interacted. In the North Atlantic, the Triangular Trade between Africa, America, and Europe integrated the spatially separate slave and free sectors of Western European empires.[3] Enslaved Africans were purchased on the coast of Africa in exchange for manufactured goods produced in the free sectors of Europe (like guns, rum, and textiles). The African slaves were then transported across the Atlantic to European colonies in the Americas and the West Indies (not Europe), where they were put to work on slave plantations producing raw materials like sugar and cotton. The raw materials were then shipped to the free sectors of Europe to be used in the production of manufactured goods (like processed sugar, rum, and cotton textiles). Raw sugar ranked first or second in the value of English/British imports for more than a century (from at least 1699 to 1824). Cotton ranked third between the American Declaration of Independence in 1776 and the ratification of the US Constitution in 1789, but then skyrockets to first place shortly thereafter (Berg and Hudson 2023, p. 59).

Findlay (1990), inspired by Darity (1982), develops a simple general equilibrium model of the Triangular Trade that helps us identify which sector is driving expansion of the system, and when. The model is a steady-state model, meaning it specifies conditions under which there are no tendencies for the system to change. It treats African-American slaves as an asset that planters hold in the Americas, valued as an investment, like in Conrad and Meyer (1958). Given an equilibrium slave population in the Americas, the flow of slaves across the Atlantic is a replacement flow to maintain the equilibrium slave population. The steady-state slave population produces a steady-state amount of raw sugar or cotton, which is shipped to the free sector for the production of a steady-state quantity of manufactured goods (sugar, rum, or cotton textiles).

The essence of the model can be depicted in our simple supply-and-demand graph (Figure 6.4). Quantity is now the stock of slaves in the Americas. To integrate the slave and free sectors, the price is now a ratio of prices (raw material/manufactured). The demand curve for slaves (Demand 1) is now a derived demand for slaves that "illustrates the fact that the higher the price of the raw materials, the less will be the demand for it in the manufacturing center, therefore the less will be the derived demand for a slave labor force in America" (Findlay 1975, pp. 9–10). Likewise, the supply curve (Supply 1) now "illustrates the fact that the higher the price of raw materials in terms of manufacturers, the more profitable will it be to hold slaves as an asset in America" (p. 8). Given the input–output coefficients in the slave and free sectors, equilibrium in the international slave market determines an equilibrium stock of African-American slaves, an equilibrium quantity of raw material produced in the slave sector, an equilibrium amount of manufactured goods produced in the free sector, and an equilibrium price ratio.

Simple comparative statics can now be read off the graph. Expansion of the system could be driven by expansion in either the slave or free sectors, or both. For example, the gun–slave cycle described in the previous chapter reduced the supply price of slaves on the coast of Africa. This increased the profitability of holding slave as assets in the Americas, especially between 1699 and 1740. This would shift the supply schedule to Supply 2, increasing the equilibrium stock of slaves in the Americas, increasing the production of raw materials in the slave sector and ultimately increasing the size of the manufacturing sector. Steady-state equilibrium is reestablished at a *lower* price ratio. The same comparative static applies to technological changes in the slave sector that improve the profitability of holding slave assets, or improvements in slave productivity, or changes in slave management practices that increase slave productivity.

Alternatively, expansion could be driven by increases in the demand for manufactured goods, or technological change in the manufacturing sector. Hicks-neutral technological changes increase the derived demand for raw materials and slaves. The derived demand for slaves shifts out to Demand 2, increasing the desired stock of slaves in the Americas, and the size of the slave and free sectors. Steady-state equilibrium is reestablished at a *higher* price ratio.

WHEN SLAVERY FED FREEDOM

We can now identify the drivers of expansion. If expansion of the slave sector is driving the expansion of manufacturing, then the ratio of raw material to manufactured prices should *decline.* If expansion in manufacturing is driving expansion in the slave sector, then the ratio of prices should *increase.* Both sectors could be expanding at the same time. It is the relative speed or distance of the shifts that determines the direction of movements in the price ratio.

Figure 7.1 reports the raw and processed prices for sugar in London between 1674 and 1869. They follow similar trends but they converge and diverge several times. Most of the imported raw sugar was semi-processed muscovado, and London became the center for further processing into an array of sugar varieties and qualities (Berg and Hudson 2023, pp. 60–71). "Much of the imported sugar went on to further processing. Sugar houses and sugar bakers in London … carried out the more sophisticated refining and process" (p. 63). Grocery stores stocked their shelves with sugars of different quality and sugar bakeries emerged to convert processed sugar into edibles of all kinds.

We are interested in the ratios of the prices, which are reported in Figure 7.2. Movements in the price ratio reveal several distinct cycles. In the early eighteenth century, the trend is sharply downward, indicating

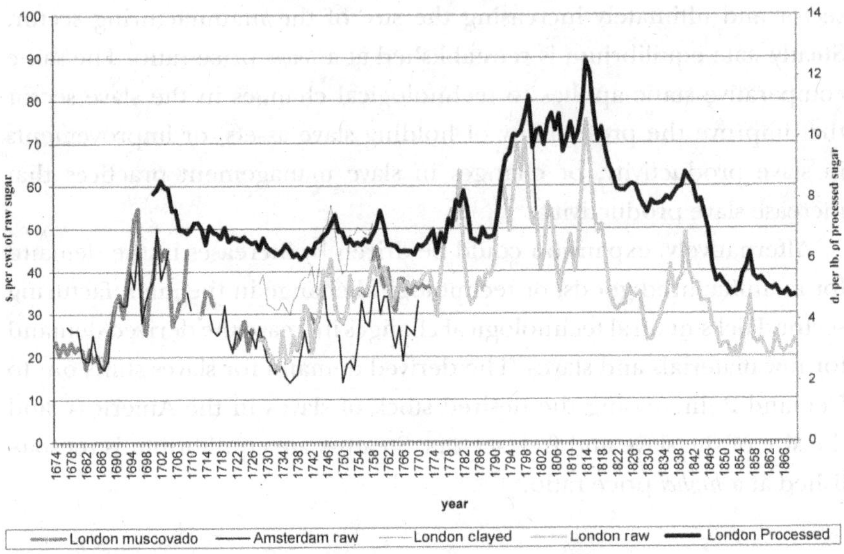

7.1 The prices of raw and processed sugar in London, 1674–1869. Data sources: Sugar prices are taken from Deerr (1950), pp. 530, 531. The London price for processed sugar is taken from Clark (2005).

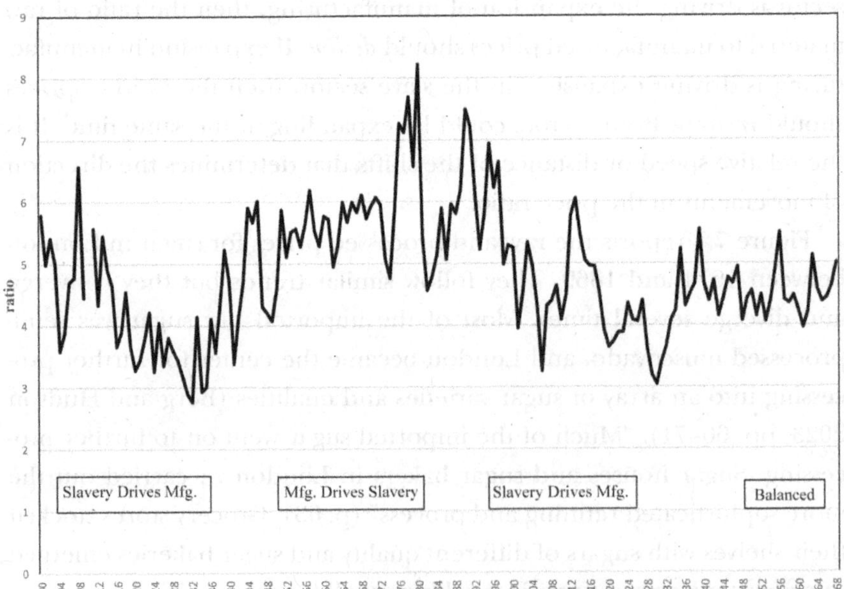

7.2 The ratio of raw to processed sugar prices in London, 1700–1869. Data sources: The raw sugar price is for London muscovado between 1700 and 1775 and for London raw between 1776 and 1869. The processed sugar is the London retail price taken from Clark (2005).

that expansion in the slave sector was driving the expansion of sugar processing. This is the period of increases in British slave supply following the introduction of the European gunpowder technology into Africa.

After approximately 1740, the price ratio reverses and begins a prolonged period of increase, indicating that expansion in the demand for manufactured sugar or technological change in sugar processing are driving the expansion of slavery. According to Berg and Hudson (2023) sugar made the "shift from a luxury to an everyday commodity from the beginning of the seventeenth century to the end of the eighteenth century, and *especially during the mid to late eighteenth century*" (pp. 64–65; original emphasis). Sugar became indispensable in hot drinks and tea and as a preservative for fruits. By 1800, consumers were willing to pay 10 percent or more of their income to maintain their sugar consumption (p. 68). Looking at probate records, de Vries (2008) reports similar diffusions of teaware in colonial Maryland and Antwerp (pp. 149–52). Rum making moved from the backyard still to large distilleries.

Approaching the end of the eighteenth century, the price ratio turns down again, indicating that expansion in the slave sector was again driving expansion of manufacturing. Perhaps this expansion reflects renewed expansion in British sugar slavery following the collapse of sugar production in Haiti. Alternatively, it could reflect a rush to purchase slaves ahead of the 1807 prohibition on imports. The data suggest, more importantly, that British slavery was profitable and expanding on the eve of prohibition, and not because the demand for processed sugar was growing but because the slave system itself was growing. After 1807, the price ratio shows no trend one way or the other.

Figure 7.3 reports similar prices ratios for cotton, available from 1784 to 1835, during the heyday of the Industrial Revolution in Britain. They report US raw cotton prices relative to British textile prices. The price of raw US cotton declines throughout the period. Textile prices come from Harley (1998) and Esteban (1999) and are estimated in radically different ways. Harley claims that the early Estaban prices are too high and then decline too fast, which explains why the ratio for Esteban declines less than Harley's. The price ratios fluctuate widely, but both series exhibit a decline following the diffusion of Eli Whitney's cotton gin in 1794, which allowed US cotton slavery to expand westward off the coast.

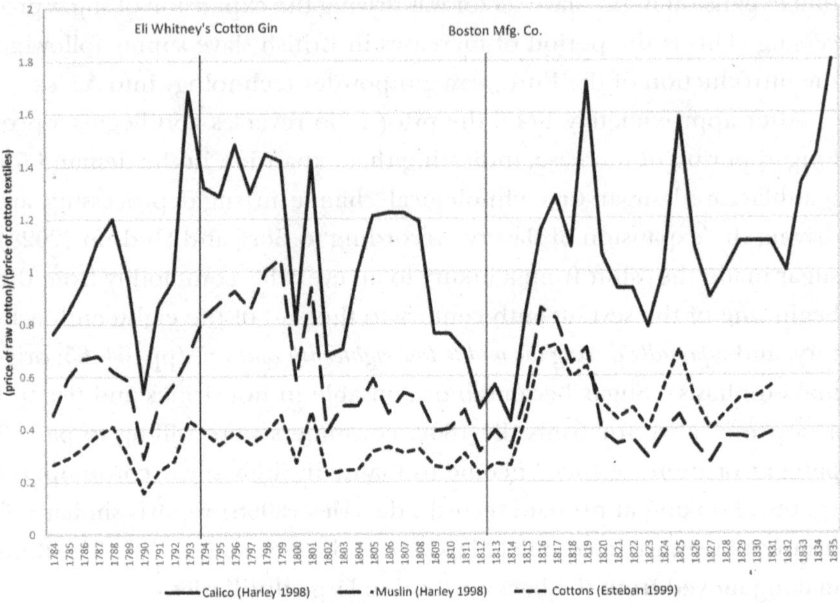

7.3 The ratio of raw US cotton prices to manufactured British textile prices. Data sources: British textile prices are from Harley (1998), p. 78, and Esteban (1999), p. 755. Raw US cotton prices are from Haines (2006).

The British price ratios begin to increase in the early nineteenth century, after the United States entered large-scale textile manufacturing, beginning with the founding of the Boston Manufacturing Company in Lowell, Massachusetts in 1814.

Both sugar and cotton reveal shifting dynamics between the slave and free sectors. While the interpretations call for more investigation, they appear to be consistent with the broad outlines of the sugar and cotton industries – both the brutal and relentless exploitation of slaves on sugar and cotton plantations emphasized by the new history of capitalism, and the relentless technological innovation emphasized by economic historians. Both price histories begin with the slave sector driving the manufacturing sector, so one might be tempted to argue that the slave sector "got things going," as in primitive accumulation; or be tempted to argue that the early flashes of liberalism in the Netherlands and Britain might have died out had slavery not given them a boost; or be tempted to argue that Western slavery explains why Western Europe got a 200-year head start on China. One could argue that.

CHAPTER 8

Into the Interior of Africa

THE NEED FOR SPEED

The transatlantic slave trade was everywhere in the eighteenth century, driving the expansion of manufacturing and being driven by the expansion of manufacturing, especially where escape velocity was mounting. But what about Africa? What was happening in Africa when all of this revolutionary change was mounting in Western Europe and its offshoots? Did exposure to the slave trades change societal norms and institutions in Africa too? Did exposure to the slave trade spread slavery as a social norm and institution in Africa? What were some of the African solutions to the first problem of slavery? How well did African slave systems preserve slave wealth?

Most Africans lived inland, away from coastal slave ports, so distance from ports offered some protections. The best available measure of distance is travel time, which has been shown to outperform other measures of distance and can identify details of institutional changes that other measures miss (Whatley 2022a).[1] Travel time measures proximity to the nearest port serving any of the four international slave trade – the transatlantic, Indian Ocean, trans-Saharan, and Red Sea ports – so it captures exposure to international slave trades in general. Travel time essentially quantifies some of the general features of the precolonial transportation technology in Africa, like walking, portage, canoe, horse, and camel.[2] Enslaved Africans were always transported by foot or by river down to the coast. Travel time accounts for the effects of groundcover type (e.g., rainforest versus desert), terrain (uphill or downhill), river velocity, headload, and local knowledge about the best path forward.

Parameters rely on hydrological studies, survey maps, hiking and head-load studies, and latitude: longitude readings by early European ambassadors, missionaries, and explorers.

To get good measures of travel time across Africa, this chapter visits early nineteenth-century Metropolitan Asante, where "place marked time." We then catch passage to industrializing Europe, where "time marked place." Then, back to Africa, where we measure travel time again, this time using the latest scientific technology produced by the Industrial Revolution. Along the way, we learn how to make a mosaic that captures local history, feel the burden of headload that many Africans had to endure, see how rivers unite and mountains divide, and appreciate the importance of relying on local knowledge about the best path forward. We can know all of this now thanks to modern GIS (Geographic Information System) computer software. If you are not interested in visiting these places, or learning about the ecology of Africa, or seeing how the Industrial Revolution changed the concept of time, you might want to skip this chapter. The next chapter, however, will use travel time to measure societal exposure to international slave trades.

A GUIDE ACROSS THE LANDSCAPE

For those of you who want to visit these places, we will be looking for *travel time* = $T \times V$, where T is the time to travel across a flat square kilometer cell of the earth's surface, and V is a correction for slope, over land and water. Travel by horse or camel is captured by the tsetse fly suitability index.

On land, T is influenced by land cover type. Map 8.1 maps the 27 FAO land cover types (Mayaux et al. 2003). The dark section at the continent's center (along the equator) is the Congo Basin, a thick rainforest with a swamp in the middle. Surrounding the rainforest is a land cover class called mosaic, where some forest has been partially cleared for cropland, the first indication that land was not abundant everywhere. North of the rainforest is a band of woodlands transitioning into savannah and grasslands before turning into desert. This east–west strip of transitional ecology is called the Sahel or the coast of the desert. Southwest of the Congo Basin is more desert. The Great Rifts are east of the rainforest, running

Map 8.1 FAO Land Cover Classifications, Africa. Data source: Mayaux et al. (2003).

north–south, where the topography and ecologies vary, with mountain kingdoms and populous valleys supported by large inland lakes, savannah, grassland woodlands, and mosaics.

Table 8.1 reclassifies the twenty-seven FAO land cover types and reports the estimated walking speeds used to calculate travel time. The remainder of this chapter describes how this is done.

NINETEENTH-CENTURY ASANTE: WHERE PLACE MARKED TIME

The best available data on walking speeds in Africa come from Wilks (1975, pp. 1–31), who estimates the time to walk the Great Roads of Asante in the early nineteenth century. The Great Roads were public

Table 8.1 Hours to walk a kilometer, by twenty-seven FAO Land Cover Classifications

		Hours per km	
FAO land cover class	**Reclassification**	**No load**	**With load**
Closed evergreen lowland forest	Rainforest	0.880	1.06
Degraded evergreen lowland forest	Rainforest	0.880	1.06
Sub-montane forest (900 to 1500 m)	Forest	0.417	0.500
Montane forest (greater than 1500 m)	Forest	0.417	0.500
Swamp forest	Water	0.216	0.216
Mangrove	Water	0.216	0.216
Mosaic forest/cropland	Mosaic forest	0.368	0.442
Mosaic forest/savannah	Mosaic forest	0.368	0.442
Close deciduous forest	Forest	0.417	0.500
Deciduous woodland	Forest	0.417	0.500
Deciduous shrubland with sparse trees	Field	0.329	0.395
Open deciduous shrubland	Field	0.329	0.395
Closed grassland	Field	0.329	0.395
Open grassland with sparse shrubs	Field	0.329	0.395
Open grassland	Field	0.329	0.395
Sparse grassland	Field	0.329	0.395
Swamp bushland and grassland	Water	0.216	0.216
Cropland (greater than 50 percent)	Field	0.329	0.395
Cropland with open woody vegetation	Field	0.329	0.395
Irrigated croplands	Field	0.329	0.395
Tree crops	Field	0.329	0.395
Sandy desert with dunes	Desert	0.255	0.306
Stony desert	Desert	0.255	0.306
Bare rock	Desert	0.255	0.306
Salt hard pans	Desert	0.255	0.306
Water bodies	Water	0.216	0.216
Cities	Field	0.329	0.395

Source: Estimates of hours per kilometer comes from Wilks (1975, pp. 1–31), Constance (2009), Smith (1970, p. 523), and Stanley (1891, p. 98). Headload factors are based on a formula found in Pandolf, Giovani, and Goldman (1977). See footnote 9 for a description.

roads that radiated out from the capital city of Kumasi. The central government maintained eight Great Roads to extend its political and military authority, to administer state affairs, and to facilitate commerce. These were among the best roads in precolonial sub-Saharan Africa. They traversed three land cover classes (forest, savannah, and mosaic). In addition, the terrain in this region is relatively flat, minimizing contamination from variations in elevations, which we add later.

Each Great Road had a series of appointed "halting places." Each halting place was a seat of authority where lodging could be secured, provisions replenished, and banditry reported. Wilks describes the travel time between each halting place as "equidistant," in the sense that they were separated by a conventional measure of a journey (in the Twi language, a *kwansi*, literally "part of the road"). Each journey (interpreted as a day's journey) was further divided into "watches" or "hours" or *kwansimma* (or little *kwansin*). A *kwansin* consisted of seven *kwansimma* or seven travel hours.[3]

Many halting places along the Great Roads survive today as towns and villages. Wilks uses Ghana Ordnance Survey Maps to compute the approximate straight-line distances between halting places. He estimates an average of ten and half miles per seven-hour day in the forest and 13.3 miles per seven-hour day in the savanna (p. 31). As a check, he reports time estimates recorded in the journals of two British ambassadors who were residents in Asante in the early nineteenth century, Bowdich (1819) and Dupuis (1824). Bowdich estimates an average linear distance of ten miles per day in forest and 13.3 in savannah, almost precisely what Wilks estimates.[4] Table 8.1 reports the speeds estimated by Wilks in kilometers per hour, converted at a rate of 1.6 kilometers per mile and seven hours of travel per day.

EXTREMES AND MAKING A MOSAIC

Mosaic land cover combines forest and savannah or forest and cropland. It is a widespread land cover type in sub-Saharan Africa because the expansion of agriculture often required the conversion of rainforest and forest into arable land. According to Wilks, it took 500 person-days to clear the 1,250 tons of vegetation from an acre of Akan Forest, or eighty-three sixty-hour weeks (1.5 years) to clear ten acres (Wilks 1993, pp. 44–61). Grollemund et al. (2015) estimate that carving civilization out of the rainforest slowed the Bantu migration by an average of 300 years. For mosaic regions, we take the mean of savannah and forest. According to Wilks, this equals 11.9 miles per day.

For desert, we estimate 27.5 kilometers per seven-hour day, or 0.233 hours per kilometer. The estimate comes from Constant (2009), who walked across the Sahara desert and often commented on her pace. Some of her quotes include the following:

> For the first time in the desert, I will simply have to walk between twenty-five and thirty kilometres per day in order to keep to schedule (3438) ... He sets a fast stride and maintains it, for at least 30 kilometres over rough terrain. (4107) ... 30 kilometres per day (4281) ... plodding through prickles and over hills for twenty-five, thirty kilometres – then camp, eat, sleep ... Every day when I check our location and mark the kilometers on the map, I can see that we are covering good ground. (4870) ... I walk over 25 kilometres every day (4964) ... 25 to 30 kilometres a day walking (6142).

Her guide said he did 50 per day, but he was riding camels and donkeys.

For rainforest, we use the average daily estimate of 0.88 hours per kilometer found in Henry Morton Stanley (1891):

> The next day left the track and struck through the huge towering forest and jungle with undergrowth by compass ... Naturally penetrating a trackless wild for the first time the march was at a funeral pace, in some places at the rate of 400 yards an hour (.366 km per hr. or 2.73 hours per km), in other more open portions that is of less undergrowth, we could travel at a rate of half, three quarters, and even a mile per hour (.625 hours per km) – so that from 6:30 AM to 11 AM when we halted for lunch and rest, and from 12:30 PM to 3 o'clock or 4 PM and from 6 to 7 hours per day, we could make a march of about 5 miles (.880 hours per km). (p. 98)

For mangroves, swamps, and waterbodies with no water current (no slope), we use the estimate of 2.9 mph (0.216 hours per kilometer) found in Smith (1970, p. 523), who reports average rowing speeds in the lagoons along the Lower Guinea coast in the early nineteenth century.[5] The average observed time for modern-day canoe and kayak travel is also 3.0 mph. Table 8.1 converts all of these estimates into hours per kilometer using 1.6 kilometers per mile and seven hours per day.

THE BURDEN OF HEADLOAD

The last column of Table 8.1 adds an adjustment for headload. Ergonomic tests conducted by the US Army report that carrying load by head is more efficient than carrying load by arms because arms rely on small muscle groups that tire quickly. S. J. Legg (1985) reports: "In the head-carriage method, the stress is born by the vertebral column and the legs. The limiting factor in carrying heavy loads on the head is not energy cost but rather the mechanical load tolerated by the musculature. Movement of the body as a whole is restricted, but the method is very suitable for repeated short distance carries" (p. 199).

Stanley (1878, vol. I, pp. 81–82) describes how he used this principle to allocate the 18,000 pounds of his caravan among his 300 porters:

> each man's load was given to him according as we judge to his power of bearing burthen. To the man of strong sturdy make, with a large development of muscle, the cloth bail of 60 pounds was given … to the short compactly formed man, the bead sack of 50 pounds weight; to the light use of 18 or 20 years old, the box of 40 pounds.

The additional energy would need to be replenished with food and rest. In addition, "movement of the body as a whole is restricted," which should reduce walking speed. To account for load-related effects on speed, rest, and additional headload, I add a load factor of 20 percent to the walking rates.[6]

NINETEENTH-CENTURY BRITAIN: WHERE TIME MARKED PLACE

Travel times from Asante have pluses and minuses. They apply to several land cover types and for relatively flat terrain (so elevation effects can be systematically added later). Still, it is a sample of travel times for a somewhat confined region of Africa and for a politically centralized state, so one can question their application to the entire continent. A good check would be a sample that is more representative of the continent, where travel times were scientifically recorded by actual travelers carrying actual headloads over actual terrains.

European explorers left precisely this record, but not until the nineteenth century. Here, the record is not distances between daily checkpoints, like in Asante, but scientific latitude and longitude readings. European explorers were interested in cataloging the world and its peoples and, perhaps more importantly, recording how to get back.

The problem of knowing where you were on the surface of the earth was known as the "longitude problem," a problem that occupied some of the greatest minds of the time. It was not solved satisfactorily until the late eighteenth century, and the technology was not generally available to explorers until the mid-nineteenth century. Mungo Park explored the Niger River from the Atlantic coast in the 1790s, but he did not carry recording technology. When he got back to Britain, cartographers used his descriptions of places to make educated guesses about his locations. By the 1850s, however, David Livingstone and Henry Barth are carrying the best recording devices available. By the time Henry Morton Stanley trekked across Africa in the late 1870s, the technology was so ubiquitous that he hardly mentioned having it, yet he took daily readings of his location.

Knowing latitude was relatively easy. The earth rotates every twenty-four hours around a magnetic axis that tilts through the north and south poles. The latitudes, or parallels, mark equal distances to these poles, with the equator as the prime meridian separating the northern and southern hemispheres. Astronomers and cartographers have known these facts since circa AD 150 when Ptolemy plotted them in his first world atlas. By the end of the fifteenth century, maritime navigators could rely on increasingly accurate tools to find their latitude. On a starry night in the northern hemisphere, a mariner could quickly determine latitudes by measuring the angle between the North Star and the horizon. On fair days, the sun provided reliable readings. The sextant is an instrument invented to measure these angles precisely.

It is not so easy with longitudes. Here, the placement of the prime meridian is a purely political decision. Ptolemy ran it through the Canary and Madeira Islands off the northwest coast of Africa. Later mapmakers moved it to the Azores, to the Cape Verde Islands, as well as to Rome, Copenhagen, Jerusalem, St. Petersburg, Pisa, Paris, and Philadelphia, among other places, before settling down in Greenwich, England (Sobel 1995, p. 5). Longitudes are not parallel to each other like latitudes but meet at the poles and mark the twenty-four hours of each rotation of the earth around its axis.

Getting lost at sea drove innovations because the costs here were tremendous. Water and food were rationed. The threat of scurvy increased with time, and getting lost increased the risk of running aground on rocks and reefs. As the saying goes, "if you want to learn to pray, go to sea." Prizes for solutions were offered by Spain in 1598 and the Dutch Republic two years later, designed to stimulate the best scientific minds of the time. Galileo competed for two prizes in the seventeenth century, offering an astronomical and a clock solution.[7]

A widespread astronomical method was the lunar distance method, based on the well-known fact that the moon changes its position against the background of the sky and stars reasonably quickly, moving the distance of its diameter in an hour, a distance called a "lunar." The technique was adopted widely by mariners in the late eighteenth century. Newton pointed out that the lunar approach would establish location within two or three degrees, or about 138–207 miles at the equator, and to get this close required a complex set of mathematical calculations and volumes of tables (Burton and Nicholas 2017, p. 23). Nor was it useful during overcast skies.[8]

As early as 1714, Newton described the problem that would ultimately be solved: "One [method of finding longitude] is by a Watch to keep time exactly. But, by reason of the motion of the Ship, the Variation of Heat and Cold, Wet and Dry, and the Difference of Gravity at different Latitudes, such a watch hath not yet been made." Theoretically, since the earth rotates fifteen degrees around its axis every hour, longitude can be found by comparing the time at a fixed longitude (say Greenwich) with the local time at your current destination. Local time can be measured by the location of the sun. To know the time at Greenwich, one needed an accurate timepiece onboard ship that kept Greenwich time. To know where you were, you had to know when you were there.

The loss of a British fleet in 1707 near the Scilly Isles provoked British political interest in finding a solution. In 1714, the British parliament passed the Longitude Act, which offered a series of prizes for solutions: £10,000 (worth the equivalent of over £1.46 million in 2019) for anyone who could demonstrate accuracy within one degree (sixty nautical miles at the equator); £15,000 for a demonstration within forty minutes; and £15,000 for within half a degree. Between 1735 and 1772, an English carpenter and watchmaker named John Harrison built five prototype sea clocks that convincingly demonstrated the feasibility of accurate timekeeping at sea. Prototypes H4 and H5 were watches. Eric Bruton (2000), in his book *The History of Clocks and Watches*, describes prototype H4 as "probably the most remarkable timekeeper ever made" (p. 93). They were ingenious devices but difficult and costly to reproduce accurately. Still, they guided the work of later watchmakers, whose modifications became known as marine chronometers.

Harrison's design was perfected in the 1770s, but it took decades of incremental advances before it became commercially feasible (Burton and Nicholas 2017, p. 26). Harrison's chronometer cost £450 to construct in 1769. By 1840, a chronometer could be produced for as little as £14 (p. 35). The British Admiralty tested chronometers and marked the best with the designation "maker to the Admiralty" (p. 24).

This explains why Mungo Park, as late as the 1790s, did not carry tools for taking longitude readings. He took a few latitude readings, so he likely had a sextant, but he does not mention having one. He typically described his locations as best he could, sometimes using distance (like "a day's journey south") to help establish his position relative to some marker, like a city or a waterfall. Back in England, Major Rennell, a famous cartographer, fed Park's descriptions and names into his encyclopedic knowledge of maps and essentially guessed where Park had been (Park 2000, Appendix Chapter I–VII, pp. 315–96). The result is the drawing of a map published at the end of Park's travelogue *Travels into the Interior Districts of Africa.* Thirty years later, Hugh Clapperton (2005, 1829) still followed Mungo Park's practice of recording a place of departure and the general direction of a day's travel.

By the 1850s, explorers like Henry Barth and David Livingstone were carrying pocket chronometers, sextants, telescopes, and compasses. David Livingstone (1858), for example, had a bag for clothes, a bag for medicine, and "a third for books, my stock being a Nautical Almanac, Thompson's Logarithm Tables, and a Bible ... The sextant and artificial horizon, thermometer, and compass were carried apart" (p. 250). He then describes, with great pride, his portable laboratory as the best technology money could buy:

> The instruments I carried, though few, were the best of their kind. A sextant, by the famed maker Troughton and Sims, of Fleet Street; a chronometer watch, with a stop to the secondhand – an admirable contrivance

> for enabling a person to take the exact time of observation: it was constructed by Dent, of the Strand for the Royal Geographical Society, and selected for the service by the president, Adm. Smythe, … Besides these, I had a thermometer by Dollond; a compass from the Cape Observatory, and a small pocket one in addition; a good small telescope with a stand capable of being screwed into a tree. (Livingstone (1858, pp. 250–51)

In 1850, Henry Barth (1890) described how he carried "a good sextant, a good chronometer, tolerably good compasses, a thermometer, and an aneroid barometer" (p. 8). When he was warned that the depths of a river exceeded the height of his horse, he declined to cross because "in so doing I should not be able to keep my chronometer and my compass dry; for these were now the most precious things which I had on earth, and could not be replaced and repaired so easily as gun and pistol" (pp. 393–94). He wore his chronometer and compass fashionably attached to his waist (p. 444).

In 1876, Henry Morton Stanley (1878) carried a chronometer (p. 48) and a sextant (p. 122). By then, the art and technology of recording latitude and longitude were so common that Stanley hardly mentions his tools, yet he used them almost daily to record his location. His table of readings published at the end of volume II (Stanley 1879) is the best available data on travel time across many different regions of Africa. Stanley trekked across the entire continent from east to west while scientifically recording his locations.

HENRY MORTON STANLEY'S TRAVEL LOG

As a check on the walking rate reported in Table 8.1, Table 8.2 reports rates collected from the published logs of Henry Morton Stanley's multi-year expedition through Africa between 1874 and 1876 (Stanley 1879, volume II, pp. 516–50). Stanley was the first European to march inland from "Zanj" on the east coast of Africa up to Lake Victoria in the Highlands, southward along the Rift Valley, westward again through a portion of rainforest in the Congo Basin, before floating down the Congo River to Isangila Falls, and from there overland to the Atlantic Ocean. At the end of volume II, which documents this expedition,

Table 8.2 Henry Morton Stanley's travel logs

	Observed from Stanley's logs				Estimates (with and without load)
	Average for all days		Average for travel days		Average for travel days
	hr/km	Obs.	hr/km	Obs.	hr/km
Stanley's wanderings	(1)	(2)	(3)	(4)	(5)
Overland to Lake Victoria	0.591	50	0.42	26	0.329, 0.395
Circumnavigation of Lake Victoria	0.282	53	0.240	47	0.216
Overland in Uganda	1.281	17	0.425	8	0.329, 0.395
Overland from Nyanza Muta-Nzige to Ujiji	0.694	102	0.422	62	0.329, 0.395
Circumnavigation of Lake Tanganyika	0.295	64	0.245	58	0.216
Overland to Lualaba River near Nyangwe	0.695	40	0.417	26	0.368, 0.442
Congo River to Isangila Falls (minus cataracts)	0.380	21	0.265	4	0.216
Overland from Isangila Falls to the Atlantic Ocean	0.703	7	0.841	4	0.88, 1.06

Notes: The source is Stanley (1878, pp. 516–61). Columns (1) and (3) report the hours per kilometer assuming seven-hour days. Column (1) includes non-marching days used for rest and re-provisioning. Column (3) reports average travel times that do not include rest days (only observations with consecutive dates). Column (5) reproduces the estimates from Table 8.1 that match the dominant land cover type of each of Stanley's wanderings.

Stanley published a travel log that records location, dates, name of country, name of station, village or camp, distance between (in miles), and remarks. Three hundred fifty-five entries in these logs report distance and date.

Table 8.2 reports the average travel times by water and land for what Stanley calls "wanderings," or sections of his trek across Africa. Columns (1) and (3) report hours per kilometer assuming seven-hour days. The hourly travel rates reported in column (1) include non-marching days for rest and re-provisioning. Care is taken to exclude off-days used for other purposes, like the 1875 royal visit to the Kingdom of Buganda (in current Uganda).[9] Column (2) reports the number of observations used in these calculations. Column (3) reports average travel times that do not include rest days. It contains only observations with consecutive dates and so cannot include days of rest. These observations are most comparable to the estimates in Table 8.1, the major exception being the impact of the earth's slope. Column (5) reproduces the Wilks estimates that match the dominant land cover type of each of Stanley's wanderings.

Wilks' estimates of travel times in Asante are comparable to Stanley's. Differences reflect the fact that Stanley's elevations were more varied. Stanley traveled over mountain passes, up to the highland lake region, and into the surrounding valleys before reaching the Congo River. Stanley also took longer to travel by water. Lake Victoria and Lake Tanganyika are bodies of relatively calm water, so their rates should be similar to those observed in the lagoons of the Lower Guinea coast. Stanley's vessel, *Lady Alice,* was constructed in Europe, dismantled into three parts, transported to the African coast, and carried overland to the lakes and rivers of the interior. Pictures show it to be significantly broader and heavier than the average African canoe. Stanley repeatedly refers to the swiftness of the African canoes he encountered on the Congo River and the elegance of their construction. While circumnavigating Lake Victoria and Lake Tanganyika, Stanley was interested in exploring and documenting as many bays, inlets, and rivers as possible, which also slowed progress.

RIVERS AS NATURAL HIGHWAYS

Rivers attract traders. They serve as natural highways across the landscape. Compared to overland transportation, rivers have advantages and disadvantages. They are not available everywhere, and they often flow in a different direction than one might want. On the plus side, water reduces friction and facilitates the transformation of human energy into velocity. When a paddler manipulates an appropriately constructed vessel, the buoyancy of water can transport comparable weight faster than an overland porter. Roberts (1987, pp. 73–74) discusses the relative carrying capacities of canoes and caravans in the nineteenth-century Middle Niger Valley. A twenty to thirty-ton freight canoe could transport as much produce as a caravan of 1,000 porters (0.025 tons per porter). Stanley (1878, volume I, p. 64) used 300 porters to carry eight tons of bulk, a comparable capacity for porters (0.026 tons per porter).[10]

The quality and size of canoes were dictated by the availability of trees and the economic returns to trade. Canoes were dug out of trees by hand using iron axes and adze-like tools. As early as 1506, Fernandes writes about "huge canoes carrying 120 warriors" on the Sierra Leone

River (Smith 1970, p. 518). As early as 1682, Barbot describes canoes along the Gold Coast as seventy feet long and seven to eight feet wide (Smith 1970, p. 518). In the late eighteenth century, Mungo Park (2000) observed a canoe composed of two log sections attached end to end that ferried four horses and several men across the river (p. 293). By the end of the nineteenth century, Murdock's *Ethnographic Atlas* records guilds of specialized boat-makers along the Niger River and on the western shore of Lake Victoria. Stanley (1879, p. 392) sketches the variety of canoes he observed during his trek across Africa in the 1870s. War and trade spurred developments in the technology (Smith 1970).

There may have been economies of scale in the canoe technology, but according to Roberts (1987, pp. 73–74) and Stanley (1879, volume II, p. 270), this was not the case in the Middle Niger or the Congo River.[11] Economies of scale did exist in the size of caravans, on land and water, to protect from attack when traveling through hostile territory. States sometimes provided public goods on water, similar to the halting place along the Great Roads of Asante. Mountains divide, and rivers unite, the saying goes.[12] Here, the advantage may be with river transport because it may have been cheaper to protect waterways than to maintain and protect roads. In addition, canoes pull double duty. When not used for trade, they could dispatch troops, blockade enemies, and wage war (Smith 1970, pp. 525–32).

These are local economic considerations, but in a global sense the most significant advantage of river transportation is speed – the combination of rowing tonnage on flowing water. Not all rivers were navigable at all times. Shallow streams could not support a canoe full of people and trade goods. Some rivers dried up during the drier seasons. Some flowed faster than others, and some were wider or deeper.

All of these features of rivers find expression in the hydrological identity for river velocity:

$$\text{Velocity (meters/sec)} = \frac{\text{Discharge rate } (\text{m}^3/\text{sec})}{\text{Cross-sectional area } (\text{m}^2)}.$$

Velocity is the rate of flow measured in meters per second. It is a function of the rate at which the river system discharges its volume of water, divided by the cross section (width × depth) of the riverbed through which the water is released. The Global Runoff Data Centre (Global

Runoff Data Center 2009) maintains a GIS dataset containing volumetric discharge rates for 687 major river systems worldwide. Based on the concept that a river basin covers all land that drains to the point of lowest elevation, the estimation procedure starts at river outlets (pour points) that coincide with either a confluence with a river, a mouth into an ocean, or an endorheic sink (like Lake Chad). The basins above the pour points are mapped using the flow direction data in the HYDRO1k Elevation Derivative Database. The procedure identifies 405 river basins and 687 river networks around the world.

The GRDC dataset also contains data on discharge rate, measured as the average volume of water discharged per second from the basins, recorded at 3,843 gauging stations between 1961 and 1990. The dataset splits river polylines into equidistant 0.25-length units. The WaterGAP 2.1 program assigns a discharge rate to each river segment. Andreadis et al. (2013) estimate river width and depth using well-established geomorphic relationships between discharge rates and drainage areas (p. 7164).[13] Their estimates of river width are evaluated using satellite imagery.

I convert the resulting estimates of river velocity into hours per kilometer to make them comparable to the walking rates. Africa's estimated mean river velocity is 0.44 hours per km (2.3 kilometers per hour). The standard deviation is 0.11. Some 68.2 percent of the river segments flow at an estimated rate between 1.82 and 3.0 kilometers per hour. The fastest river segment flowed at 6.6 kilometers per hour and the slowest at 1.05 kilometers per hour. Segments are removed if they contain a significant waterfall or rapids.[14] Travelers must portage through these cells.

The GRDC readings on discharge rates between 1961 and 1990 generally apply to precolonial Africa. Alsan (2015, online appendix) reports paleoclimatic data that show no change in African temperature between 1500 and 1900. Fenske and Kala (2015, online appendix) reported observed temperatures for Benguela and Whydah between 1725 and 1875 that show no trend. Nohara et al. (2006) carried climate change models back to 1900. The rapid economic growth scenario produced little change in mean precipitation and river discharge. However, the variance among the individual models is substantial. The models' weighted ensemble mean statistic shows more variance in climate change around the equator than elsewhere (Nohara et al. 2006, p. 1081). There is certainly direct evidence of a southward expansion of the Sahara Desert. Timbuktu was a great medieval city situated at the bend of the Niger River. The town is now well within the desert. Travel time does not account for local changes in river discharge and land cover.

USING LOCAL KNOWLEDGE ABOUT THE BEST PATH FORWARD

River velocity already captures the effect of the earth's slope, which is gradual along the runoff. Discontinuous sections like waterfalls and rapids have been removed using available maps, forcing travelers to portage around. The estimated walking rates in Table 8.1 assume a flat surface. The calculation must be adjusted using a digital elevation model because it is more difficult to walk uphill than downhill or along a flat surface. Traders will have access to guides and local knowledge about the best path forward, hoping to avoid scaling cliffs, steep mountains, or canyon walls, or falling off one.

The vertical factor for walking handles these issues. It is derived from Waldo Tobler's (1993) hiking function, a function commonly used to account for the impact of slope on walking velocity.

$$V = 6e^{-3.5|s + 0.05|}$$

"*V*" measures walking velocity (measured in kilometers per hour), and "*s*" measures the slope of the terrain. *V(s)* equals approximately five kilometers per hour on flat terrain. At a slope of fifty degrees, the predicted walking rate (*V*) is virtually zero. At thirty degrees, it is 0.5 kilometers per hour. On the downside, the drop in velocity is approximately 0.5 kilometers per hour less at each absolute slope value, so at a slope of –30 percent, the walking velocity drops to around 1.0 kilometer per hour rather than 0.5.[15]

A maximum slope can be imposed beyond which the vertical factor is infinity. Setting a maximum slope is like assuming travelers find a way around cliffs and steep mountains. A 6 percent slope is the maximum slope allowed for an interstate highway in the United States. Safe building access ramps are between 7 and 15 percent. Stair slopes are between 30 and 35 percent. The steepest gradient in San Francisco is on Filbert

Street at 31.5 percent. According to the *Guinness Book of World Records*, Baldwin Street in New Zealand, about 3.5 kilometers (2.2 miles) northeast of Dunedin's city center, is the world's steepest residential street, a 350-meter street with a 35 percent slope section.

In our estimate of travel time, *V* captures changes in average altitude between two square-kilometer cells. Setting a maximum slope of 30 percent assumes that a trading caravan facing a kilometer-long path as steep as a staircase will find an alternate route. It is reasonable to think traders will avoid kilometer-long stretches steeper than a steep building access ramp (15 percent), especially if porters are carrying loads. Low maximum slopes are synonymous with assuming that travelers use local knowledge to find the best paths forward.[16]

TRAVEL TIME AS A MEASURE OF EXPOSURE

These data are used to estimate travel time in precolonial Africa. The data projection is Africa Equidistant Conic, a secant projection with standard parallels at latitudes of approximately 20 and –23, which is the appropriate projection for calculating distances in sub-Saharan Africa because it straddles the equator. Cell sizes are set to the cell size of the digital elevation model.

First, a cost raster F_i is calculated that measures the time to walk across cells. The vertical factor (VF) and its limit are then applied to F_i. If a cell in F_i contains a river, then the value is set to zero. This prevents double counting when the river velocities in raster F_j are added to F_i to form $F_{ij} = F_i + F_j$. The ArcGIS Cost Distance Tool is used to estimate travel times to the nearest slave port, assuming a maximum vertical factor of 20 percent and a minimum navigable river velocity of 0.27 hours per kilometer.[17]

Map 8.2 displays the average travel times between each society in Murdock's *Ethnographic Atlas* (circa 1900) and the nearest slave port. Ports serving the transatlantic and Indian Ocean slave trades are taken from the Trans-Atlantic Slave Trade Database.[18] Ports serving the trans-Saharan or Red Sea slave trades are taken from Austen (2010, p. 29). Each society's travel time is the average weighted travel time for all of the cells contained within the society's borders.[19]

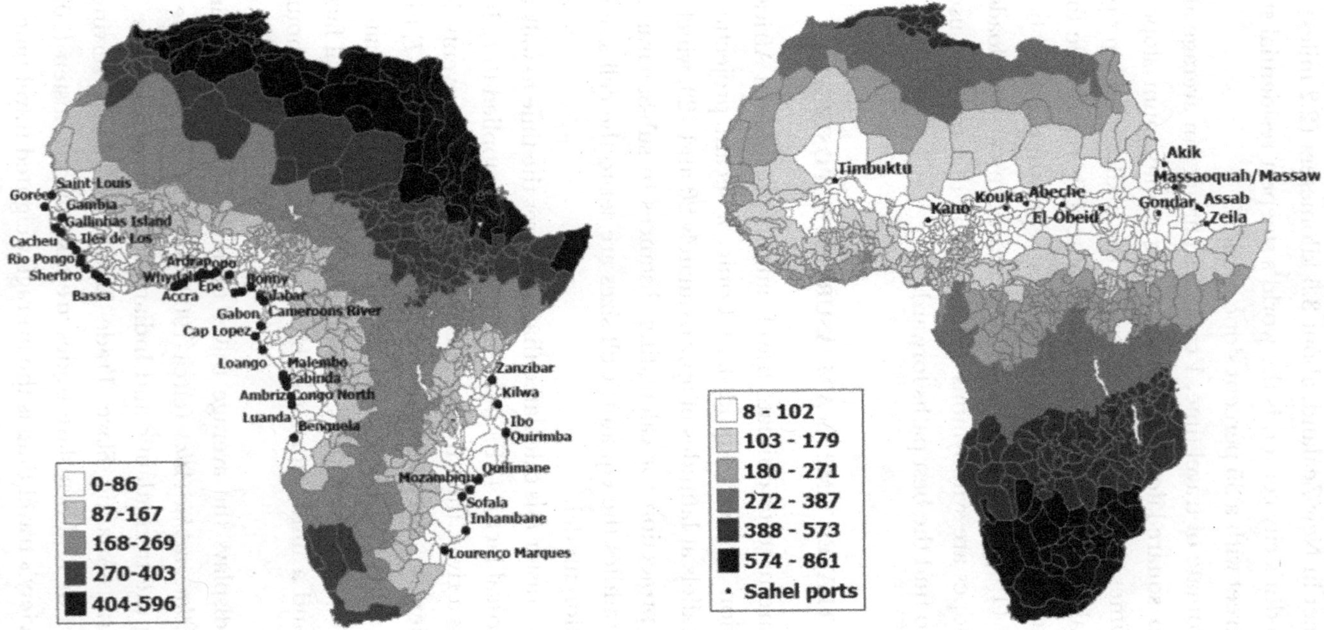

Map 8.2 Average travel times to the nearest major slave port. Data source: Whatley (2022a, pp. 413–14).

Traders could sometimes travel by horse or camel. Enslaved Africans were always transported by foot or canoe, but information about market conditions and load could travel by horse or camel. The tsetse fly suitability index developed by Alsan (2015) captures the general availability of horses and camels.

CHAPTER 9

How the Slave Trades Underdeveloped Africa

> The 15th and 16th centuries were ones of momentous change in Europe ... An ancient Mediterranean economy was giving way to a modern Atlantic. The same centuries were also ones of momentous change in West Africa. Old systems not unlike the feudalism of Medieval Europe were falling apart ... They were replaced by nothing of their kind, and the future lay with the regional absolutisms that were to emerge in the next century: Oyo, Dahomey, Ashanti, and the rest. The political economy began to change. *The diagnosis eludes us still*, but the symptoms are apparent. Status is derived from wealth as well as birth, and the networks of credit and debt as well as of kinship become important in maintaining the social fabric. Everything – even people – acquires a transactional value, and the slave trade becomes the commercial triumph and moral shame of Europe and West Africa alike. The two subcontinents, inextricably linked within the Mediterranean economy in the beginning of the 15th century by virtue of the gold trade, emerged inextricably linked within the Atlantic economy by the beginning of the 17th century by virtue of the slave trade. There is, in all of this, a great debate to be pursued.
>
> Ivor Wilke's (1982a), *Wangara, Akan and the Portuguese in the 15th and 16th Centuries. 1. The Matter of Bitu*

THE FUNDAMENTAL IMPACT

This chapter pursues this debate. The proposed diagnosis is exposure to international slave trades, an exposure that incentivized the reallocation of resources toward enslaving people, and acquiring and maintaining

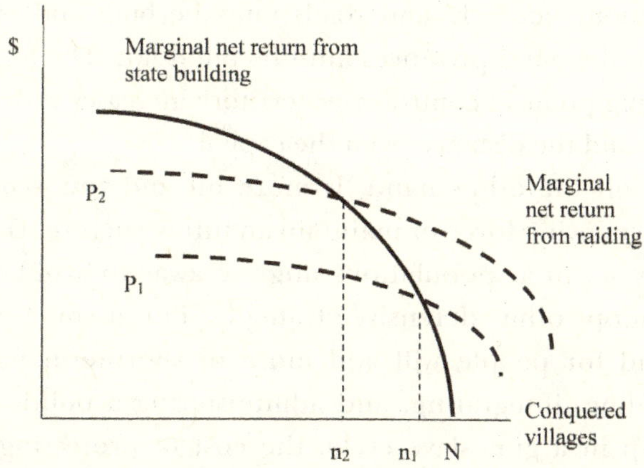

9.1 The fundamental impact of exposure to slave trades. Source: Whatley and Gillezeau (2011a).

slave wealth. The pace quickened with the gun–slave cycle, which acted like a slave export multiplier at the regional level.

Figure 9.1 is a stylized depiction of the typical regional political economy before and after exposure.[1] The players are the rulers of nations and villages. Nations can attack villages to either conquer the village or raid for people. Villages can form alliances but at the cost of power-sharing with other elites. Define *war* as aggression to acquire both people and territory (state-building). Define *raiding* as aggression to acquire people only.

Villages and nations are absolutist in the sense that elites (elders, chiefs, or kings) have the authority to make decisions for their people regarding war, raiding, and forming alliances. This assumption has several important implications. First, decisions are made to maximize the elites' welfare, not the welfare of their people. These are not democracies. Second, if a village is captured in a war, the victor claims the right to the land by disposing of the elite. In other words, the chief is beheaded. Raiding is for people's bodies, but war is for elites' heads.

Finally, assume the economic returns to raiding initially decline slower than the economic returns to war. This is a reasonable assumption because territory annexed by war must be protected from outside aggressors, policed, and administered internally. Taxes must be collected.

Communications networks and roads must be built and maintained. Rebellions in the outer provinces must be put down. The marginal cost of maintaining political control over territory increases with the size of the territory and the distance from the capital.

Raiding, on the other hand, is more hit and run – no need to deploy an occupying force or maintain an infrastructure. Diminishing returns may set in as populations migrate away to avoid capture or as victims adopt other defensive strategies, but at some point, traveling to raid for people will add more to short-term net revenue than defending, integrating, and administering a political outpost. If caught up in a gun–slave cycle, the cost of protecting land and people increases exponentially, pushing the region further into a slave-raiding equilibrium.

Before exposure, the nation in Figure 9.1 will want to conquer N villages. An increase in the economic returns to raiding (from higher slave prices or imported weaponry) will reduce the nation's size (say to n_1) and increase the number of unconquered villages (N–n_1). Raiding increases, with a permanent reallocation of resources away from state-building and toward slave raiding. As the economic returns to raiding increase (say, from P_1 to P_2), nations will generally be smaller and ethnic diversity greater (more outside villages). Exposure to a slave trade even reduces the incentive for village elites to form defensive alliances because exposure reduces the probability that a village will be conquered and the elites beheaded. The model generates a positively sloping slave supply curve. It also predicts smaller nations and greater ethnic diversity in exposed areas (Whatley and Gillezeau 2011a, 2011b).

One last implication of the model. Imagine the villages and the nation located spatially along a line that runs from the coast into the interior. When a coastal nation conquers villages, it will be expanding toward the interior. When an interior nation conquers villages, it will be expanding toward the coast. Net slave prices increase as one expands toward the coast because transport costs decline. Interior nations, therefore, have an incentive to push toward the coast, and coastal nations have an equal incentive to defend their position, but less of an incentive to push into the interior.

TWO EXTREMES THAT PROVE THE RULE: ASANTE AND ARO

This simple model is flexible enough to explain cases as different as politically centralized Asante and politically decentralized Aro. Asante was a large militarized and bureaucratic state that emerged behind the Gold Coast of Africa (present-day Ghana) at the beginning of the eighteenth century. Eventually, all roads led to Kumasi, the capital city located about 200 miles inland and encircled by an efficient farming sector that supported the military and bureaucratic classes. The Asante were powerful enough to defend against British invasion for almost 100 years. They were one of the largest and most powerful states in West Africa.

Our model predicts that slave capture discouraged state-building. How, then, could Asante have developed into such an impressive state at the height of the transatlantic slave trade? Wilks, Hunwick, and Lawler (1996) refer to this as the enigma of Asante: "The importance of Asante is most apparent from its sheer geographic extent. At the height of its power in the early nineteenth century, Asante's empire extended not only over all of present-day Ghana with the exception of the far northwest, but also over large parts of what is now Ivory Coast and smaller parts of what is now Togo" (p. 27).

What were the incentives to conquer so much territory in the era of the slave trade? Part of the answer is the common Akan ancestry. This reduced the cost of power-sharing, which made alliance formation more likely. Asante emerged from an alliance of Akan chieftaincies that defeated Denkyira, the dominant Akan chieftaincy, in the late seventeenth and early eighteenth century. According to Wilks (1975), "There was no Asante tribe. Asante was a creation of the Kumasis, Dwabens, Nsutas, and so forth, all of whom became Asantes under the new dispensation" (p. 28).

What explains the timing of the alliance and the geographic expanse of Asante? The key factors can be seen in Figure 9.2, which depicts the military campaigns that produced territorial Asante in the first half of the eighteenth century (Wilks 1975, p. 19). When the campaigns are projected onto a geological map of gold fields found on page 30 of Dumett (1998), the answer to the question becomes transparent: Asante was interested in territorial expansion because there was gold in

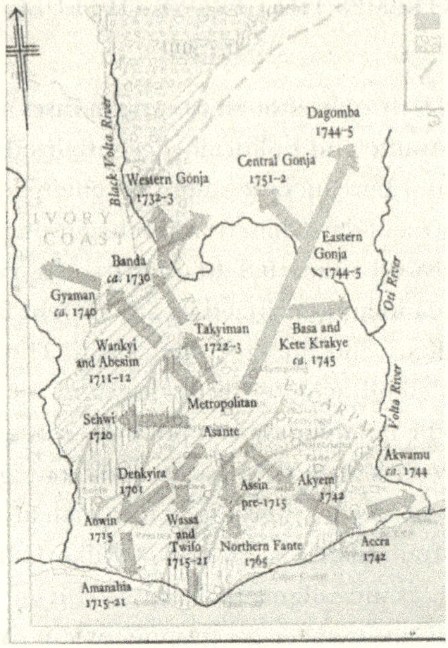

9.2 The origins and expansion of Asante. Sources: Geological map of gold fields comes from Dumett (1998, p. 30). The map of Asante military campaigns comes from Wilks (1975, p. 19).

the territories. Early military campaigns followed the gold, or the gold mines. Northern expansions beyond the gold fields were not annexed but became tributaries, where elites retained semi-autonomy if they made annual tribute payments to Kumasi, most often in captives.

Common heritage helps explain the Akan alliance, and gold helps explain the impulse to conquer territory. The model, however, also predicts that, while significant, Asante would have been larger had there been no slave trade. This appears to be what happened. According to Wilks (1975, p. 18), "the campaign which destroyed the independent power of Asante's neighbors to the north, south, east, and west occurred for the most part in the half-century 1700–1750." As the model predicts, Asante territorial expansion halted after 1750 because the export price of enslaved people started its sharp upward climb. It became more profitable to raid for slaves than to expand the kingdom.

Finally, the model predicts that Asante, an inland nation, would expand toward the coast while coastal nations defend their position. In Asante's history, this is called the "southern problem," where peace was elusive, and rebellion and re-conquest were a recurrent pattern (Wilks 1975, pp. 26–28). In the 1750s, Dutch and English merchants interested in securing peaceful trade to the coast tried to initiate a peace treaty between Asante and the coastal nations of Wassa, Twifo, Denkyira, and Akyem. The negotiations fell apart. Asante conquered the coastal city of Accra from Akyem, but Akyem continued to revolt (Wilks 1975, p. 28). Wilks argues that the case of Akyem was not unique (p. 28). The border between Asante and the coastal states became a kind of catchment zone where nobody controlled territory for very long, but where everyone extracted captives. Coastal states continued to rebel, but their posture was always defensive. This was the pattern along the Guinea coast from the Gold Coast all the way to the Bight of Benin.

At the other extreme is the politically decentralized Aro trading group that organized the African slave trade in Igboland behind the Bight of Biafra. The Aro coordinated the production and trade of slaves over a vast territory but without a centralized state. This outcome is even more curious because the hinterland behind the Bight of Biafra had one of the highest population densities in Africa. Still, it lacked a centralized state structure until the colonial era. (Northrup 1978, p. 118)

This is where Olaudah Equiano, the famous British abolitionist, grew up. The political structure consisted of many villages co-existing in a heightened state of conflict, producing enslaved people for Aro traders. Today, it boasts the highest degree of ethnic diversity in Africa. Klein (2001) calls clusters of politically decentralized societies like these "catchment zones," where centralized societies typically raided for slaves. In Igboland, decentralized villages raided each other.

How was the systematic enslavement of people for export sustained among politically decentralized villages? Why didn't an alliance of villages emerge, like Asante, to form a state that could control violence and trade and protect its people? Moreover, why didn't the uncoordinated violence prevent the transport of captives to the coast?

The literature here emphasizes a self-ordering network that organized the violence and trade – the network of Aro traders. According to Northrup, "at a time when most inhabitants of the hinterland considered traveling beyond the confines of their native villages a foolhardy and possibly fatal venture, the Aro moved in relative freedom across the myriad political units and through the no-man's lands between them. Their forte was the slave trade, much of which passed through their hands before reaching the coast" (Northrup 1978, p. 114). And:

> Given their wealth and control of the arms trade, they might have set out to create a territorial empire, but there is no indication that state building was ever their goal ... The Aro used arms to defend themselves and their allies and, in some places, for limited territorial gain, but their trading operations were not dependent on conquest nor their routes on armies. Their trading network could not have thrived without military measures, but it was not built or sustained by aggression. (Northrup 1978, p. 139)

What explains this "slave trade without rulers?" Our model characterizes this as a situation where the elites of decentralized villages chose not to form alliances to defend their people against slave raiders, but instead chose to protect themselves from beheading. The best description is offered by Equiano himself, who describes, in stark economic terms, how Aro traders co-opted village elites:

> From what I can recollect of these battles, they appear to have been irruptions of one little state or district on the other to obtain prisoners or booty. Perhaps they were incited to this by those traders who brought the European goods I mentioned amongst us ... When a trader wants slaves, he applies to a chief for them, and tempts him with his wares. It is not extraordinary, if on this occasion he yields to the temptation with a little firmness, and accepts the price of his fellow creatures' liberty, with as little reluctance as the enlightened merchant. Accordingly he falls on his neighbor, and a desperate battle ensues. (Equiano and Allison 1995, p. 40).

The traders mentioned by Equiano are most likely Aro traders or their agents. Rather than form alliances, village chiefs created pretexts for raiding neighbors, like the feuding predicted for segmented societies (Moscona, Nunn, and Robinson 2020). Our model predicts this type of equilibrium will occur when elites maximize their welfare over the welfare of their people. When chiefs are absolutist, their welfare may be higher in the slave-raiding equilibrium than in the alliance equilibrium. In the alliance equilibrium, they share power but still risk being conquered and losing their heads. Absolutist chiefs may prefer the slave-raiding equilibrium so long as they can protect themselves from capture.

I do not mean to imply that village chiefs sold people to save their heads. The literature is replete with examples of mechanisms Aro traders used to co-opt village elites, which is why Nwokeji (2010) likens the Aro network to a state. Equiano mentions economic incentives, and the Aro certainly controlled the lucrative coastal trade with Europeans, positioning themselves as the supplier of desirable merchandise, including firearms (Northrup 1978, Chapter 5).

They used other mechanisms as well. The Aro used ruthless headhunters to enforce the equilibrium – threatening to unleash an even greater terror than slave raiding. The Abam mercilessly massacred any village or alliance seeking to withdraw from the Aro network. The Aro also used religion. They became the interpreters of the divine will of the religious oracle of Arochukwu, giving them the power to punish crimes and perpetrate all kinds of superstitions for the benefit of their network and trade. The Aro also propagated a secret society of "insiders" called Ekpe, whose members participated in public ritualistic displays of power and elitism. Initiates were the most influential segments of societies and allied with the Aro. Members were also exempt from capture. The Aro used all of these mechanisms – trade, terror, religion, and elitism – to "persuade" elites to their cause and to sustain a network of hierarchical villages locked in a slave-raiding equilibrium.

THE IMPACT OF EXPOSURE ON NORMS AND INSTITUTIONS

We can generalize the model by thinking of exposure as a treatment that affects the institutions of African societies. Suppose the locations of international slave ports were chosen independently of pre-existing institutions of African societies. If so, any correlations between proximity to ports and African institutions capture the impact of exposure on African institutions. Travel time to the nearest international slave port is our measure of exposure.

Even as late as the nineteenth century, international slave traders still knew very little about the locations and characteristics of inland African societies, so it is unlikely they located slave ports close to known stocks of enslaved people. In 1620–21, Richard Jobson (1932) traveled 400 miles up the Gambia River looking for gold, but as late as the 1790s, Mungo Park's *Travels in the Interior Districts of Africa* (2000) were still not far into the interior, confined primarily to the Sahel region around the Niger Bend, only venturing as far southeast as Bussa, where he was ambushed or died in the rapids.

Port locations were determined primarily by the geography of the coast. Islands off the mainland were protected trading posts throughout the slave trade era. Examples include Cape Verde off the Upper Guinea coast, Sao Tome off the Lower Guinea Bights, and Pemba, Madagascar, and Zanzibar off the east coast. On the mainland, traders established trading posts at the mouths of rivers, like the Senegal, Gambia, Niger, Congo, and Zambezi River systems. Ports were also located in the expansive Niger Delta and the lagoons along the Lower Guinea coast. A few forts were established upriver, on islands, and in protected bays. The Portuguese established upriver forts along the Zambezi River system, although Livingstone believed they did not know the path from one coast to the other. Agents, goods, and information about international slave trades reached inland societies along these rivers, through dense forests, and over mountain passes. The idea is that travel time correlates with the cost of transporting goods and people between inland societies and coastal slave ports. Once exposed, people and societies coordinate a response.[2]

Society must choose to interact or not, and in the raid-or-be-raided equilibrium, they often had little choice but to interact. Once engaged, societies must solve the first problem of slavery – who is free and who is slave. They must recognize enslaved people as a form of wealth, where the rules governing the inheritance of social status influence the rate at which the wealth is preserved. Patrilineal societies have more difficulty preserving slave wealth than matrilineal ones, where leakage stems from the constraint patriliny places on free men's sexual interactions with enslaved women. The Western solution (matriliny for slaves and patriliny for free) solves this problem. Non-Western slave systems preserved slave wealth at a lower rate.

In all slave systems, however, the reproduction of slave wealth reinforces patriarchy by concentrating slave wealth within male-headed nuclear families as opposed to the lineage, the clan, or the tribe. Even in matrilineal societies, the social status of offspring is inherited from the slave mother, so the offspring of a free father and a slave mother is a slave with no recognized kin other than the father. In patrilineal societies, the social status of offspring is inherited from the father, so the offspring of a free father and a slave mother should be free. Here, however, there is a conflict between the patriliny of the social order and the desire to preserve slave wealth. According to Meillassoux (1991, pp. 130–40), this explains why patrilineal societies seldom condone marriage between free men and slave women, but instead incorporate slave women as concubines. The offspring then have no recognized kin other than the father.

Miers and Kopytoff (1977) summarize the results of centuries of this type of pressure on inherited slave status in Africa. They conclude that the "position of the second generation is least ambiguous in matrilineal societies ... Most patrilineal societies, however, made some distinction between the various children of 'free' men, based on the status of their mother" (p. 33). Lovejoy (1983), focusing on the property aspect of inherited slave status, concludes that the incorporation of enslaved people "enabled wealthy men to establish large households that were dependent upon them and not some larger kinship unit" (p. 123).

Was exposure to international slave trades behind these types of transformations? To address this question, we estimate the impact of proximity to the nearest international slave port on the probability that a society was organized around the preservation of slave wealth. The bundle of institutions includes slavery as a property right over people, polygyny as a property right over women, inheritance rules that favor the retention of wealth within the nuclear family, and hereditary succession in local politics.

Figure 9.3 graphs the impact of exposure on the probability of observing an African slave system by the end of the slave trade era (see Whatley (2022a) and the Appendix Table A9.1 for the underlying regression coefficients). In each case, the likelihood of observing an African slave system is significantly higher for societies adjacent to a major slave port, with the probability declining as one moves away.

Across Africa (on the east coast, the west coast, and the Sahel), exposure encouraged the spread of slavery joint with polygyny. The connection was so strong and so universal that one might call them inseparable. The first sentence of the volume on *Women and Slavery in Africa*, edited by Robertson and Klein (1983), explains why. It reads: "Most slaves in sub-Saharan Africa were women" (p. 3).

But we should not expect the impact of exposure to be the same across Africa. The relationship between international slave trading and African slavery has a long, complex, and nuanced history. While African trade in the Indian Ocean dates from the Middle Ages (Subrahmanyam 2019; Horton and Middleton 1988, pp. 72–87), according to Lovejoy (1983, pp. 226–51) the major transformation in East African slavery dates from the late eighteenth and early nineteenth centuries, with the expansion of European, Omani, and Swahili slave plantations on the mainland and its islands. Kilwa expanded as a slave port in the 1780s under French encouragement to supply the sugar plantations of the Mascarene Islands and Madagascar. Mombasa also developed plantations during the late eighteenth century, and by the early nineteenth century clove plantations expanded on Pemba and Zanzibar where slaves were used to clear the land and work the fields.

On Zanzibar, clove exports increased from 140 tons in 1839 to 3,100 tons in 1859 (Martin 1991, p. 451). The plantation sector spread to the mainland opposite Zanzibar, especially along a 110 kilometer-wide stretch of coast from Mtwapa to Mambrui, but also included other places as far north as the Banadir coast and as far south as Mozambique (Lovejoy 1983, p. 230). By the 1830s, Arab merchants reached the inland commercial center of Tabora, halfway between the east coast and Lake Tanganyika. By the 1870s, Muslims, including Arabs, Swahili, and converts among the Nyamwezi and Yao, dominated a vast network of trade routes that stretched beyond the Highland Lakes and into the Congo Basin, establishing a network of inland slave plantations to supply their caravan trade. This is the inland route that David Livingstone and Henry Morton Stanley followed.

Trade off the west coast of Africa was limited or nonexistent before the middle of the fifteenth century, then the lateen sail enabled Portuguese caravels to sail further down the coast. There is evidence of pre-existing coastwise trade along the lagoons of the Lower Guinea coast, between the Kingdom of Benin and the Akan of the Gold Coast, but no trade into the Atlantic. Then came the discovery and settling of the Americas, the decimation of American populations and the transplantation of slave codes across the Atlantic. In the mid-seventeenth century, an old and

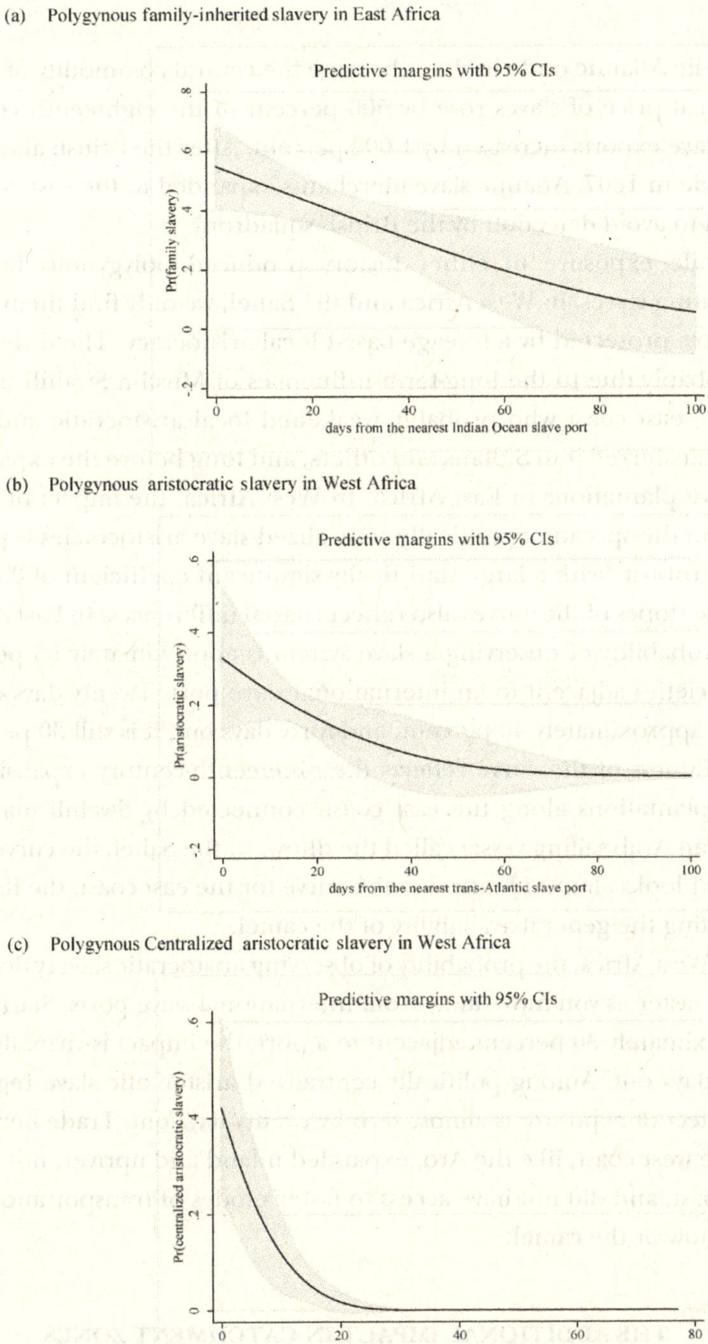

9.3 African slave systems by proximity to slave ports. Data sources: see Appendix Tables A9.2a and 2b and A9.3a and 3b.

sporadic Atlantic trade in slaves became the central commodity of trade. The real price of slaves rose by 500 percent in the eighteenth century and slave exports increased by 1,000 percent. After the British abolished its trade in 1807, Atlantic slave merchants expanded to the east coast of Africa to avoid detection by the British squadron.

While exposure to either history produced polygynous families inheriting slaves, in West Africa and the Sahel, we only find them when they are protected by a lineage-based local aristocracy. The difference is probably due to the long-term influences of Muslim Swahili traders on the east coast who probably weakened local aristocratic authority and transferred it to Sultans and others, and long before the expansion of slave plantations in East Africa. In West Africa, the impact of exposure on the spread of politically centralized slave aristocracies is particularly robust (with a large statistically significant coefficient of 0.227).

The slopes of the curves also reflect coastal differences. In East Africa, the probability of observing a slave system is approximately 55 percent for societies adjacent to an international slave port. Twenty days out, it is still approximately 40 percent, and forty days out, it is still 30 percent. The flatness of the curve reflects the nineteenth-century expansion of slave plantations along the east coast, connected by Swahili mariners using an Arab sailing vessel called the dhow. In the Sahel, the curve (not shown) looks almost identical to the curve for the east coast, the flatness reflecting the general availability of the camel.

In West Africa, the probability of observing aristocratic slavery declines much faster as you move away from international slave ports. Starting at approximately 30 percent adjacent to a port, the impact is virtually zero forty days out. Among politically centralized aristocratic slave regimes, the effect of exposure is almost zero by twenty days out. Trade networks on the west coast, like the Aro, expanded inland and upriver, not along the coast, and did not have access to faster modes of transportation like the dhow or the camel.

THE ADDITIONAL IMPACT IN CATCHMENT ZONES

Some societies were exposed to slave capture in addition to slave trading. The kinds of social conflict that produced enslaved people did not

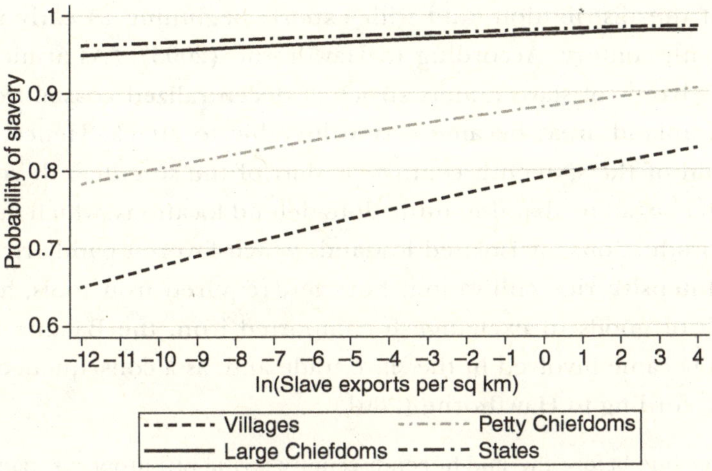

9.4 The additional impact in catchment zones. Source: Whatley (2022a, 2022b).

always have clear winners and losers, and the importation of new weapons of war pushed entire regions into a prisoners' dilemma arms race of raid or be raided, with belligerents sometimes winning, sometimes losing. These effects are in addition to exposure to the trade of captives on their way to the coast.

Figure 9.4 shows how exposure to capture increased the probability that a society would recognize slavery by the end of the slave trade era (Whatley 2022a). Societies that were politically decentralized at the end of the period were impacted most, as one might expect. Historical case studies show how the probability of capture transformed kinship-based societies into bands of young cadets and warriors who used new acquired slaves to raid the countryside for more recruits.[3] Similarly, along the southern shores of the Sahara desert, eighteenth and nineteenth-century Islamic jihads began as defensive movements to protect against enslavement, only to become justifications for enslaving others (Lovejoy 2016).

Decentralized societies engaged in a variety of strategies to protect themselves – like building walls, moving further away, forming coalitions, and changing crop patterns (Diouf 2003). The decentralized patrilineal Balanta, for example, responded by moving into large, tightly packed villages for protection. In our dataset, slave exports from Balanta were 5.6 per square kilometer, which places them in the upper tail of the distribution, and with exports beginning as early as the sixteenth century. According to Hawthorne (2003): "As armies and roving bands of slave raiders struck at decentralized coastal populations, upland areas became very vulnerable to attack. Hence, from the end of the sixteenth century or start of the seventeenth century Balanta began to abandon difficult-to-defend locations, which favored yam production, for isolated lowlands which favored paddy rice" (p. 14). Intensive rice cultivation, however, required iron tools, and in search of goods to exchange for imported iron, the Balanta themselves became involved in the slave trade and, as a consequence, slavery. According to Hawthorne (2001):

> sometime before the mid-fifteenth century arrival of Europeans, paddy-rice farming techniques were developed in coastal Guinea by Mande speakers. However, it was only after coastal populations began to bear the brunt of the slave raids that fed an expanding Atlantic economy and Europeans began to supply the Guinea-Bissau region with iron that Balanta began to cultivate large quantities of rice. (p. 21)

As for the associated political transformation: "As the distance between households diminished, Balanta refashioned their stateless social and political structures to foster broader, village-wide identities. Through those structures, the heads of households, b'lante b'ndang, organized large bodies of laborers to exploit the environment effectively" (Hawthorne 2001, p. 19).

Another example comes from the Bambara of the Middle Niger Valley in the eighteenth century, which exhibits a full-blown transformation. According to Roberts (1987, 1980), the traditional Bambara economy was based on cereal agriculture augmented by hunting. Age-sets institutionalized the intergenerational transfers of surplus. Membership was open to all children of the same age, regardless of clan and often regardless of ethnic origin. The bachelor age-set was the site of the most intense intergenerational conflict. Young men, wanting access to wives, were most conscious of the restrictions on marriage and access to eldership.[4]

Around the beginning of the eighteenth century, Mamari Kulubali led his bachelor group through a series of altercations with elders. The elders eventually excommunicated him, but the sanction backfired as Mamari convinced many other bachelors to follow him. After some initial successes through raids and battles, slaves and other young people joined Mamari in what amounted to the transformation of an agricultural age-set into an offensive and militarized unit capable of reproducing itself.

The resulting Segu Bambara state apparatus was dependent upon warfare and produced little, if any, food, instead producing enslaved people and professional warriors who disdained agricultural production. Fulbe herders, dependent upon Segu for protection, sent tribute in the form of cattle and enslaved people. Some were recruited into the military; others were sold to Maraka merchants or sent directly to Kangaba or Jenne in exchange for horses, firearms, flints, sulfur, cloth, and other luxury consumption goods. Maraka cities paid substantial taxes to the Segu Bambara state for protection, behind which they coordinated a slave plantation sector geared to the commercial production of cotton and cereals.

Where warfare and raiding had limited success, a trade diaspora could exploit intra-societal conflict and mobilize inside agents to do their bidding. The most important were the Luso-African traders of the upper Guinea coast (Green 2012), the Aro in the Bight of Biafra (Nwokeji 2010; Northrup 1978), the Maraka in the Senegambia region (Jobson 1932; Roberts 1987), the Bobangi in the Congo River Basin (Harms 1981), and the Swahili along the east coast (Horton and Middleton 1988; Sheriff 2010). The Aro, like many of these trade diasporas, did not raid for slaves but acquired enslaved people to facilitate trade and to protect those who wanted protection (having access to imported weapons). They bought and sold enslaved people and provided trade goods in exchange for them.

REVOLUTIONARY TIMES

Recalling Wilks's (1982a) quote, "these were revolutionary times," but we now have a diagnosis – exposure to international slave trades, where "status is derived from wealth as well as birth, and the networks of credit and debt as well as of kinship become important in maintaining the social fabric. Everything – even people – acquires a transactional value, and the slave trade becomes the commercial triumph and moral shame of Europe and West Africa alike" (p. 333).

How deep did the slave trade rip into the fabric of African societies? We have seen how it spread the norm of slavery and institutions that concentrated slave wealth in polygynous male-headed households. In that sense, the slave trades strengthened patriarchy.

What about more fundamental norms, like lineage, the foundation of clan and aristocratic rule? Did the slave trades alter fundamental lineage and descent rules and practices? To political scientists like Bates (2010) lineage rules enforced a kind of pre-state "rule of law" at the village level, sometimes called customary laws, like those in Europe before the Papal Revolution. Táíwò (2010, 2021) argues that aristocratic rule in Africa was being contested by Africans, but was brought to an abrupt halt by colonial efforts that legitimize aristocratic authority for its own purposes of maintaining order and collecting taxes.

Did the slave trades destabilize or strengthen lineage and descent rules and practices? An insightful test is found in Murdock (1949), based on the long-standing idea in anthropology that firmly established lineage systems converge on kin-naming conventions that reflect their descent rules and practices, like whether or not you can marry your second cousin or whose property you will inherit. These are the parameters of social life in a clan – your rights, obligations, and expectations.[5] Generations of stable clan life converge on a corresponding "equilibrium" kin-naming convention that reflects these rights, obligations, and expectations. In long-standing matrilineal systems, the equilibrium-naming convention is called Crow. For patrilineal systems, it is called Omaha.[6]

Useful information about a group's recent past is preserved and captured by the incongruencies between kin-naming conventions and lineage rules and practices. If a clan's lineage rules and practices change, so will its kin-naming convention, but with a lag. According to Murdock (1949): "Adaptive changes in kinship terminology … are frequently not completed until the new rule of descent has become established, and sometimes not for a considerable period thereafter, so that they may continue for some time to reflect the previous form of social organization" (Murdock 1949, pp. 221–22). Since changes in kin-naming conventions lag behind changes in descent rules and practices, lingering kinship terminology from a different descent system is evidence of recent changes in lineage rules and practices.

Did exposure to slave trades alter African lineage rules and practices? To reiterate, long-standing matrilineal societies converge on the Crow naming convention, and long-standing patrilineal societies converge on Omaha.[7] A simple test is run on all societies that did not have the long-standing patrilineal kin-naming convention (i.e., not Omaha) to see if proximity to slave ports altered the probability that they nonetheless practiced patrilineal descent and inheritance by the end of the slave trade era. The test is also run on all societies that did not have the long-standing matrilineal naming convention (not Crow) to see if proximity to slave ports altered the probability that they nonetheless practiced matrilineal descent and inheritance by the end of the slave trade era.

The results are reported in Table 9.1. Proximity to a slave port increased the probability of disequilibrium between lineage rules and kin-naming conventions. There is evidence of this across all of sub-Saharan Africa. In West Africa, the transatlantic slave trade discouraged patrilineal descent and encouraged matrilineal inheritance of land and movable property. Exposure to the trans-Saharan slave trade had the opposite effect, encouraging patriliny and discouraging matriliny.

These two results are consistent with sex selectivity in slave exports encouraging the spread of descent and inheritance rules based on the sex that is least disrupted by the slave trade. The transatlantic slave trade exported a surplus of men, in some areas by a ratio of two to one. The Muslim trans-Saharan slave trade exported a surplus of women, primarily as concubines. Sex selectivity in the slave trades may have disrupted the ability to track lineage, and the associated expectations about how well the old lineage pattern predicted current and future rights to property and social status.

Alternatively, sex preferences in exports could have been influenced by African sex preferences for slaves. Sex selection in exports varied more across regions of Africa than regions of the Americas (Eltis 1986), and we have already seen how matrilineal societies had an added incentive to incorporate female slaves because it strengthened patriarchy, which might explain why the fewest females were exported out of matrilineal regions like the Matrilineal Belt in South Central Africa and the matrilineal Akan behind the Gold Coast (Eltis 1986; Eltis and Engerman 1992; Geggus 1989).[8] Patrilineal Islamic influence might explain the

Table 9.1 How the slave trades changed African lineage systems

Impact of slave trading on lineage systems

	(1)	(2)	(3)	(4)	(5)	(6)
	Encourages patrilineal lineage in:			Encourages matrilineal lineage in:		
Proximity to:	Descent	Land	Movable	Descent	Land	Movable
West Africa						
Transatlantic Port	-0.045***	-0.004	-0.004	0.017	0.020***	0.020***
	(0.014)	(0.009)	(0.009)	(0.012)	(0.006)	(0.006)
Trans-Sahara Port	0.044***	0.037***	0.037***	-0.045***	-0.039***	-0.039***
	(0.011)	(0.007)	(0.007)	(0.010)	(0.008)	(0.008)
East Africa						
Indian Ocean Port	0.010	-0.001	-0.001		0.251***	0.251***
	(0.019)	(0.007)	(0.007)		(0.023)	(0.023)
Red Sea Port	0.023**	0.022***	0.022***		-0.025**	-0.025**
	(0.010)	(0.006)	(0.006)		(0.012)	(0.012)
Societies	68	54	55		63	63

Impact of slave capture on lineage systems

	(1)	(2)	(3)	(4)	(5)	(6)
	Encourages patrilineal lineage in:			Encourages matrilineal lineage in:		
Proximity to:	Descent	Land	Movable	Descent	Land	Movable
West Africa						
Transatlantic captives	-0.159***	-0.026	-0.026	0.091*	0.103***	0.103***
exported per kilometer	(0.029)	(0.042)	(0.042)	(0.055)	(0.038)	(0.038)
Societies	110	86	87	112	86	86
East Africa						
Indian Ocean captives	0.055	-0.004	-0.001		0.326***	0.326***
exported per km	(0.088)	(0.032)	(0.031)		(0.015)	(0.015)
Societies	68	54	55		63	63

Sources and notes: see Table A9.2a and 2b in Appendix 9.

trans-Saharan and Red Sea results, but not the Indian Ocean results. Exposure to capture had the same effects as exposure to trade.

Whatever the explanations, proximity to a slave port altered African customary laws that governed the inheritance of social status and property. Murdock (1949), like Wilks, describes the outcome without attributing cause. Based on a complex cross-sectional analysis of his data, Murdock identified what he calls a transitional lineage system in Africa that he coined the "Guinea-type" because of its prevalence in West Africa:

> This type, which is named for its prevalence in West Africa, is transitional ... It is devised to accommodate those tribes which formerly belonged to one of the stable bilateral types, Eskimo and Hawaiian, and which have evolved patrilineal descent rules on the basis of patrilocal residence without having yet undergone the adaptive modifications in cross-cousin terms necessary to achieve a more typical patrilineal structure. (Murdock 1949, pp. 235–36)

Murdock identified another African case as the "Sudanese-type" – communities using distinct descriptive names for almost every possible kin relationship. These societies "occur mainly in a band across central Africa from west to east on both sides of the boundary between the Bantu and Sudanese linguistic areas. Although many tribes in the same area do not exhibit use of descriptive terminology, the distribution nevertheless suggests that some obscure historical or linguistic cause has been operative" (pp. 238–39).

Murdock, like Wilks, did not speculate on causes. Table 9.1 provides evidence that it had something to do with exposure to international slave trades. The empirical results in Table 9.1 call into question any view of African kinship and lineage systems as a stage in human development frozen in time, or evolving linearly from one stage to the next. By the end of the slave trade era, many earlier lineage systems of authority were being transformed into something else. These were indeed revolutionary times!

THE MACROECONOMICS OF UNDERDEVELOPMENT

We can now take a macro-level view of how international slave trades underdeveloped Africa. Again, the transatlantic trade offers the best view because capitalists' records are so good. For similar reasons, we can best track underdevelopment by focusing on gold-exporting West Africa. Figures 9.5 and 9.6 provide the view.

The top (broken) line in Figure 9.5 is the annual number of enslaved people exported from West Africa (meaning the upper and lower Guinea coasts, excluding West Central Africa). Exports increase

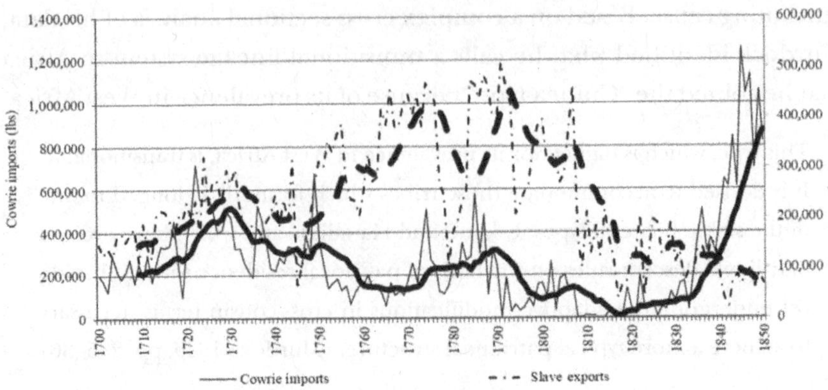

9.5 The macroeconomics of underdevelopment, West Africa, 1700–1850. Data sources: slave exports from the Trans-Atlantic Slave Trade Database (2009) www.slavevoyages.org/voyage/database. Cowrie imports from Hogendorn and Johnson (1986), pp. 58–60, 67.

sharply during the eighteenth century, especially after 1740, peaking at an average of 40,000 per year for the thirty-seven years between 1770 and 1807. At an average real price of £25 per slave (valued in 1699 prices), export earnings from slave exports amounted to approximately £1.0 million per year.[9] If West Africans consumed 80 percent of this, the export multiplier increased equilibrium permanent incomes by [1/0.2] × £1.0 million = £5 million per year.

How much additional money was needed to circulate this additional product? The quantity theory of money is based on the identity $MV = PQ$, where M is the West African money supply, V is the velocity of its circulation, P is the West African price level, and Q is the West African real gross national product. If slave exports generate ΔQ = £5.0 million per year (in 1699 prices), then the money supply or the rate it circulated must increase to keep West African prices from falling. A general decline in prices would eventually depress domestic investment and income.

The bottom (unbroken) line in Figure 9.5 measures additions to the West African money supply (M). Cowrie shells circulated widely as money in West Africa. As a small-denomination currency, "a pocket full of shells could have been easily spent as money in coastal Burma or Timbuktu, in Benin or Bengal, and on long stretches of the Ganges River or the Niger. They were used in the territories of several strong central governments and in hundreds of smaller polities as well" (Hogendorn and Johnson

1986, pp. 1–2). The cowrie did not circulate everywhere in West Africa, but "most major African shippers of slaves were eventually included in the zone (p. 104)."

The shells were mined in the Maldive Islands in the Indian Ocean. British and Dutch traders used them as ship ballast on their return voyages from India, and then re-exported them to Africa, which is why they appeared in European markets and customs records. Hogendorn and Johnson (1986) collect the available data on re-exports to West Africa (pp. 58–60, 67), and these are graphed in Figure 9.5. They show that cowrie imports did not add much to the West African money supply in the eighteenth century. In fact, cowrie imports declined as slave exports increased and rebounded only after slave exports declined in the nineteenth century.

Increases in gold circulating as currency could have added to the West African money supply. We do not have systematic data on West African gold imports, gold production, or industry capacity. There is some evidence of gold imports recorded in the contracts of eighteenth-century slave traders. Between 1707 and 1754, British traders along the Gold Coast of Africa were encountering Brazilian gold smugglers looking to avoid the Portuguese tax on Brazilian gold exports. The Portuguese were using the smuggled gold to buy skilled African gold miners to work the Brazilian mines (Verger 1964, 1976). The 1770s trade books of Richard Miles, one of the largest British traders in West Africa, record gold imports in 16 percent of his trades (Metcalf 1987b). The contracts analyzed by Johnson (1966) show similar gold imports around the middle of the eighteenth century.

Johnson (1966), Metcalf (1987a), Polanyi (1964), and Curtin (1984) all infer from these contracts that the demand for gold in West Africa must have increased around mid-century, presumably to circulate the growing incomes from slave exports. The eighteenth-century devaluation in the value of gold also could have increased the supply of gold circulating as money, but declining cowrie imports suggest a decline in the demand for money. Which is correct?

Gold could have substituted for cowries, but the two currencies serviced different trades, and there is no evidence that gold appreciated against cowrie shells in the eighteenth century. Between 1700 and 1820,

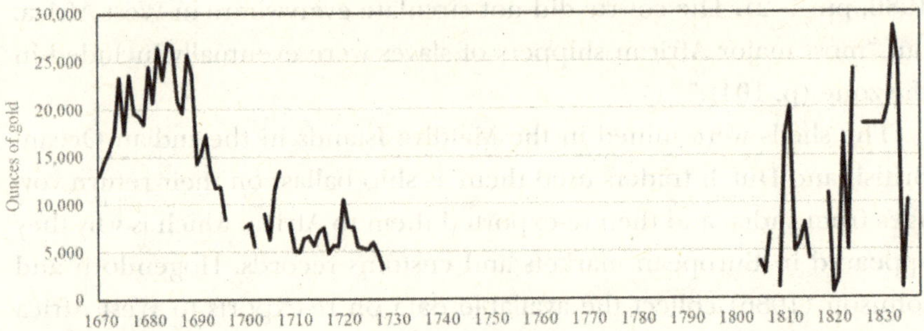

9.6 West African gold exports, 1670–1840. The series before 1730 is taken from Curtin (1983) and includes the West African gold exported by the Royal African Company and the Dutch West India Company. The series after 1800 is taken from LaTorre (1978) and includes all gold exported from "British Settlements in West Africa."

the cowrie gold exchange rate in the Niger Bend was a steady 20,000 cowries per troy ounce of gold (Hogendorn and Johnson 1986, pp. 129–33). Cowrie was a small-denomination currency, heavy and difficult to transport across markets, being limited primarily to local circulation, with gold servicing longer-distance trades.

While we do not have direct evidence of gold in circulation, we do have estimates of gold exports. Gold exports from West Africa never exceeded 30,000 ounces a year for any period between the late fifteenth century and the late nineteenth century, and suggest an annual industry capacity.[10] Figure 9.6 reports annual gold exports from West Africa between 1670 and 1835. Gold exports began to decline around 1690, following the increases in firearms imports and slave exports. Gold exports were nonexistent after 1730, following the large Brazilian discoveries, and they recover after 1807, when slave exports decline.

What is most revealing about Figure 9.6 is the low levels of gold exports in the early nineteenth century. West Africans had just lost slave export earnings equal to £1 million per year (in 1699 prices) and permanent income approaching £5 million per year (for thirty-seven years), and all the economies could muster to replace it was a maximum export of 25,000 ounces of gold, or £50,000 per year (valued at 1699 prices). In crisis times like these, one would expect West African gold mines to approach capacity and for people to be taxed at their maximum to recover as much of the lost export revenue as possible. The amount of gold in circulation must not have been that great. Local specialization and trade using cowrie shells had collapsed, and enslaved people as wealth substituted for gold in the expanding slave trade.[11] Pawns did the same (Lovejoy and Richardson 2001).

In short, there is little evidence of advances in Smithian-style specialization and trade in eighteenth-century West Africa. Relative to the seventeenth-century Age of Trade, specialization and trade retreated. This is the opposite of the trade pattern driving Western European development in the eighteenth century, where export earnings drove specialization and trade. The African pattern is more like underdevelopment, where export earnings from slave production, slavery, and slave trading reduced local and regional specialization and trade. Thriving cities like Begho get sacked. Militarized states "eat the countryside." And villagers flee to the hills.

Viewing eighteenth-century African economies as underdeveloping economies also helps explain the position of West Africa in the eighteenth-century globalization of the textile industry. At the beginning of the eighteenth century, India held a clear competitive advantage over Britain. Britain raised tariffs to protect its high-wage industry but could not penetrate third markets. The continent of Africa, between Britain and India, became the site of an evolving global competition for dominance. Over the eighteenth century, more than 60 percent of British cotton exports and 80 percent of British re-exports of Indian textiles were sold in Africa.[12]

Initially, Indian textiles dominated the cargoes of British slave ships, seen in the Anglo-African Trade Statistics reported in Figure 9.7. According to Broadberry and Gupta (2009), competition between British and Indian textiles for the African market induced early labor-saving technological changes in the British textile industry. After the mid-century explosion in transatlantic slave exports, the Indian advantage in Africa virtually disappears, and both British cotton and re-exported Indian pieces penetrated deep into the African market (see Figure 9.7).

However, technological change and competitive advantages outside of Africa cannot be the whole story because African textile imports were paid for with African slave exports. As Thornton (1998) observes, Africa had a thriving textile industry in the seventeenth century, exporting

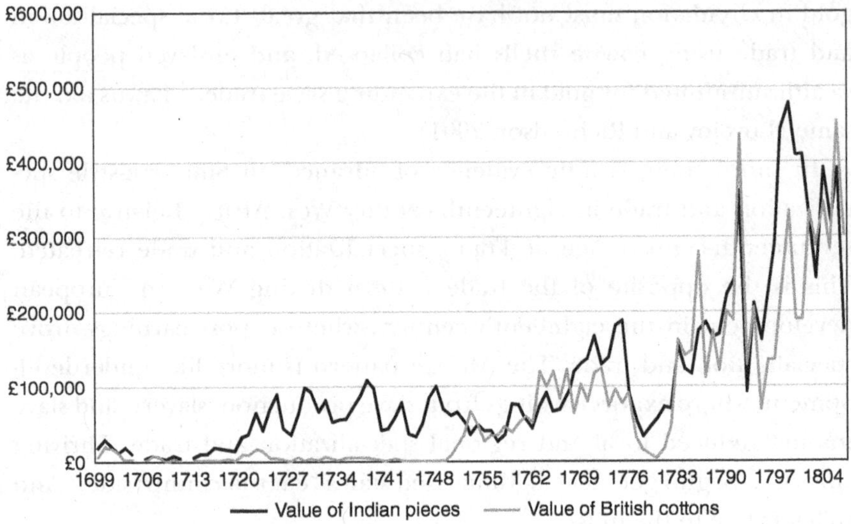

9.7 Underdevelopment's version of import substitution, textile imports, 1699–1807. Data source: The Anglo-African Trade Statistics (1990).

textiles across regions and oceans. But it is too easy to attribute, as he does, the eighteenth-century influx of foreign textiles to conspicuous consumption among Africans, especially without evidence (pp. 46–53). Contractions in the demand for money point to a disruption in specialization and trade, effectively plugging the "Mandinka leak" that early Portuguese textiles could not plug.

Inikori (2009), for example, describes how Muslim economies in the savanna regions around the Niger Bend and Lake Chad, presumably in the seventeenth-century Age of Trade, were putting out large quantities of textiles and leather, and selling them southward to places like Benin and Begho to be processed and exchanged for a variety of goods that were being traded northward, including processed iron, gold, bronze, palm oil, shea butter, wood, and kola nuts (an acceptable stimulant in the Muslim north). Inikori argues that the negative externalities of expanding slave production in the eighteenth century disrupted this interregional trade, reallocated resources toward slave raiding, and reduced the aggregate demand for money (pp. 101–4). Imported British and Indian textiles filled the gap – underdevelopment's version of "import substitution."

CHAPTER 10

Past, Present, and Future

WHATEVER HAPPENED TO PRESTER JOHN?

By 1492, freedom in Western Christendom had been paying dividends for centuries, enough to begin reclaiming territory in Islamic Iberia. The Age of Exploration started with Portuguese explorers sailing down the coast of West Africa looking for three things: trade, the sources of African gold, and Prester John, a mythical Christian priest on the other side of Islam who possessed a mirror that reflected the world. In 1497, Vasco Da Gama began his famous voyage around the southern cape of Africa, up its east coast, and across the Indian Ocean to India, where Prester John was initially thought to reside. Bartholomew Dias must have named the southern tip of Africa the Cape of Good Hope because of the abundance of wealth and information on the other side, including the whereabouts of Prester John.

The diary of Vasco Da Gama's voyage up the east coast is a first-hand account of East African development before European contact (Axelson 1998). Like gold, the observations offer context for counterfactual speculations about what could have been. The diary first describes the abundance of "cattle, oxen and cows" (p. 28), which thrived south of the tsetse fly zones. When the expedition reached the southern edge of the copper-circulating, gold-exporting vicinity of Great Zimbabwe, in Inhambane Bay, Mozambique, about 600 miles northeast of the current city of Pretoria, the ships anchored for five days to take on water.

> This land, it seems to us, is densely populated. There are in it many Senhores. The people of this land greatly prize linen cloth, and they gave

> us much of this copper for as many shirts as we cared to give ... To this land we gave the name Terra da Boa Gente (The Land of Good People) and to the river Rio de Cobre. (Axelson 1998, pp. 32–33)

After another week's sail up the coast, they reached an island called Mocobraquy (Mocambique), north of the city of Sofala, where the Senhor was called Sultan, and the people were

> of the Mohammedan faith, and they speak like Moors. Their clothes are of very thin linen and cotton, of many colors and stripes; they are rich and embroidered. They all wear toques on their heads with piping of silk worked with gold thread. They are merchants, and they trade with white Moors, four of whose vessels were here at this place, carrying gold and silver, cloves, pepper and ginger, rings of silver with many pearls, and seed pearls and rubies and the like ... It seems to us from what they said that all these things were transported here, and that the Moors brought them, except the gold. (Axelson 1998, pp. 35–36)

Here, they met Moors who brought "two Indian Christian captives" and assured them that Prester John was further up the coast but far inland. They secured two pilots for "30 meticals of gold and two hooded cloaks" each, and eventually reached the African port of Mombasa "where there are many ships, all beflagged with their standards" (p. 42).[1] They were drawn into local conflicts between Christians and Muslims and eventually departed from the port of Malindi on Wednesday, April 26, for the crossing to India. That Sunday, they spotted the North Star, "which we had not seen for a long time," and on May 20, they anchored off the coast of Calcutta in the state of Kerala (p. 48).

The Portuguese initially thought Prester John resided in India, but we can be 100 percent certain that Da Gama did not find him there. If he had, he would have told us. Instead, the diary is dead silent for the four and a half months of their stay, except for occasional reconnaissance on local trade and politics. We now know that Da Gama found a thriving matrilineal society in Kerala that had normalized a degree of freedom for women that would have certainly perplexed him, if not shocked him. In Kerala, the matrilineal inheritance system had normalized a degree of women's control over their property and their bodies that European

Christendom had abolished long ago. Certainly, Prester John would not have allowed this.

Information about Prester John's whereabouts in Ethiopia was more promising. Franciscans had been coming overland to Ethiopia through Muslim Egypt since 1440. The Catholic Church would eventually establish four ecclesiastic jurisdictions in Africa from which they would launch religious and military incursions (Kenny 1982). By 1513, Portuguese Christians had captured Kilwa, Mombasa, and Soquotra (an island inhabited by Christians off the Horn of Africa), Hormuz at the mouth of the Persian Gulf, Muscat in Uman, and Gao in India. In a counter-offensive, the Ottoman government of Egypt armed a jihad against Ethiopia and occupied the country from 1531 to 1543. "Churches were pulled down, their riches plundered, their books and paintings burnt, and the clergy massacred" (Kenny 1982, Chapter 1). Ethiopia then asked for Portuguese assistance to expel the Muslims, which they did. Bad move. By 1634, Ethiopia's relations with Portugal also soured. The Jesuits were expelled, and Ethiopia sought Muslim assistance to keep the Portuguese Christians out. "For 100 years the Portuguese had searched for the legendary Prester John, for 100 years they tried to convert him, then separated in failure" (Kenny 1982, Chapter 1; Kiros 2005, Chapter 2).

Born into these tumultuous times was an Ethiopian philosopher named Zara Yacob (1599–1692). Yacob wrote half a century before Kandiaronk visited Europe, the Iroquoian-speaking statesman and protagonist of what Graeber and Wengrow (2021) call the indigenous critique of European Christendom, a critique that helped spark the Enlightenment questions of the eighteenth century. Zara Yacob did the same in Ethiopia, except his philosophy would critique both Christian and Muslim justifications for social inequality, what Kiros (2005) calls an indigenous African Enlightenment: "While Ethiopians were taught that they were living in the center of the universe, the birthplace of Christianity, the Portuguese convinced themselves that Ethiopians needed an authentic Christian credo since the Gospels (according to them) did not sprout in Ethiopia" (Kiros 2005, pp. 33–34, parenthetical comment added).

In Ethiopia, the legacy of Pauline Christianity had come face-to-face with the Christian legacy of the Nag Hammadi Scriptures (Meyer 2008) and the Dead Sea Scrolls (Eisenman 1998). Christianity did exist on the other side of Islam – it always had. Ethiopians inhabited the center of that world, a worldview that Zara Yacob would critique – Prester John's world.

In Yacob's philosophy, rationality was the creator's gift to humans and was required of all justifications of their world, like self-evident truth. According to Yacob, Islamic polygamy violated the creator's natural fairness between men and women because "we do not see eight or ten women for every man" (quoted in Kiros 2005, p. 21). On Christian monastic celibacy, Yacob wrote, "our intelligence tells us and confirms to us without proof that marriage springs from the law of the creator; and yet monastic law renders this wisdom of the creator ineffectual since it prevents the generation of children and extinguishes mankind" (quoted in Kiros 2005, p. 20). Likewise, slavery "cannot come from the creator of man who made us equal, like brothers, so that we call our creator our father" (quoted in Kiros 2005, pp. 21–22). Descartes would require rational proof of God's existence before having faith, but for Yacob rationality itself was proof of God's existence (pp. 38–48), what Kiros calls "rationality of the human heart."

Unfortunately, and understandably, the mountain Kingdom of Ethiopia and the legacy of Prester John would eventually isolate itself from the world. It would be the only African culture able to resist colonial occupation in the nineteenth and twentieth centuries. Today, along with Nigeria and South Africa, it is one of three federalist systems in Africa. Like the federalist system of the United States of America, Ethiopia struggles to maintain democratic governance among ethnically diverse regional states. We should all wish them, and the USA, luck.

HOW SLAVERY AND POLYGYNY SOLVE THE MATRILINEAL PUZZLE

A growing body of literature is beginning to investigate how family and kinship systems (like polygyny and matriliny) influence social outcomes, like access to family planning services, women and child welfare, women's political participation, and more.[2] While it is too early to generalize from these findings, many of the cases come from sub-Saharan Africa, particularly the matrilineal belt in Central Africa. Why?

First, matriliny itself needs to be explained. The matrilineal puzzle, generally speaking, is the following: Why does matrilineal inheritance survive in an evolutionary sense if patrilineal inheritance is more efficient at guaranteeing the survival of offspring? Matrilineal inheritance systems distribute wealth along the matriline, to maternal uncles and their children rather than to one's own children. Matrilineal systems also transfer some of the child-rearing responsibility to maternal uncles. Both weaken the intergenerational link between parent and child and the probability of survival of one's offspring. Patrilineal inheritance, on the other hand, distributes wealth directly from parent to child.

There may be many reasons for the origins of matrilineal descent, but why would it persist when patriliny is evolutionarily more efficient? The "paternity threshold" model emphasizes female cuckoldry and how it can reduce paternity certainty to the point where transferring wealth to sisters' children (known to be related) provides a higher reproductive return. However, the lowest recorded paternity certainty (approximately 0.8) is substantially higher than the paternity certainty threshold (0.3), below which matriliny produces a higher reproductive return (Fortunato 2012).

The analysis presented in this book suggests two social and economic reasons why matrilineal systems might persist. First, matriliny preserves slave wealth better than patriliny. In matrilineal societies, the child of a slave woman is a slave regardless of the status of the father. Free fathers in matrilineal slave systems can produce free and slave offspring. In patrilineal societies, free fathers cannot produce slave offspring without calling into question the existing norms that govern the inheritance of social status.

Second, patriarchy, where men have the power to enforce rules that benefit men at the expense of women, can solve the matrilineal puzzle even in the absence of slavery if the matrilineal society is also polygynous. Rather than spreading wealth across the matriline, men in polygynous matrilineal societies inherit wealth from the matrilines of their wives (their brothers-in-law), so the more wives the better. In the 1920s, after bowing to British colonial pressure, the Nayars of Kerala passed laws abolishing matrilineal inheritance. Men supported abolition in their lineages (from which they inherited nothing) but they opposed abolition in the matrilines of their wives (Fortunato 2012). In short, matrilineal descent and inheritance can survive in the long run, especially if the matrilineal society is a polygynous slave society, like many of the social systems produced in Africa by exposure to international slave trades.

The more interesting matrilineal puzzle is this: What happens to free women in these societies? Even in Asante, a polygynous matrilineal slave society, free women had the right and the freedom to marry slave men. In matrilineal Kerala, women enjoyed sexual freedoms and divorce rights that surpassed those of many modern societies (Pilai 2015, pp. 179–88). The key was female access to the wealth of the matriline (like the house into which they were born) and the independence it offered in marriage markets and household bargaining between husband and wife, or, as in the case of matrilineal Kerala, between temporary partners.

In addition, bride wealth is seldom exchanged in matrilineal societies. When it is, it is minimal, so stipulations about its return following the dissolution of a marriage do not constrain divorce (Goody and Tambiah 1973). Contemporary evidence suggests that women in matrilineal societies have increased rates of political participation, are less likely to believe domestic violence is acceptable, have greater autonomy in healthcare decisions, produce better child welfare outcomes, and close the education gap (see the citations at the beginning of this section). Kerala, poor by most standards, has India's highest human development index and a world-renowned public health system.

KING COTTON: THE WEALTHIEST SLAVE SYSTEM IN HUMAN HISTORY

Slavery has been observed in many places around the world and throughout history. It normalizes the right to possess others, a right that finds economic expression as slave wealth. Western slave culture produced two related but distinct slave systems, one ancient and one modern. The substantive difference between the two is the peculium as an institutionalized form of upward mobility in the ancient system and race as a constraint on upward mobility in the modern system.

America's King Cotton may well have been the wealthiest slave system the world has ever known. As a Western slave culture, it minimized generational leakages. As a racial Western slave culture, it minimized leakages through manumission and escape. Not only did it separate the slave and free sector, but it fed the freedom dividends through interregional trade rather than the more expensive international trade that Europeans had to pay.

It should, therefore, be no surprise that the origin of the United States (with its free and slave sectors) was a proclamation of liberty by slaveholders. Thomas Jefferson, James Madison, and George Washington were all Virginia slave holders, but according to Edmund Morgan (1972), "It was an axiom of current political thought that republican government required a body of free, independent, property-owning citizens" (p. 8). In the New World, economic independence was the foundation of liberty, thus Jefferson's opposition to debt (and Hamilton), artificers, and landless urban workers "who could lay claim to freedom without the independence to go with it" (p. 9). In times of crisis, when employment and income were scarce, these elements might be tempted to overthrow the republic, as in Bacon's Rebellion, and the state would have to increase repression to preserve liberty, not a good look for a republic.

A short-term solution might have been the redistribution of land, but there was another – African slavery:

> A solution, which allowed Virginia's magnates to keep their land, yet arrested the discontent and the repression of other Englishmen, a solution which strengthened the rights of Englishmen and nourished that attachment to liberty which came to fruition in the Revolutionary generation of Virginia statesmen. But the solution put an end to the process of turning Africans into Englishmen. *The rights of Englishmen were preserved by destroying the rights of Africans.* (Morgan 1972, p. 24; emphasis added)

Like the Medieval Germanic tribes that practiced a Western-style slavery but also advanced self-governance among the free, in the United States of America, "As the tide of slavery rose between 1680 and 1720 Virginia moved towards a government in which the yeoman farmer had a larger share. In spite of the rise of Virginia's great families on the black tide, the power of the council declined; and the elective House of Burgesses became the dominant organ of government" (Morgan 1972, p. 28).

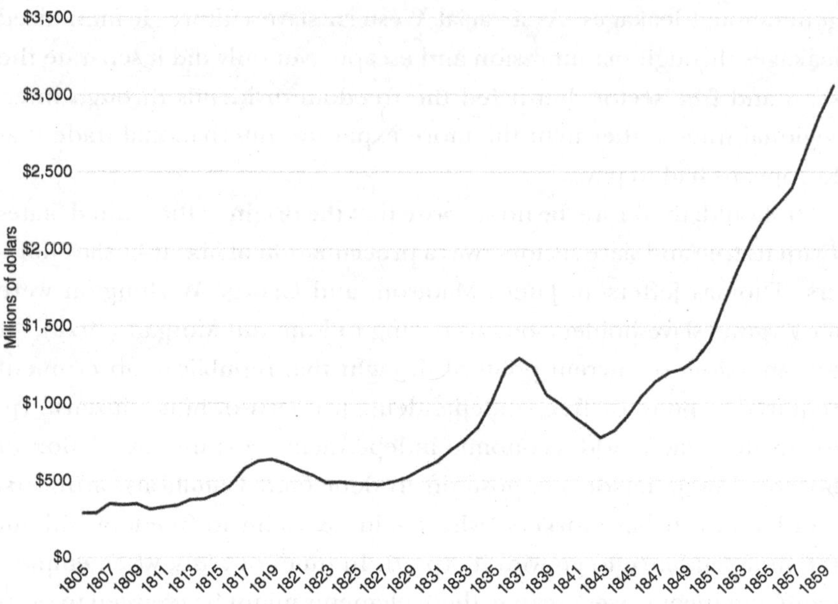

10.1 The appreciation of slave wealth in King Cotton. The figure shows the market value of the US slave population. Data source: Sutch (2018).

Piketty (2014, pp. 160–61) estimates that between 1770 and 1810, US slave wealth was half of all southern wealth. In 1850, it was more than a quarter of the total wealth of the United States. Figure 10.1 displays the growth in the market value of the slave population of the United States following the prohibition on imports in 1808. Before the prohibition, the market value was approximately $300 million. By 1849, less than two generations later, it was $1.2 billion, and just ten years later, on the eve of the Civil War, it exceeded $3 billion. This is a remarkable internal rate of return, and at a time when the purchase price of new slaves on the west coast of Africa had fallen from a peak of $159 in 1807 to $54 in 1850 (Lovejoy and Richardson 1995). No wonder southern slaveholders opposed reopening the international slave trade, and fought a costly Civil War to preserve their slave wealth (Wright 1978, Chapter 4).

ON REPARATIONS FOR SLAVERY

One cannot write a book about slavery and freedom without addressing the controversial issue of reparations for slavery, the transgenerational claim by the descendants of slaves to restore, or repair, the injustices perpetrated on their ancestors. The injustices are not hard to list. Slaves were beaten, raped, forced into dangerous, brutal, and unhealthy jobs, malnourished, degraded, dishonored, traded, despised, and denied the hopes and dreams of family and freedom. One can debate whether or not slavery was a crime in the slave cultures that legalized it, but we have seen how that hair was split. In Western European Christendom, the enslavement of fellow Christians was a sin, the enforcement of which unleashed freedom dividends throughout Europe and its offshoots. The enslavement of others, however, was still a property right, one that fed freedom dividends through international and interregional trade. The expansion of free trade, in this sense, nullified the freedoms of others.

The persistence of the transgenerational claim is rooted in the fact that modern slavery was a racial slavery, the second large-scale Western slave system, where the ideology of racial inferiority emerged to justify the enslavement of African Americans. The transgenerational claim would disappear if racial identity had no social and economic value (Darity, Mason, and Stewart 2006). Justifications for the transgenerational claim are rooted in the fact that free people did not repair the injustice when they could have and continued the injustices for at least another century. The history of failed Reconstruction and the Jim Crow segregations and discriminations that followed is American history, what Darity and Mullen (2020) call the failure to "de-Confederate" the United States.

Reparations purport to repair the injustice, what Robin Kelley (2002) calls the "radical dream" of social equality, and what Darity and Mullen (2020) describe as racial equality within capitalism. Olúfémi Táíwò (2022) is skeptical of the possibility of racial equality under capitalism and calls for worldwide reparations claims to combat the global effects of climate change. According to him, global reparations are justified because the slave sectors of European empires fed the Industrial Revolution, where the adverse effects of climate changes disproportionately affect Africans and African Americans. Those who benefited least from the Industrial Revolution suffer the most from its negative externalities.

This book takes a longer view of slavery, freedom, and development, so it may have something to add to these debates. It locates the origin of racial identity in Europe (as in Western European Christendom), which unleashed freedom dividends that, half a millennium later, created the conditions for the emergence of an African identity. Hundreds of ethnic identities from the continent of Africa, commingling as slaves on American plantations, reconstructed their identities by searching for common African cosmologies, creating similar creole languages, and adapting family structures to the reality of Black life under White rule.[3] The same economic history produced Europe and Africa as mirror images of each other. By the dawn of the twentieth century, that mirror image would crystallize into a Western eugenics movement that would come home to roost in Nazi Germany. If Western slavery birthed Western freedom, then Western freedom birthed racial identity.

Are reparations for slavery a way out? This book has shown that Western freedom and White racial identity are related, a historical fact that still motivates White Christian nationalism. How could Black racial identity, through settling reparations claims for the injustices of racial slavery, unleash new freedom dividends? I believe that is possible if, and only if, the settlement ends racial identity politics and the racial blame game on both sides of the culture war. In the final analysis, ending the blame game is a necessary condition for any just settlement. In a very real sense, it is the whole point of the exercise, the only end that justifies the means. Political minefields and headwinds are everywhere, none more potent than the patriarchy of big-man minority rule and its culture wars, like those currently raging in the United States of America.

Eternal vigilance, however, is the price of freedom. In the United States, the reparations claim (currently approximately $15 trillion and growing) could be used to birth new freedom if it was used to finance something like universal "baby bonds," where every child born to a US citizen receives a trust fund that grows in value over time, to be available in adulthood to invest in wealth-generating assets like education, home ownership, or retirement.

Baby bonds were first introduced at the federal level by Senator Cory Booker (D-NJ) and Republican Ayanna Pressley (D-MA-7). Since 2022, at least seven states and the District of Columbia have considered launching programs (Markoff, Radcliff, and Hamilton 2024). Cory Booker's plan proposed investing $1,000 at birth and up to a maximum of $2,000 each year thereafter, depending on household income (investments should depend on wealth, but that is harder to measure, and easier to game). The investments are deposited in a low-risk portfolio managed by the Treasury to generate an expected average return of 3 percent per year. At age 18 a young adult could access the fund to invest in wealth-generating assets like education, home ownership, or retirement. The program's cost would be approximately $82 billion per year, less than the existing annual costs of subsidizing similar wealth portfolios through tax codes, like tax deferrals on contributions to retirement accounts, or tax breaks on capital gains income. In 2010, Hamilton and Darity (2010) proposed a program where investments would be wealth-tested. "If the average trust is set at $20,000 per child and three-quarters of all newborns (3 million) are eligible, the cost was about $60 billion per annum" (p. 215).

These are not budget-busting numbers, even if you allow for the incentive to increase fertility, which needs to be studied. In FY 2022 the federal budget was $6.75 trillion. In addition, the figure of between $60 billion and $89 billion a year is the gross cost of the program. It does not take into account savings from reductions in public spending on poverty programs and education subsidies, not to mention reductions in crime, abortion, incarceration, and drug abuse. Zewde (2019), using the Panel Study of Income Dynamics, estimates that baby bonds could reduce the median racial wealth gap from a factor of 16 to a factor of 1.2. This does not address the gross racial inequality at the upper end of the wealth distribution, but baby bonds could equalize the wealth experiences of the vast majority of Americans – Black, White, and other.

$82 billion per year add up to $15 trillion in 190 years! A reparations settlement could fund approximately nine cohorts of twenty-year-olds, or six thirty-year generations of families. The fund would need to be safe and independent of political influence (the hard part), but six generations of new freedom is a lot of economic growth and welfare enhancement. Call the fund the Second Reconstruction Bank, or something similar, or not, but this time, pay it forward. Rather than cut a check to the generation of descendants who agitate for reparations, refocus the agitation for the welfare of the next generation. Paying it forward is precisely what we are asking our ancestors to do. It is the righteous way to honor their legacy.

I am not suggesting that reparations pay for a universal baby bonds program of this scale and magnitude. That is a political issue, not a scholastic or abstract one. The American Civil Liberties Union (2023) has reported polling data on baby bonds showing nearly universal net favorability (support minus opposition) across age, geography, race, even political party. Net favorability increases when the question adds stipulations on how the funds can be spent. The poll, however, does not ask if respondents favor a larger and longer program that ends the racial blame game. I suspect net favorability would increase again, but by how much? The people, I dare say, have not been asked. The answer might surprise us. The deal might be a bargain!

For Africa, the reparations issues are different. Exposure to international slave trades underdeveloped Africa in all the ways documented in this book: large-scale slavery, ethnic stratification, decentralized political systems, large patriarchal polygynous households, inherited aristocracies, and retreats from specialization and trade. As in all slave systems, insider-outsider marked the boundaries between slave and free, but Western-style slavery (with patriliny for the free and matriliny for slaves) never took hold in Africa. Justifications took many forms but seldom as racialized immutable human differences. That would come later, with European colonial occupation in the nineteenth and twentieth centuries.

While the abolition of slavery was a stated justification for European colonization of Africa, colonial authorities quickly realized that precolonial traditions of authority were required for political stability, infrastructure development, and revenue enhancement.[4] Rather than encourage competitive markets in labor and land, colonial authorities strengthened indigenous chiefly authority over "customary" laws and lands, and enlisted allied chiefs in the collection of taxes and the recruitment of labor for the colonial effort.[5]

Colonial-era efforts to abolish African slavery may have even intensified gender-based exploitation by making wife pawning a more acceptable form of property rights in people. Lovejoy and Falola (2003) document that most pawns in the colonial era were women, and that pawning rose substantially in the colonial era, although they caution that this might be a reflection of better recordkeeping (pp. 1–26). Douglas (1964) describes how the pawning of wives in Central Africa converted matrilineal rights in land into inheritable patrilineal rights in the pawned wife and her children. Vansina (2010) describes a similar dynamic among the matrilineal Kuba in colonial Congo.[6]

Post-colonial African nation-states have claimed reparations from colonizers, perhaps because each state had their own history of beneficiaries and victims of slavery and slave trading (Howard-Hassmann 2008; Táíwò 2022). This book documents a prisoner's dilemma arms race of raid or be raided that few Africans could escape, even if they wanted to. Recognizing this fact might reduce internal claims for reparations, one ethnic group from another, and strengthen external ones, whatever they might be.

Another implication of the book is that indirect colonial rule sanctioned and legitimized as "customary authority" the kinds of authority that emerged out of the slave trade era.[7] The colonial sanctioning of this authority must have changed the local distribution of rights, otherwise the colonial policy would not have stabilized the situation. Either labor gained rights to stay on the land (or protections from displacement) or landlords gained powers to control labor mobility. According to Domar (1970) the outcome depends on the prevailing strength of the aristocracy. Strong aristocracies will control labor mobility while weaker ones will permit greater freedoms. Indirect rule strengthened aristocracies.

Today, slavery in Africa is officially dead, but customary authority lives on.[8] Táíwò (2021) argues that the authority of customary chiefs cannot be liberal because their authority derived from colonial powers interested in pacifying subjects, not advancing liberties and freedoms. He also argues that liberalism was advancing in Africa before colonial occupation put a stop to it (Táíwò 2010). If left to their own devices to question and restructure power relations, Africans would have "figured it out" and moved toward modernity. Perhaps. Perhaps not. Counterfactuals like that are hard to confirm, but the evidence presented here, on the simultaneous disruption in lineage systems and the strengthening of the aristocracies that rely on them, is an indication that the foundations of political authority were being contested before colonial authorities strengthened aristocracies.

Legal scholars will continue to debate the future of customary authority in a modern democracy, but there is no debating the fact that customary authority in Africa today is a mechanism that discriminates against migrants (aliens) and women, and their rights to own and inherit property.[9] Reparations for slavery in Africa could begin here, in challenging and restructuring local institutions and customary authority in ways that advance freedom and development at the local level. Political minefields and headwinds are everywhere, none more potent than the patriarchy of big-men minority rule and its culture wars, like those currently raging in Africa. Eternal vigilance, however, is the price of freedom – and development.

Appendix to Chapter 5

Table A5.1 The impact of the tsetse fly on the probability of observing polygyny, centralization, and slavery, circa 1900

	(1)	(2)	(3)	(4)	(5)	(6)
VARIABLES	Polygyny	Polygyny	Centralization	Centralization	Slavery	Slavery
Tsetse fly exposure, circa 1900	0.334***	0.591***	−0.289***	−0.092	0.387***	0.250
	(0.092)	(0.201)	(0.080)	(0.176)	(0.109)	(0.238)
Region_North	−1.634***	−1.582***	0.678**	0.543	0.439	0.203
	(0.359)	(0.386)	(0.315)	(0.351)	(0.449)	(0.435)
Region_South	0.069	−0.264	0.645**	0.581*	−0.821**	−0.597
	(0.374)	(0.345)	(0.290)	(0.309)	(0.336)	(0.404)
Region_East	−0.046	−0.013	0.063	0.049	−0.317	−0.334
	(0.224)	(0.230)	(0.197)	(0.200)	(0.243)	(0.251)
Region_West	0.255	0.336	0.146	0.162	0.555**	0.551**
	(0.210)	(0.217)	(0.178)	(0.178)	(0.280)	(0.277)
Date of observation	−0.002	−0.000	−0.002	−0.002	−0.006	−0.007*
	(0.004)	(0.004)	(0.003)	(0.003)	(0.004)	(0.004)
Fly exposure (×) exposure to coastal port		0.007		−0.004		−0.008
		(0.005)		(0.004)		(0.006)
Fly exposure (×) exposure to Sahel port		−0.011***		−0.004		0.008**
		(0.004)		(0.003)		(0.004)
Constant	4.730	1.461	3.800	2.988	12.891*	15.080**
	(7.655)	(8.043)	(6.187)	(6.486)	(7.294)	(7.655)
Observations	376	373	382	379	340	337

Notes: Coefficients are the estimated coefficients from the probit specification. Robust standard errors are in parentheses. *** $p < 0.01$, ** $p < 0.05$, * $p < 0.1$. The dependent variables are from the *Ethnographic Atlas*. Centralization is "Large Chiefdom" and above. Slavery is "Never Slavery." Tsetse fly exposure, circa 1900, is the tsetse fly suitability index from Alsan (2015). Tsetse fly exposure, before exposure to slave trades removes the correlation between the tsetse fly suitability index and travel time to the nearest slave post (in days). Controls are regional indicators and observation date, taken from the *Ethnographic Atlas*.

Appendix to Chapter 6

Here, I estimate a simple supply-and-demand system of equations using eighteenth-century British data.

$$P = S(Q, X_s)$$

$$P = D(Q, X_d)$$

P is the price that British merchants pay for enslaved Africans on the coast of Africa. *Q* is the number of enslaved Africans boarding those ships. X_d is a set of demand shifters (*CARGO* and *WARS*), and X_s is a supply sifter (*GUNPOWDER*).

We set $D(Q, X_d) = S(Q, X_s)$ and solve for the equilibrium Q^* as a function of the shifters. $Q^* = H(X_d, X_s)$. We then totally differentiate the relationship to express changes in the equilibrium quantities of $SLAVES_t$ as a function of changes in demand-and-supply shifters.

$$dQ^* = \sum_i \frac{\partial H}{\partial X_i} dX_i$$

The estimated coefficients reported in Tables A6.1 and in Table 6.2 in Chapter 6 are estimates of the partial derivatives. They capture the marginal impact of changes in the shifters on changes in the number of enslaved people boarding British ships.

We have data to estimate the following partial derivatives:

$$dSLAVES = \alpha_1 d(CARGO) + \alpha_2 d(SugarRev) + \alpha_4 d(WAR) + \alpha_5 d(GUNS) + \varepsilon$$

GUNS measures the annual pounds of gunpowder shipped to Africa on British ships, which should influence the number of enslaved people

Table A6.1 The impacts of supply and demand shifters on changes in British slave exports, before and after 1740

Dependent variable = Change in British slave purchases						
	Unweighted gunpowder			Weighted gunpowder		
	1699-1807	1699-1739	1740-1807	1699-1807	1699-1739	1740-1807
VARIABLES	(1)	(2)	(3)	(4)	(5)	(6)
Δ(t) ln(lb. of	0.169**	0.214**	0.069	0.112*	0.178*	0.006
gunpowder)	(0.074)	(0.101)	(0.104)	(0.063)	(0.098)	(0.070)
Δ(t-1) ln(lb. of	0.034	0.014	0.022	0.089**	0.130*	0.051
gunpowder)	(0.053)	(0.081)	(0.071)	(0.044)	(0.070)	(0.058)
Δ(t-2) ln(lb. of	0.032	0.036	0.021	0.011	-0.057	0.017
gunpowder)	(0.047)	(0.083)	(0.061)	(0.045)	(0.075)	(0.056)
Δ(t) ln(sugar	0.047	0.030	0.073	0.095	0.173	0.067
revenue)	(0.085)	(0.145)	(0.122)	(0.087)	(0.117)	(0.125)
Δ(t) ln(cargo)	0.418***	0.236***	0.561***	0.466***	0.277**	0.612***
	(0.072)	(0.085)	(0.088)	(0.073)	(0.102)	(0.082)
Δ(t) Wars	0.029	0.066	-0.020	0.032	0.086	-0.024
	(0.056)	(0.105)	(0.059)	(0.051)	(0.074)	(0.055)
Constant	-0.012	-0.009	-0.013	-0.015	-0.006	-0.014
	(0.018)	(0.030)	(0.021)	(0.017)	(0.027)	(0.020)
F-Stat	21.51	5.70	25.09	26.35	5.93	26.84
Observations	106	38	68	106	38	68

Sources: See text.
Notes: Natural logs are stationary. Newey-West standard errors in parentheses, with max lag(1).
*** $p < 0.01$, ** $p < 0.05$, * $p < 0.1$.

captured and marched to the coast.[1] Think of gunpowder as an input in the production of slaves, one that might give slavers an advantage over those they seek to enslavers. Gunpowder imports are also lagged because it may take time for additional gunpowder to produce additional slaves for export. British gunpowder could be used to produce slaves that other nations buy, or British slave traders might buy African slaves that were captured using other nations' gunpowder imports. To reduce these kinds of leakages and injections in the observed British gunpowder–slave relationship, columns (4)–(6) of Table A6.1 weight British gunpowder by the degree of British monopoly in major British trade ports (see Whatley 2018). *SugarRev* is gross revenue from sugar produced on British plantations in the Americas and should influence the British demand for enslaved people (see Whatley 2018). *WAR* controls for the impact of British wars on British demand.[2]

Results are reported in Table A6.1. Over the 107 years (column 1), an increase in *GUNS*, as a supply shifter, increased equilibrium *SLAVE* exports. Columns (4)–(6) remove some of the leakages and injections in the British gun–slave relationship and reveal how it also took time for changes in British gunpowder to produce more British slave purchases.

Appendix to Chapter 9

Table A9.1 reports probit estimates of the impact of proximity to port on the probability that an African society was organized to preserve slave wealth by the end of the slave trade era. The bundle of institutions includes slavery as a property right over people, polygyny as a property right over women, inheritance rules that favor the retention of wealth within the nuclear family, and hereditary succession in politics. The first panel reports results for all of Africa, the second panel for West Africa, and the third panel for East Africa.[1] The conditional predicted probabilities graphed in Figure 9.3 are obtained by the inverse probit transformation, where the predicted probabilities vary over the distribution of covariates.

First, consider the all-Africa sample. The impacts on family structure are reported in columns one to three. Column one reports the coefficient on the joint outcome of slavery and polygyny and shows that proximity to ports spread the institution of slavery joint with the institution of polygyny.[2] This result is found for all of Africa, and for East and West Africa. The connection between slavery and polygyny is so strong and so universal that one might call them inseparable. The first sentence of the volume *Women and Slavery in Africa*, edited by Robertson and Klein (1983), explains why. It reads: "Most slaves in sub-Saharan Africa were women" (p. 3).

The trade of enslaved people also created slave wealth. Columns two and three report exposure effects on the joint outcome of slavery and inheritance rules that favor wealth retention within the nuclear family.[3] The estimated coefficients in the all-Africa sample are large and statistically significant for capital (including enslaved people) and land.[4] To the

Table A9.1 Estimated impact of exposure to slave trade on bundles of African institutions

	Slavery joint with					Bundles of institutions		
		Own children inherit						
	Polygyny	Capital	Land	Hereditary political succession	Political centralization	Cols. (1)–(3)	Cols. (1)–(4)	Cols. (1)–(5)
	(1)	(2)	(3)	(4)	(5)	(6)	(7)	(8)
				All of Africa				
Proximity to port	0.029***	0.017**	0.015**	0.000	−0.010*	0.015*	0.024**	0.029*
	(0.005)	(0.008)	(0.006)	(0.005)	(0.006)	(0.008)	(0.011)	(0.016)
McFadden Pseudo R^2	0.281	0.214	0.187	0.137	0.072	0.198	0.236	0.151
Observations	333	275	273	261	337	244	181	181
				West coast				
Proximity to port	0.032***	0.002	0.008	−0.006	−0.006	0.005	0.035*	0.227**
	(0.010)	(0.012)	(0.007)	(0.010)	(0.011)	(0.017)	(0.021)	(0.101)
McFadden Pseudo R^2	0.289	0.219	0.159	0.154	0.101	0.183	0.122	0.356
Observations	228	182	179	171	232	161	109	109
				East coast				
Proximity to port	0.048***	0.030**	0.042***	0.014	0.004	0.029**	0.031	0.005
	(0.017)	(0.014)	(0.012)	(0.011)	(0.022)	(0.014)	(0.021)	(0.016)
McFadden Pseudo R^2	0.248	0.317	0.366	0.123	0.034	0.331	0.354	0.073
Observations	105	93	94	90	105	83	72	72

Notes: Robust standard errors in parentheses clustered by ethnolinguistic affiliation. *** $p < 0.01$, ** $p < 0.05$, * $p < 0.1$. Estimated probit specifications.

Sources: Proximity = – travel time. Institution variables come from Murdock's *Ethnographic Atlas*: Slavery (V70), polygyny (V9), children inherit (V74, V76), and hereditary local headship (V72). Political centralization includes large chiefdoms and states (V33). Controls include patrilineal descent (V43), political hierarchies (V33), tsetse fly suitability from Alsan (2015), and the agricultural suitability index from Michalopoulos and Papaioannou (2013). Region controls are north, south, east, west, and central, and come from Michalopoulos and Papaioannou (2013). West coast includes the north, west, and central regions. East coast includes the east and south regions. The date of observation comes from Murdock's *Ethnographic Atlas* (V102). Data on ethnolinguistic affiliation were taken from Alsan (2015).

author's knowledge, this is the first empirical evidence showing that the international slave trades altered patterns of intergenerational wealth accumulation in Africa, encouraging the concentration of wealth within the nuclear family as opposed to the lineage, the clan, or the tribe.

The last three columns go further and report results for bundles of institutions. Column six bundles slavery, polygyny, and the inheritance of wealth within the nuclear family. In the all-Africa sample, proximity to port encouraged the spread of polygynous family-inheriting slavery – i.e., slavery and polygyny as integral components of family structure, with wealth accumulated within the nuclear family over generations. Column seven adds hereditary political succession at the local level and finds that proximity to port encouraged the spread of family-based polygynous slavery under inherited local political control. Call this polygynous aristocratic family-inheriting slavery. Column eight adds the level of political centralization beyond the local level and finds that proximity to port also encouraged the spread of polygynous family-inheriting slavery under the protection of politically centralized aristocracies.

These are the results for all of Africa. They mask essential differences between East and West Africa. In all areas of Africa, proximity to ports encouraged the spread of slavery, joined with polygyny, but this is where the similarities end. Column six shows that in East Africa, proximity to port encouraged the spread of polygynous family-inheriting slavery independent of political institutions, which is consistent with the driving force being the expansion of export-oriented slave plantations in the late eighteenth and early nineteenth centuries. Columns seven and eight show that the effects of exposure were very different in West Africa. Here, polygynous family-inherited slavery emerges only under the protection of a lineage-based local aristocracy, which is consistent with West African slavery evolving out of the adaptations of lineage systems to long-term exposure to slave trades. In West Africa, the impact of proximity on the spread of politically centralized slave aristocracies is extremely robust, with a statistically significant coefficient of 0.227.

Table A9.2a Impacts of exposure to slave trading on descent and inheritance systems, West Africa

	(1)	(2)	(3)	(4)	(5)	(6)
	Patrilineal descent	Patrilineal land	Patrilineal moveable property	Matrilineal descent	Matrilineal land	Matrilineal moveable property
Proximity to coastal port	-0.045***	-0.004	-0.004	0.017	0.020***	0.020***
	(0.014)	(0.009)	(0.009)	(0.012)	(0.006)	(0.006)
Proximity to Sahel port	0.044***	0.037***	0.037***	−0.045***	−0.039***	−0.039***
	(0.011)	(0.007)	(0.007)	(0.010)	(0.008)	(0.008)
Centralization	−0.023	0.188	0.179	0.462***	0.163	0.163
	(0.200)	(0.158)	(0.152)	(0.179)	(0.238)	(0.238)
Agricultural suitability index	1.163	2.270***	2.311***	−1.725	−0.977	−0.977
	(0.940)	(0.853)	(0.859)	(1.705)	(1.413)	(1.413)
Tsetse suitability index	0.236*	−0.131	−0.124	−0.118	−0.061	−0.061
	(0.142)	(0.158)	(0.155)	(0.121)	(0.101)	(0.101)
Date observed	0.016	−0.004	−0.004	−0.008	−0.008	−0.008
	(0.010)	(0.008)	(0.008)	(0.016)	(0.016)	(0.016)
Constant	−29.979	8.553	7.795	13.251	13.435	13.435
	(20.094)	(14.753)	(14.819)	(32.562)	(30.761)	(30.761)
Observations	110	86	87	112	86	86

Table A9.2b Impacts of exposure to slave trading on descent and inheritance systems, East Africa

VARIABLES	(1) Patrilineal descent	(2) Patrilineal land	(3) Patrilineal moveable property	(4) Matrilineal descent	(5) Matrilineal land	(6) Matrilineal moveable property
Proximity coastal port	0.010	−0.001	−0.001	119.146	0.251***	0.251***
	(0.019)	(0.007)	(0.007)	(0.000)	(0.023)	(0.023)
Proximity Sahel port	0.023**	0.022***	0.022***	−8.277	−0.025**	−0.025**
	(0.010)	(0.006)	(0.006)	(0.000)	(0.012)	(0.012)
Centralization	−0.346	0.382	0.435	−139.768	0.589***	0.589***
	(0.425)	(0.576)	(0.592)	(0.000)	(0.209)	(0.209)
Agricultural suitability index	−2.111*	1.209	1.228	4,394.181	13.943***	13.943***
	(1.183)	(1.407)	(1.412)	(0.000)	(2.443)	(2.443)
Tsetse suitability index	−0.745**	−0.463***	−0.449***	−129.102	−0.252	−0.252
	(0.297)	(0.147)	(0.147)	(0.000)	(0.216)	(0.216)
Date observed	−0.019***	0.000	0.001	15.538	0.037**	0.037**
	(0.006)	(0.005)	(0.005)	(0.000)	(0.015)	(0.015)
Constant	40.075***	0.077	−1.057	−31,702.914	−77.948**	−77.948**
	(11.731)	(9.596)	(9.299)	(0.000)	(30.786)	(30.786)
Observations	68	54	55	77	63	63

Notes: Robust standard errors in parentheses clustered by ethnolinguistic affiliation. *** $p < 0.01$, ** $p < 0.05$, * $p < 0.1$. Estimated probit specifications. Capture regressions are 2-stage IV probit specifications, where slaves per kilometer is instrumented using proximity to the nearest coastal port.
Sources: Proximity = – travel time. Institution variables come from Murdock's *Ethnographic Atlas*: Slavery (V70), polygyny (V9), children inherit (V74, V76), and hereditary local headship (V72). Political centralization includes large chiefdoms and states (V33). Controls include tsetse fly suitability from Alsan (2015), and agricultural suitability index from Michalopoulos and Papailoannou (2013). Region controls are north, south, east, west, and central, and come from Michalopoulos and Papailoannou (2013). West coast includes the north, west, and central regions. East coast includes the east and south regions. The date of observation comes from Murdock's *Ethnographic Atlas* (V102). Data on ethnolinguistic affiliation were taken from Alsan (2015).

Table A9.3a Impacts of exposure to capture on descent and inheritance systems, West Africa

	(1)	(2)	(3)	(4)	(5)	(6)
VARIABLES	Patrilineal descent	Patrilineal land	Patrilineal moveable property	Matrilineal descent	Matrilineal land	Matrilineal moveable property
ln_slaves per km	−0.159***	−0.026	−0.026	0.091*	0.103***	0.103***
	(0.029)	(0.042)	(0.042)	(0.055)	(0.038)	(0.038)
Proximity Sahel port	0.022**	0.037***	0.037***	−0.036**	−0.036***	−0.036***
	(0.009)	(0.008)	(0.008)	(0.015)	(0.009)	(0.009)
Centralization	0.059	0.181	0.172	0.353	0.152	0.152
	(0.221)	(0.171)	(0.163)	(0.250)	(0.286)	(0.286)
Agricultural suitability index	0.244	2.091***	2.127***	−1.235	−0.522	−0.522
	(0.689)	(0.708)	(0.715)	(1.266)	(1.339)	(1.339)
Tsetse suitability index	0.290**	−0.097	−0.090	−0.197	−0.143	−0.143
	(0.124)	(0.160)	(0.155)	(0.140)	(0.122)	(0.122)
Date observed	0.011	−0.004	−0.003	−0.008	−0.008	−0.008
	(0.009)	(0.007)	(0.007)	(0.014)	(0.012)	(0.012)
Constant	−20.978	7.070	6.303	15.352	13.981	13.981
	(16.849)	(14.200)	(14.097)	(28.536)	(24.474)	(24.474)
Observations	110	86	87	112	86	86

Table A9.3b Impacts of exposure to capture on descent and inheritance systems, East Africa

	(1)	(2)	(3)	(4)	(5)
VARIABLES	Patrilineal descent	Patrilineal land	Patrilineal moveable property	Matrilineal land	Matrilineal moveable property
ln slaves per km	0.055	−0.004	−0.001	0.326***	0.326***
	(0.088)	(0.032)	(0.031)	(0.015)	(0.015)
Proximity Sahel port	0.019***	0.023***	0.023***	−0.039**	−0.039**
	(0.007)	(0.005)	(0.005)	(0.016)	(0.016)
Centralization	−0.343	0.369	0.420	0.387*	0.387*
	(0.412)	(0.589)	(0.604)	(0.204)	(0.204)
Agricultural suitability index	−1.994*	1.271	1.281	3.693***	3.693***
	(1.048)	(1.425)	(1.431)	(1.112)	(1.112)
Tsetse suitability index	−0.757***	−0.491***	−0.478***	0.047	0.047
	(0.252)	(0.157)	(0.158)	(0.115)	(0.115)
Date observed	−0.018***	0.000	0.001	0.008	0.008
	(0.007)	(0.005)	(0.005)	(0.006)	(0.006)
Constant	38.245***	−0.257	−1.339	−18.752	−18.752
	(12.275)	(9.649)	(9.332)	(12.280)	(12.280)
Observations	68	54	55	63	63

Notes: Robust standard errors in parentheses clustered by ethnolinguistic affiliation. *** $p < 0.01$, ** $p < 0.05$, * $p < 0.1$. Estimated probit specifications. Capture regressions are 2-stage IV probit specifications, where slaves per kilometer is instrumented using proximity to the nearest coastal port.
Sources: Proximity = - travel time. Institution variables come from Murdock's *Ethnographic Atlas*: Slavery (V70), polygyny (V9), children inherit (V74, V76), and hereditary local headship (V72). Political centralization includes large chiefdoms and states (V33). Controls include tsetse fly suitability from Alsan (2015), and agricultural suitability index from Michalopoulos and Papaioannou (2013). Region controls are north, south, east, west, and central, and come from Michalopoulos and Papaioannou (2013). West coast includes the north, west, and central regions. East coast includes the east and south regions. The date of observation comes from Murdock's *Ethnographic Atlas* (V102). Data on ethnolinguistic affiliation were taken from Alsan (2015).

Notes

1 REINTERPRETING AFRICAN ECONOMIC HISTORY

1. This is the "turn" in Western Europe described by Acemoglu, Johnson, and Robinson (2005) and in Africa told by Wilks (1982a, 1982b), Green (2019), and others.
2. See McCann (2005), Miracle (1966), and Cherniwchan and Moreno-Cruz (2019).
3. See Garrard (1980), Johnson (1966), Metcalf (1987a), Curtin (1984), or Polanyi (1964).
4. See Brooks (1993), Conrad and Frank (1995), and Abby (2011).
5. For a sample of different ways to measure exposure and their relative power, see Nunn (2008), Nunn and Wantchenkon (2011), Whatley and Gillezeau (2011), Obikili (2016), and Bhattacharyya (2009), and Whatley (2014, 2022a).
6. Data are missing for 1705 and 1712. These years are estimated by taking the average of the bracketing years.
7. See Richardson (1991) for a discussion of countervailing biases in the Anglo-African Trade Statistics. On the one hand, Customs Office records underestimate British exports to Africa. Ships took on additional goods at non-British ports, at Channel Island, and the Isle of Man; and between 1713 and 1730 many ships outbound for Madeira eventually sailed on to Africa. On the other hand, the Customs Office did not record imports of gold from Africa. No official British record of gold imports exists. No attempt has been made to correct for these omissions. After careful assessment, Richardson concluded that the two omissions probably cancelled each other out.
8. The most prominent examples are Thornton (1998), Curtin (1975b), and Eltis (1987). Joseph Miller (1976: 1–10) described this tendency as a self-conscious effort to critique the "Hamitic Myth" that African state-formations had been imposed by outsiders.
9. "Stolen from Africa, brought to America" like Bob Marley's Buffalo Soldiers; or "recollections" in the Works Progress Administration Slave Narratives (Berlin, Favereau, and Miller 1998; Gomez 1998).
10. The slope also slides into a critique of reparations claims in the West. In a *New York Times* op-ed "Slavery Reparations? Healing the Wounds of the Past" (23 April, 2010), Henry Louis Gates, Jr. set off a firestorm by asserting – correctly – that Africans (a racialized Western concept) enslaved other Africans. However, he erroneously infers

that all Africans should be blamed for the crimes of a few and that all Europeans should be held harmless. This book demonstrates that the fundamental cause of Africans enslaving Africans was the extraordinarily high price that Europeans paid them to do so, often in the form of weapons to do it better – so fingering African accomplices does not exonerate Europeans. The African poor may well be the greatest victims of the slave trades as they, too, became victims of slavery.

11. For a full elaboration of this critique, see Clarkson (1786), his award-winning Oxford essay that launched his career as a major figure in the British abolition movement. Also see Patterson (1982), who calls the process of enslavement "social death" regardless of justification.
12. Rodney (1972, p. 135): "It is clearly ridiculous to assert that contacts with Europe built or benefited Africa in the precolonial era ... The truth is that a developing Africa went into slave trading and European commercial relations as into a gale-force wind, which shipwrecked a few societies, set many others off course, and generally slowed down the rate of advance."
13. Thornton (1998, p. 73): "When Rodney presented his conclusions on the negative impact and hence special status of the slave trade as a branch of trade, it was quickly contested by J. D. Fage, and more recently the transformation thesis has been attacked by David Eltis. As these scholars see it, slavery was widespread and indigenous in African society, as was, naturally enough, a commerce in slaves. Europeans simply tapped this existing market, and Africans responded to the increased demand over the centuries by providing more slaves."
14. Goody (1971, p. 39): "It is necessary to remind the reader that, in talking of pre-colonial states, I do not imply that such states were uninfluenced by the advent of Europeans to the coastal areas of Africa. The import of guns and the external demand for slaves encouraged the war-like proclivities of centralized government and consequently the nature of their interaction with other people." Also see Stefano Fenoaltea (1999) and Gemery and Hogendorn (1990).
15. "... there have been times in history when social groups have grown stronger by raiding their neighbors for women, cattle, and goods, because they then use the 'booty' from the raids for the benefits of their own community. Slaving in Africa did not even have that redeeming value. Captives were shipped outside instead of being utilized within any given African community for creating wealth from nature" (p. 100).
16. "[i]f the prisoners were to develop into a true serf class, then those prisoners would have had to be guaranteed the right to remain fixed on the soil and protected from sale" (p. 118).
17. "... developing Africa went into slave trading and European commercial relations as into a gale-force wind, which shipwrecked a few societies, set many others off course, and generally slowed down the rate of advance" (1972, p. 135).
18. For a sample of this growing literature, see Nunn (2008), Nunn and Wantchekon (2011), Obikili (2016a, 2016b), Whatley and Gillezeau (2011b), Whatley (2014), Dalton and Leung (2014), Boxell (2019), and Levine, Lin, and Xie (2020).
19. See Nunn (2009), Fenske (2010), and Michalopoulos and Papaioannou (2020) for reviews.

2 GOING BEHIND THE MIRROR IMAGE

1. The color white denotes "missing data," where the *Ethnographic Atlas* did not record information on this characteristic for this ethnic group. The institutions of slavery and polygyny are depicted in black. The increasing shades of gray illustrate the levels of political hierarchy above the local level.
2. According to the APA Dictionary of Psychology, a social norm is:

> any of the *socially determined consensual standards* that indicate (a) what behaviors are considered typical in a given context (descriptive norms or what people actually do) and (b) what behaviors are considered proper in the context (injunctive norms or what people should do) … social norms include an evaluative quality such that those who do not comply and cannot provide an acceptable explanation for their violation are evaluated negatively. Social norms apply across groups and social settings, whereas group norms are specific to a particular group.

3. Burke and Payton do not distinguish between a social norm and a social convention, where the latter is typically referred to as conformity that a third party enforces: "there is a constellation of internal and external mechanisms that hold norms in place, and the salience of these factors varies from one situation to another" (p. 315).
4. For evidence on widespread slavery and other forms of human bondage remaining in the world today, see Quirk (2009), Lawrence and Roberts (2012), and the annual surveys by Free (2023).
5. North Korea is the only modern state that has not officially abolished slavery.
6. www.oed.com/dictionary/liberty_n1?tab=meaning_and_use#39406838. I thank Deirdre McCloskey for pointing out the distinctions.
7. See Rio (2021) and the discussion in Chapter 4 of this book.

3 LESSONS FROM SLAVERY IN WORLD HISTORY

1. Also see the discussions in Sheridan (1958), and Berg and Hudson (2023).
2. This is not the value of freedom from slavery (Hornbeck and Logan 2023), which also included the income a person would pay to avoid slavery. From an economic perspective, that also includes creativity, innovation, and the opportunities of freedom. Fenoaltea (1984) argues that using the stick (pain or the threat of pain) rather than the carrot (say, delayed self-purchase) tends to increase slaves' comparative advantage in occupations that require routine and repetition (e.g., unskilled) and reduces their comparative advantage in occupations that require caring and discretion (the precondition for innovation).

4 ON THE ORIGINS OF WESTERN FREEDOM AND DEVELOPMENT

1. See *Dawn of Everything* (Graeber and Wengrow 2021) and *Sapien* (Harari 2015) for discussions of earlier societies.
2. According to Rio (2021), the Romans outlawed self-sale because the person seeking it did not understand the meaning of freedom and did not deserve to sell it. The

Carolingians/Franks experimented with part-time self-sale. They turned the act of buying poor people's freedom for food into a Christian charity, and those unwilling to do so were failing in their duty of compassion.

3. Berman (1983) describes the centralized Catholic Church as state-like in no uncertain terms.

   "After Gregory VII, however, the Church took on most of the distinctive characteristics of the modern state. It claimed to be an independent, hierarchical, public authority. Its head, the Pope had the right to legislate, and in fact Pope Gregory's successors issued a steady stream of new laws, sometimes by their own authority, sometimes with the aid of Church councils summoned by them. The Church also exercised its laws through an administrative hierarchy, through which the Pope ruled as a modern sovereign ruled through his or her representatives. Further, the Church interpreted its laws, and applied them, through a judicial hierarchy culminating in the papal curia in Rome. Thus, the church exercised the legislative, administrative, and judicial powers of a modern state. In addition, it adhered to a rational system of jurisprudence, the canon law. It imposed taxes on its subjects in the form of tithes and other levies. Through baptismal and death certificates it kept what was in effect a kind of civil register. Baptism conferred a kind of citizenship, which was further maintained by the requirement – formalized in 1215 – that every Christian confess his or her sins and take holy Communion at least once a year at Easter. One could be deprived of citizenship, in effect by excommunication. Occasionally, the church even raised armies" (pp. 113–14).

4. At universities following the Papal Reform, the Justinian Codex was widely debated – a "long lost" codification of Roman Law ordered in the sixth century by Justinian I, the Eastern Roman emperor in Constantinople.
5. Henrich (2020) refers to the Catholic Church's Marriage and Family Policy (MFP), its breakup of clans and the spread of individualistic psychology as the "dark matter of the Enlightenment" (pp. 427–29). Here I referred to the dark matter of the freedom dividend, equally hard to quantify but definitely a precondition for both individualistic psychology and human capital acquisition.
6. Berman (1983) sees this as progress, especially the work of economic historians:

   A new millennial history of the West, which traces the development of Western institutions from the 11th to the 21st century, has in fact emerged in recent decades ... Economic historians in particular have written books to explain "the rise of the West" as a great economic power in the world, and have traced that rise partly to the commercial revolution in the 11th and 12th centuries and two subsequent revolutionary periods of rapid economic growth, and partly to the development of systems of law that facilitate such growth ... Now that leading economic historians, taking a millennial view, have recognized that changes in the legal institutions have played a key role in the economic development of the West, it remains for legal historians to show that changes in the belief system have played a key role in the development of these legal institutions. (p. 23)

7. When I was in graduate school at Stanford in the late 1970s, my choices for classes were American economic history and European economic history. Today, the choices are much broader, in that they now focus on world inequality and why the world is not as

developed as Europe and its offshoots. The shift from European to world economic history began with the Eurocentric critique, into the Great Divide and a series of articles by Acemoglu, Robinson, and Johnson on the colonial origins of inequality and the reversal of fortune (2001, 2002, 2005).

8. See, for example, McCloskey (2010) and Mokyr (1990, 2017, 1977).
9. Eltis and Engerman (2000), Acemoglu, Johnson, and Robinson (2005).
10. O'Brien and Engerman (1993), Solow (1985), Inikori (2002), Wright (2020), Berg and Hudson (2023).
11. See, for example, Johnson (2013), Baptist (2014), Beckert (2014).
12. Hilt (2017), Olmstead and Rhode (2018), Wright (2020), Rhode (2024).

5 AFRICAN DEVELOPMENT BEFORE THE TRANSATLANTIC SLAVE TRADE

1. The McEvedy and Jones *The Atlas of Population* (MJ *Atlas*) has 1,953 citations in Google Scholar, but more importantly, the data have been cited in some of the most influential studies of long-term economic development published in the past two decades, receiving literally hundreds of thousands of citations in the literature on the economic rise of Europe and its offshoots, the Great Divergence between East and West Eurasia, and the origins of global economic inequality in general, even tests of the new unified growth theory. To say that the MJ *Atlas* has been an influential and fundamental piece of information in the modern economic development literature would be an understatement. Economic historians, however, are more skeptical (see Guinnane, 2023).
2. See Frankema and Jerven (2014) and Manning (2010).
3. How does Thornton (1977) reconcile large slave exports from Kongo with a rapidly growing population of Kongo? "All this indicates that while Kongo rulers did participate in the slave trade, they generally did not export their own subjects" (p. 528). More recent research does not support this view. Estimates of slave exports from Kongo were built up from Kongo's own ethnicities found in the Americas.
4. See Olsson and Hibbs Jr. (2005), Currie and Mace (2009), Turchin, Adams, and Hall (2006), and Laitin and Moortgat (2012).
5. The trade ounce has been identified and discussed by a number of historians. For a representative sample see Polanyi (1964), Johnson (1966), and Curtin (1984).
6. Johnson (1966), Curtin (1984), and Polanyi (1964) vary in their interpretations of this evidence, but they all see the fixed "ounce" prices of the earlier period as a reflection of the dominance of "Africanism" in coastal trade, which passed away with the spread of European trade culture in the eighteenth century.

6 THE TRANSATLANTIC SLAVE TRADE IN AFRICA

1. The Anglo-African Trade Statistics do not report trade by region, but several studies have analyzed trade books and ships' ledgers that document the regional variation in African preferences. See Metcalf (1987a, 1987b) and Eltis (2000, p. 168) for a sample.
2. The Anglo-African Trade Statistics do not record British slave purchases because slaves were shipped to the Americas and never entered Britain. *CARGO* is calculated by

taking total British commodity exports to Africa and subtracting total African exports to Britain. What is left is the real value of goods used to purchase the slaves that were shipped to the Americas.

3. For cutoffs, the British Customs Office used Christmas-to-Christmas for 1699–1771 and January 5 to January 5 for 1772–1807 (Johnson 1990, p. 13).
4. The difference being updates to the slave trade data since 1991 and the matching of $CARGO_t$ and $SLAVES_t$ by year of ship departure from Britain.
5. These are prices from invoice books listing the goods exchanged for series or lots of slaves in the lower Gambia, without any corrections for loading or transportation costs, which Curtin did for some of his other price calculations. These prices are from Curtin (1975a, Vol. II, Table A8.1, pp. 48–49; 1975b).
6. I thank David Eltis for making these data available to me. These prices are constructed from New World price quotes on slave shipments recorded in the Trans-Atlantic Slave Trade Database. See Eltis and Ricardson (2004).
7. The "W. Africa – Bean" series is an early effort by Richard Bean to cobble together slave prices calculated in a variety of ways, for different lot sizes, by different European countries, in different currencies between the 1550s and 1774, using estimates of exchange rates to convert them into pounds sterling. They fluctuate wildly between the British African and New World prices, and are not used in this study.
8. The correlations are a simple accounting procedure because, by construction, $SLAVE_t$ exports are mechanically related to slave $PRICE_t$ (since $PRICE_t = CARGO_t/SLAVES_t$).
9. Curtin (1975b, pp. 320–25); Inikori (1977); and Richards (1980).
10. Kea (1971, p. 186); Wilks (1993, p. 23); and Northrup (2002, pp. 90–98).
11. See Inikori (1977); West (1991, pp. 122–33); and Richards (1980).
12. West (1991, p. 14) describes eighteenth-century British-made gunpowder. "Not only might the gunpowder explode in transit but it was also highly susceptible to both damp, which would cause the grains to clog and become ineffective, and to damage due to violent movement which could break the grain." Kea (1971) notes that "traders of the Gold Coast carefully examined gunpowder for dampness" (p. 205).
13. Annual real values of gunpowder are found in Johnson (1990). These are converted into physical pounds of gunpowder by dividing through by the 1699 price for gunpowder – .03375 pounds sterling per pound.
14. Roberts (1980, pp. 397–99) uses this feedback loop to criticize Curtin's distinction between political and economic motivations for slaving in Africa: "In contrast to the arguments offered by ... Curtin, I will present one that involves a more dynamic view ... Instead, I will try to demonstrate the exact amount of *productive* activity which was central to the organization of warfare in the Middle Niger valley" (p. 399).
15. Examples of raid-or-be-raided dynamics can be found in Davidson (1961, pp. 142–43), Hawthorn (2003, pp. 96–98), and Klein (2001, pp. 56, 58, 61).
16. Similar results are produced by an instrumental variables estimation of the slave export equation that uses excess capacity in the British gunpowder industry as an instrument for British gunpowder exports. The guns-for-slaves-in-production result also survives seventeen placebo tests that replace gunpowder with non-lethal British imports. For example, a textiles-for-slaves result was not found.

17. The VEC model does not converge for the sub-periods before and after 1740, so we cannot use it to test for changes in the gun–slave cycle, but the model does document a gun–slave cycle as a general dynamic feature of the eighteenth-century British slave trade.
18. "In spite of the ties, strategies, and practices that facilitated the establishment of Aro settlements among the non-Aro hosts, the Aro deemed force to be particularly effective in the Igbo heartland ... Their massive and consistent application of force in this region is widely recognized as a-typical of Aro methods" (Nwokeji 2010, p. 68).
19. The Highland Plateau serves as the source of three major rivers: the Niger, the Senegal, and the Gambia rivers. The Niger flows northeastward into the Middle Niger valley. The Senegal and Gambia flow to the northwest and into the Atlantic Ocean along the Senegambia coast. Since the Middle Ages these waterways have integrated the trade and politics in the Western Sudan, producing the classic Sudanese Empires of Ghana, Mali, and Songhai. Falling southward from the highlands, towards the Sierra Leone coast, is a dense system of lesser rivers and streams that flow through forest.
20. For a sample of this literature, see Nunn (2008), Nunn and Wantchekon (2011), Obikili (2016a, 2016b), Whatley and Gillezeau (2011b), Whatley (2014), Dalton and Leung (2014), Boxell (2019), and Levine, Lin, and Xie (2020).
21. Nunn (2008) does the same for the Indian Ocean slave trades, by ethnicity and by century, but the samples are smaller. The Red Sea and trans-Saharan efforts are only at the national level.

7 HOW AFRICAN-AMERICAN SLAVERY GREW THE FREE ECONOMIES OF EUROPE

1. See the debate in the *American Economic Review.* Fogel and Engerman (1977), Haskell (1979), Schaefer and Schmitz (1979), David and Temin (1979), Wright (1979).
2. Wright (2014), Olmstead and Rhode (2018), Hilt (2017).
3. In the South Atlantic much of the trade was bilateral, directly between South America and Africa.

8 INTO THE INTERIOR OF AFRICA

1. Travel time differs from two related measures found in the literature. Ozak (2018) introduces a global measure of distances to pre-industrial technology frontiers, but the measure does not apply to the African continent because it closely tracks global distances from the equator and tropics (see Figure 4, p. 192) with corrections for variations in the earth's slope. Nunn and Puga (2012) calculate the ruggedness of terrain, which is measured as the average change in elevation around a point on the earth's surface. Travel time goes beyond ruggedness by adding finer detail to the surface raster in a way that allows ruggedness to be additive across space.
2. According to Bulliet (1990), the camel displaced the wheel from Roman Syria and North Africa. While the history is complex, significant developments include the diffusion of the north Arabian saddle (500–100 BC), the collapse of the Roman Empire

and its road system, and camel breeders seizing control of trade at Mecca by the time of Mohammad's birth (circa 570 AD).

3. Two detailed travel itineraries from the early 1840s record the actual number of hours spent by travelers as they moved between these halting places (Wilks 1975, p. 9). One itinerary records an average travel time of 6.78 hours per day, the other an average of 7.5 hours per day. Henry Morton Stanley, during his trek across Africa in the late 1870s, estimates six to seven hours as a standard day's travel time.
4. Dupuis estimates a slightly higher average – twelve miles per day in forest zones and sixteen miles per day in savannah.
5. The estimate excludes the 1.1 mph quote because that quote is for travelling upstream from Kuramo to Ikorodu where "a canoe meets the strong currents caused by the outflow of the Ogun and other rivers into the lagoon" (p. 523).
6. Pandolf, Giovani, and Goldman (1977) use the following equation to predict the energy expenditure of carrying headloads: $M = 1.5W + 2.0(W + L)\ (L/W)^2 + n(W = L)\ (1.5V^2 + 0.35VG)$. M = metabolic rate in watts; W = porters' weight in kg; L = load carried; V = walking speed in meters per second; G = grade in %; and n = terrain ruggedness. According to this equation, a 190-pound man (77 kg) carrying a 60-pound headload (27.2 kg) at a rate of 0.329 hours per kilometer would burn 23.4 percent more watts of energy than a 190-pound man carrying nothing. A 170-pound porter carrying 50 pounds would burn an additional 21 percent, and a 150-pound man carrying 40 pounds would burn an extra 23 percent. Additions are less at slower walking rates. Through rainforest (0.88 hours per kilometer), the additions are between 16.2 percent and 20.0 percent.
7. His clock was a pendulum clock, which could not keep good time on a heaving ship at sea, or be carried around by explorers on land. The balance spring (or hairspring), invented separately in 1675 by Huygens and Hooke, eventually increased the accuracy of mechanical watches from around half an hour to within a few minutes per day (Landes 1983, p. 128). This was still not accurate enough. Over the course of a month, an explorer would lose about an hour of time, equal to an error of fifteen degrees, or about 1,000 miles at the equator.
8. Miotto and Pascali (2022) use the fact that the chronometer was effective at finding longitude on overcast days to identify the effects of the innovation on the growth of coastal cities along cloudy routes.
9. Shortly after reading Stanley's description of his lavish royal reception from Muteesa I. Mukaabya Walugembe Kayiira, the thirtieth Kabaka of the Kingdom of Buganda, I found myself in a cab being driven by a woman from Uganda. "Oh," I said. "Did you know Henry Morton Stanley visited Uganda in 1876?" to which she politely replied, "I believe that was 1875." We then had a memorable conversation about the difficulty of raising children in the USA.
10. Ideally, we would like estimates of transport costs per ton-mile. Roberts (1987, p. 62) reports that "[a] colonial officer in 1892 estimated that it cost six times more to move a quantity of goods by caravan than by canoe," but we have no way of evaluating the claim or conducting an analysis for the entire continent.
11. According to Roberts (1987, pp. 73–74), a common canoe of six-to-ten-ton capacity was often manned by two crew members and a captain. A large freight canoe with a

capacity of twenty to thirty tons was often manned by a crew of between sixteen and eighteen, plus two mates and a captain. Henry Morton Stanley describes war canoes on the Congo River as large as eighty-five and ninety feet in length "with two rows of upstanding paddles, 40 men on a side" (1879, volume II, p. 270). These ratios of canoe tonnage or size relative to crew size do not suggest appreciable economies of scale.

12. Roberts discusses how the King of Segu in the late eighteenth century spaced villages fifteen kilometers apart along the Niger River in order to regularize and protect trade. The growth of Segu plantations and their grain production spurred the development (Roberts 1987, pp. 71–72). Smaller merchants who could not tie up capital in canoes could rent passage as individuals or groups (pp. 73–74). Harms (1981, Chapters 2 and 3) discusses similar halting places and sharing arrangements along the lower Congo River.
13. For a review of this literature and a discussion of similar but alternative algorithms for calculating river width, see Dai Yamazaki, Fiachra O'Loughlin, Mark A. Trigg, Zachary F. Miller, Tamlin M. Pavelsky, and Paul D. Bates (2014).
14. The project consulted online maps for the Congo River Basin, East Africa Rivers, the Niger River system, South Africa Rivers, and Sudan River Rapids. The project also consulted maps and descriptions in four books. See Livingstone (1858), Hamilton (2005), Harwood (2013), and Coppinger and Williams (1994).
15. The vertical factor (VF) enters the calculation of H as a multiplicative factor applied to F*SD. Since V(0) = 5, the vertical factor is normalized as VF = V(s)/5. Also, the vertical factor and F*SD must be in the same units. The Tobler V is measured in kilometers per hour, while F*SD is measured in hours per kilometer. The final vertical factor used in the calculation is 5/V(s), where dV/ds < 0. A 30 percent upslope generates a vertical factor of 5/.5 = 10, estimating that it takes ten times as long to walk up a thirty-degree slope as it does on a flat surface.
16. The adjustable parameters are F_i (walking rates), minimum F_j (river velocity), and max *V* (percentage slope). The ArcGIS Cost Path algorithm retains in memory a table of transition costs for all directions leading from a cell, not just the least cost direction. Imposing a maximum vertical factor forces the calculation to "backtrack" and find a path that is not blocked by the maximum vertical factor.
17. The lower limit on river velocity was set to be at least as fast as walking. The 0.27 cut-off was set early in the project to equal Dupuis's estimate of sixteen miles per seven-hour day for walking across savannah, to avoid the scene of walkers moving faster than canoes. This is also comparable to the 0.255 hours per kilometer for walking across desert. The cut-off was not chosen or recalibrated to improve analytical results.
18. Slave ports are taken from the Trans-Atlantic Slave Trade Database. They include all mainland slave ports on the West coast of Africa that exported more than 4,000 slaves between 1600 and 1865. On the East African coast, the ports included all mainland slave ports plus Zanzibar, a major island port in the Indian Ocean just off the east coast. Many of these ports predate Europeans and so capture some pre-European history and influence. The analysis misses cases where there was slavery in the distant past but abolished by the nineteenth century.

19. Days is the minimum distance to the closest Transatlantic or Indian Ocean port. The line of equal distance draws a north–south boundary that divides east from west Africa, and the transatlantic from the Indian Ocean slave trades. The minimum days to a Red Sea or trans-Saharan port draws an east–west line along the Saharan shore, or the Sahel, westward to the Red Sea. This approach was chosen for several reasons: there was little if any competition between transatlantic and Indian Ocean exposure; the "alternative" outlets for both ran along the Sahel; the slave export data are for the Atlantic and Indian trades; and it reduces the number of IVs, so it helps with the first-stage F-stat.

9 HOW THE SLAVE TRADES UNDERDEVELOPED AFRICA

1. For a game-theoretic formulation, see Whatley and Gillezeau (2011a).
2. One of the endogenous outcomes is the number of slaves captures and exported, which is why ports are not weighted by the number of exports.
3. Klein (2001), Hawthorne (2003), Roberts (1987), Meillassoux (1991).
4. Over time and through negotiated compromise, the bachelor age group gained an independent administrative structure. They elected their own leaders who controlled recalcitrant members through judicial sanctions. They also provided public labor for widows, the sick, and other family units that lacked sufficient human resources, in exchange for which they received compensations that they taxed and consumed collectively (Roberts 1980, p. 404).
5. According to Murdock, "The scientific significance of kinship systems was first appreciated by Morgan (1870) in what is perhaps the most original and brilliant single achievement in the history of anthropology" (Murdock 1949, p. 91). The claim to scientific status stems from the fact that the nuclear family and its incest taboo are universal human institutions and norms. From these universal conditions flow kin-relationships across families and generations. A kinship terminology system reduces the kin terms for the primary (8), secondary (33) and tertiary (151) kinship relations down to a manageable size. The kinship terminology system reflects the boundaries, opportunities and contractual arrangements of the kin-group. Every new anthropology student has to learn the basic kin-naming systems and the corresponding descent rules.
6. The six major kin-naming systems are Crow, Eskimo, Hawaiian, Iroquois, Omaha, and Sudanese.
7. This is confirmed in our data. The correlation coefficient between Crow kinship terms and matriliny is 0.21; for Crow kinship terms and patriliny it is –0.27. For Omaha kinship terms and matriliny it is –0.18, and for Omaha kinship terms and patriliny it is 0.24.
8. African slave cultures might also explain the high percentage of male children in the export trade. The status of the offspring of mixed parentage, if not tightly controlled, could challenge societal norms of freedom and belonging. Selling those children might relieve social pressures and help preserve the status quo.
9. Exports earnings decline sharply after 1807 because the British, French, and Dutch traders who dominated the West African trade began to abolish their slave trades, depressing prices and quantities. Portuguese exports, primarily from West South Central and East Africa continued at high levels well into the nineteenth century.

10. See the gold export data in Curtin (1983), LaTorre (1978), Ridgeway (1929), Garrard (1980), Wilks (1982b) and Feinberg (1989). Exports never exceed 30,000 ounces a year.
11. Even if the 25,000 ounces of gold were retained domestically for the thirty-seven years, the additional gold would have to circulate a minimum of five times per year to circulate the additional income from slave exports. This approaches the annual velocity of circulation of M2 in the USA in 2023, an unlikely achievement in eighteenth-century West Africa.
12. These are the value of British exports to Africa (in 1699 prices) taken from the Anglo African Trade Statistics, divided by total British exports (in 1697 prices) found in Broadberry and Gupta (2009, Table 1, p. 283).

10 PAST, PRESENT, AND FUTURE

1. "The ships of this land are large and without decks. They are not nailed and sealed tightly bound with esparto cord; and their boats the same. Their sails are of palm matting, and their mariners have Genoese needles by which to steer, and quadrants and sea-charts" (Axelson 1998, p. 37).
2. For a sample of this exciting literature, see Garenne and Van De Walle (1989), Rossi (2019), Lowes (2020), Lowes (2022), Zawaira, Matthew, and Chisadza (2022), and D'Exelle et al. (2023).
3. See Mintz and Price (1992), Gomez (1998), Raboteau (1978), Sweet (2003), and Hawthorne (2010).
4. For a sample of the voluminous literature, see Phillips (1989), Getz (2004), Miers and Klein (1999), van Waijenburg (2018), Austin (2004), Lovejoy and Falola (2003), Crowder (1978), and Bolt and Gardner (2020).
5. Bolt and Gardner (2020) present evidence that precolonial political centralization increased the taxing capacity of local native authorities. van Waijenburg (2018) concludes that "especially in the early colonial period, the invisible value of unpaid labor obligations often may have well exceeded the total size of French African budgets" (p. 74).
6. "Women pawns fetch almost ten times the amount given as ordinary bride wealth, both because the marriages could not be dissolved and because a specified number of their children would belong to the husband's lineage rather than to their own" (p. 241).
7. Whatley (2014) presents data showing a simple correlation at the state level between precolonial slave exports and the percentage of colonial court cases adjudicated in native courts.
8. The 2008 AfroBarometer survey asks several questions about customary authority as distinct from formal state authority. In Ghana, 68 percent of the respondents said traditional leaders had "primary responsibility for allocating land"; 59 percent said they had primary responsibility for "solving local disputes"; 60 percent said they should remain non-partisan, independent of government and without government salary; 65 percent said their power should be increased, and 42 percent said, "by a lot!" For the nineteen countries in the survey, on a scale of one to five, the average influence of traditional leaders was 3.30 and respondents wanted them to have 3.8 (Logan 2011).

9. See, for example, Sheleff (1999), Fenrich, Galizzi, and Higgins (2011), Bowman and Kuenyehia (2003), Burrill, Roberts, and Thornberry (2010), and Coquery-Vidrovitch (1997).

APPENDIX TO CHAPTER 6

1. Annual real values of gunpowder are found in Johnson (1990). These are converted into physical pounds of gunpowder by dividing through by the 1699 price for gunpowder – 0.03375 pounds sterling per pound.
2. I construct a dummy variable = 1 for the War of Spanish Succession (1701–1713) + the War of Quadruple Alliance (1718–1719) + the War with Spain (1727–1729) + the War of Austrian Succession (1741–1748) + Seven Years War (1756–1763) + the American Revolution (1775–1783) + the Napoleonic Wars (1792–1815).

APPENDIX TO CHAPTER 9

1. The dependent variables are dichotomous variables that takes the value zero or one. The maximum likelihood method is used for parameter estimation. The estimated coefficient is the increase in the z-score due to a one-unit increase in the independent variable. For categorical variables it is the increase in the z-score per increase in category. For $X = ln\ (EXPORTS)$ a 1 percent increase would lead to a $\beta/100$ increase in the z-score. Conditional predicted probabilities are obtained by the inverse probit transformation, where the predicted probabilities will vary over the distribution of covariates.
2. Dalton and Cheuk (2014) find this result for polygyny alone.
3. According to Murdock (1949) "the nuclear family consists typically of a married man and woman with their offspring" (p. 1). This includes both polygynous families of one man and several wives, and extended families incorporating the families of married children (pp. 1–42). Patrilineal descent controls for the fact that patrilineal societies are more likely to allow their own children to inherit property.
4. Land in precolonial Africa is often thought to be communally owned, but this was not always the case for all land rights. In Asante law, for example, "the land belongs to the chief, but the farm is mine." Improvements made to the land, including trees, belonged to the cultivator so long as the land was producing or in rotation (Rattray 1969, pp. 213–41). The cultivator could bequeath these usufruct rights to others.

Bibliography

Abby, M. T., and Rosalie Akouele. 2011. *Customary Law and Slavery in West Africa* (Trafford Publishing: United States).

Acemoglu, Daron, and James Robinson. 2012. *Why Nations Fail: The Origins of Power, Prosperity and Poverty* (Crown Business: New York).

2019. *The Narrow Corridor: States, Societies, and the Fate of Liberty* (Penguin Press: New York).

Acemoglu, Daron, and Alexander Wolitzky. 2011. "The Economics of Labor Coercion," *Econometrica*, 79: 555–600.

Acemoglu, Daron, Simon Johnson, and James A. Robinson. 2001. "The Colonial Origins of Comparative Development: An Empirical Investigation," *American Economic Review*, 91: 1369–401.

2002. "Reversal of Fortune: Geography and Institutions in Making of Modern World Income Distribution," *Quarterly Journal of Economics*, 117: 1231–94.

2005. "The Rise of Europe: Atlantic Trade, Institutional Change, and Economic Growth," *The American Economic Review*, 95: 34.

Adekunle, Julius O. 1994. "Borgu and Economic Transformation, 1700–1900: The Wangara Factor," *African Economic History*, 22: 1–18.

Allen, Robert. 2009. *The Industrial Revolution in Global Perspective* (Cambridge University Press: Cambridge).

Alsan, Marcella. 2015. "The Effect of the TseTse Fly on African Development," *American Economic Review*, 105: 382–410.

Ambühl, Rémy. 2013. *Prisoners of War in the Hundred Years War: Ransom Culture in the Late Middle Age* (Cambridge University Press: Cambridge).

American Civil Liberties Union. 2023. "Baby Bonds National Polling and Key Insights." www.aclu.org/documents/baby-bonds-national-polling-and-key-insights.

Anderson, Thomas Barnebeck, Jeanet Bentzen, Carl-Johan Dalgaard, and Paul Sharp. 2016. "Pre-Reformation Roots of the Protestant Ethic," *The Economic Journal*, 127: 1759–93.

Andreadis, K., G. Schumann, and T. Pavelsky. 2013. "A Simple Global River Bankfull Width and Depth Database," *Water Resource Research*, 49: 7164–68.

Arthur, Brian W., Yu. M. Ermolev, and Yu. M. Kaniovskii. 1983. "A Generalized Urn Problem and Its Applications," *Cybernetic System Analysis*, 19: 61–71.

Ashraf, Quamrul, and Oded Galor. 2013. "The "Out of Africa" Hypothesis, Human Genetic Diversity and Comparative Economic Development," *American Economic Review*, 103: 1–46.

Austen, Ralph A. 2010. *Trans-Saharan Africa in World History* (Oxford University Press: Oxford).

Austin, Gareth. 2004. *Labour, Land, and Capital in Ghana: From Slavery to Free Labour in Asante, 1807–1956* (University of Rochester Press: Rochester, NY).

2008. "Resources, Techniques, and Strategies South of the Sahara: Revising the Factor Endowments Perspective on African Economic Development, 1500–2000," *Economic History Review*, 61: 587–624.

Axelson, Eric. 1998. *Vasco da Gama: The Diary of His Travels through African Waters: 1497–1499* (Stephen Phillips: Somerset West).

Babcock, Theodore. 1974. "Manumission in Virginia, 1782–1806," Masters Thesis, University of Virginia.

Baptist, Edward. 2014. *The Half Has Never Been Told: Slavery and the Making of American Capitalism* (Basic Books: New York).

Barrett, Ward. 1990. "World Bullion Flows, 1450–1800." In James D Tracy (ed.), *The Rise of Merchant Empires: Long-Distance Trade in the Early Modern World* (Cambridge University Press: Cambridge).

Barth, Henry. 1890. *Travels and Discoveries in North and Central Africa: Including Accounts of Tripoli, the Sahara, the Remarkable Kingdom of Bornu, and the Countries around Lake Chad* (Ward, Lock, and Co.: London).

Bates, Robert. 2010. *Prosperity and Violence: The Political Economy of Development* (W. W. Norton: New York).

Beard, Charles A. 1913. *An Economic Interpretation of the Constitution of the United States* (The MacMillan Company: New York).

Beckert, Sven. 2014. *Empire of Cotton: A Global History* (Vintage Books: New York).

Berg, Maxine, and Pat Hudson. 2023. *Slavery, Capitalism and the Industrial Revolution* (Polity Press: Cambridge).

Berlin, Ira, Marc Favereau, and Stephen F. Miller (eds.). 1998. *Remembering Slavery: African-Americans Talk about Their Personal Experiences of Slavery and Freedom* (The New Press: New York).

Berman, Harold J. 1983. *Law and Revolution: The Formation of the Western Legal Tradition* (Harvard University Press: Cambridge).

Bertocchi, Graziella. 2015. "The Legacies of Slavery in and out of Africa." *IZA Discussion Paper.*

Besley, T., and Reynal-Querol. 2014. "The Legacy of Historical Conflict: Evidence from Africa," *American Political Science Review*, 108: 319–36.

Bhattacharyya, Sambit. 2009. "Root Causes of African Underdevelopment," *Journal of African Economies*, 18: 745–80.

Blaut, J. M. 1993. *The Colonizer's Model of the World: Geographical the Fusionism and Eurocentric History* (The Guilford Press: New York).

2000. *Eight Eurocentric Historians* (The Guilford Press: New York).

Bodenhorn, Howard. 2011. "Manumission in 19th Century Virginia," *Cliometrica*, 5: 145–64.

Bolt, Jutta, and Leigh Gardner. 2020. "How Africans Shaped British Colonial Institutions: Evidence from Local Taxation," *Journal of Economic History*, 80: 1189–223.

Bonnassie, Pierre. 1991. *From Slavery to Feudalism in South-Western Europe* (Cambridge University Press: Cambridge).

Bottero, Margherita, and Bjorn Wallace. 2013. "Is There a Long-Term Effect of Africa's Slave Trades." *Economic History Working Papers No. 30.* Economic Research and International Relations Area: Bank of Italy.

Bowdich, T. E. 1819. *Mission from Cape Coast Castle to Ashantee* (John Murray: London).

Bowman, Cynthia Grant, and Akua Kuenyehia. 2003. *Women and Law in Sub-Saharan Africa* (Sedco Publishing Limited: Accra).

Boxell, Levi. 2019. "Drought, Conflict and the African Slave Trade," *Journal of Comparative Economics*, 47: 775–91.

Brana-Shute, Rosemary, and Randy J. Sparks (eds.). 2009. *Pathways to Freedom: Manumission in the Atlantic World* (The University of South Carolina Press: Columbia).

Broadberry, Stephen, and Gupta Bishnupriya. 2009. "Lancashire, India, and Shifting Competitive Advantage in Cotton Textiles, 1700–1850: The Neglected Role of Factor Prices," *Economic History Review*, 62: 279–305.

Brooks, George E. 1993. *Landlords and Strangers: Ecology, Society, and Trade in Western Africa, 1000–1630* (Westview Press: Boulder).

Bruton, Eric. 1989. *The History of Clocks and Watches* (Crescent Books: New York).

Burbank, Jane, and Frederick Cooper. 2010. *Empires in World History: Power and the Politics of Difference* (Princeton University Press Click Save: Princeton).

Burke, Mary A., and Payton H. Young. 2011. "Social Norms." In Alberto Bisin, Jess Benhabib and Matthew Jackson (eds.), *The Handbook of Social Economics* (North-Holland: Amsterdam).

Burrill, Emily S., Richard L. Roberts, and Elizabeth Thornberry (eds.). 2010. *Domestic Violence and the Law in Colonial and Postcolonial Africa* (Ohio University Press: Athens).

Burton, Diane M., and Tom Nicholass. 2017. "Prizes, Patents and the Search for Longitude," *Explorations in Economic History*, 64: 21–36.

Center for Democracy and Development. 2009. "Afrobarometer Survey, Merged Round 4 Data (20 Countries) (2008)." www.afrobarometer.org/survey-resource/merged-round-4-data-20-countries-2008/.

Chandler, Tertius, and Gerald Fox. 1974. *3000 Years of Urban Growth* (Academic Press, Inc.: New York).

Cherniwchan, Jevan, and Juan Moreno-Cruz. 2019. "Maize and Precolonial Africa," *Journal of Development Economics*, 136: 137–50.

Clapperton, Hugh. 1829. *Journal of the Second Expedition into the Interior of Africa* (Lea and Carey: Philadelphia).

2005. *Into the Interior of Africa: Records of the Second Expedition, 1825–1827* (Koninklijke Brill N.V: Leiden).

Clark, Gregory. 2005. "The Condition of the Working-Class in England, 1209–2004," *Journal of Political Economy*, 113: 1307–40.

2007. *A Farewell to Alms: A Brief Economic History of the World* (Princeton University Press: Princeton).

2013. "What Were the British Earnings and Prices Then? (New Series)." MeasuringWorth.com. www.measuringworth.com/ukearncpi/.

Clarkson, Thomas. 1786. *An Essay on the Slavery and Commerce of the Human Species* (J. Phillips: London).

1839. *The History of the Rise, Progress, and Accomplishment of the Abolition of the Slave Trade by British Parliament* (Project Gutenberg e-book #10633s).

Cole, Ansley, and Paul Demeny. 1966. *The Regional Model of Life Tables and Stable Populations* (Princeton University Press: Princeton).

Cole, Shawn. 2005. "Capitalism and Freedom: Manumissions and the Slave Market in Louisiana, 1725–1820," *The Journal of Economic History*, 64: 1008–27.

Conrad, Alfred H., and John R. Meyer. 1958. "The Economics of Slavery in the Antebellum South," *Journal of Political Economy*, 66: 95–130.

Conrad, David C., and Barbara E. Frank (eds.). 1995. *Status and Identity in West Africa: Nyamakalaw of Mande* (Indiana University Press: Bloomington).

Constant, Paula. 2009. *Sahara: A Journey of Love, Loss and Survival* (Bantam: Sydney).

Coppinger, Mike, and Jumbo Williams. 1994. *Zambezi: River of Africa* (New Holland: London).

Coquery-Vidrovitch, Catherine. 1997. *African Women: A Modern History* (Westview Press: Oxford).

Crowder, Michael. 1978. *Colonial West Africa* (Frank Cass and Company: London).

Currie, Thomas E., and Ruth Mace. 2009. "Political Complexity Predicts the Spread of Ethnolinguistic Groups," *Proceedings of the National Academy of Sciences USA*, 106: 7339–44.

Currie, Thomas E., Andrew Meade, Myrtille Guillon, and Ruth Mace. 2013. "Cultural Phylogeography of the Bantu Languages in Sub-Saharan Africa," *Proceedings of the Royal Society B*, 280: 1–8.

Curtin, Philip D. 1975a. *Economic Change in Precolonial Africa: Senegambia in the Era of the Slave Trade* (University of Wisconsin Press: Madison).

1975b. *Economic Change in Precolonial Africa: Supplementary Evidence* (University of Wisconsin Press: Madison).

1983. "Africa and the Wider Monetary World, 1250–1850." In J. F. Richards (ed.), *Precious Metals in the Later Medieval and Early Modern Worlds* (Carolina Academic Press: Durham).

1984. *Cross-Cultural Trade in World History* (Cambridge University Press: Cambridge).

Curtin, Philip D., Steven Feierman, Leonard Thompson, and Jan Vansina. 1995. *African History: From Earliest Times to Independence* (Longman: London New York).

D'Exelle, Ben, Aurelia Lepine, Bakyono Richard, and Ludovic D. G. Tapsoba. 2023. "Fertility and Polygyny: Experimental Evidence from Burkina Faso," *Journal of Development Economics*, 164: 103134.

Daaku, Kwame Yeboa. 1970. *Trade and Politics on the Gold Coast, 1600–1720: A Study of the African Reaction to European Trade* (Clarendon Press: London).

Dalton, John T., and Tin Cheuk Leung. 2014. "Why is Polygyny More Prevalent in Western Africa: An African Slave Trade Perspective," *Economic Development and Cultural Change*, 62: 599–632.

Darity, William A. 1982. "A General Equilibrium Model of the Eighteenth-Century Atlantic Slave Trade: A Least-Likely Test for the Caribbean School," *Research in Economic History*, 7: 287–326.

1992. "A Model of Original Sin: Rise of the West and Lag of the Rest," *American Economic Review*, 82: 162–67.

Darity, William A., and Kirsten A. Mullen. 2020. *From Here to Equality: Reparations for Black Americans in the Twenty-First Century* (University of North Carolina Press: Chapel Hill).

Darity, William A., Patrick L. Mason, and James B. Stewart. 2006. "The Economics of Identity: The Origins and Persistence of Racial Identity Norms," *Journal of Economic Behavior and Organization*, 60: 283–305.

David, Paul. 1985. "Clio and the Economics of QWERTY," *American Economic Review*, 76: 332–37.

David, Paul A., and Peter Temin. 1979. "Explaining the Relative Efficiency of Slave Agriculture in the Antebellum South: Comment," *American Economic Review*, 69: 213–18.

David, Paul, Herbert G. Gutman, Richard Sutch, Peter Temin, and Gavin Wright. 1976. *Reckoning with Slavery: A Critical Study in the Quantitative History of American Negro Slavery* (Oxford University Press: London).

Davidson, Basil. 1961. *Black Mother* (Little Brown: Boston).

Davies, K. G. 1975. *The Royal African Company* (Octagon Books: New York).

de Vries. Jan. 2008. *The Industrious Revolution: Consumer Behavior and the Household Economy, 1650 to the Present* (Cambridge University Press: Cambridge).

Deerr, Noel. 1950. *The History of Sugar* (Chapman and Hall LTD.: London).

Diamond, Jared. 1997. *Guns, Germs and Steel* (W. W. Norton and Company: New York).

Dike, Onwuka K. 1956. *Trade and Politics in the Niger Delta* (Clarendon Press: Oxford).

Diouf, Sylviane A. 2003. *Fighting the Slave Trade: West African Strategies* (Ohio University Press: Athens).

Domar, Evsey D. 1970. "The Causes of Slavery or Serfdom: A Hypothesis," *Economic History Review,* 30: 18–32.

Douglas, Mary. 1964. "Matriliny and Pawnship in Central Africa," *Journal of the International African Institute,* 34: 301–13.

1969. "Is Matriliny Doomed in Africa?" In Mary Douglas, and Phyllis Kaberry (eds.), *Man in Africa* (Tavistock Publications: London).

Du Bois, W. E. B. 1903. *The Souls of Black Folk* (A. C. McClurg & Co.: Chicago).

Dumett, Raymond E. 1998. *El Dorado in West Africa: The Gold-Mining Frontier, African Labor, and Colonial Capitalism in the Gold Coast, 1875–1900* (Ohio University Press: Athens).

Dupuis, Joseph. 1824. *Journal of A Residence in Ashantee* (Henry Colburn: London).

Easaw, Joshy, and Atanu Ghoshray. 2023. "On the Trend and Variability of 18th Century British Transatlantic Slave Prices." Cardiff Economics Working Papers, Cardiff University.

Egharevba, Jacob. 1968. *A Short History of Benin* (Ibadan University Press: Ibadan).

Ehret, Christopher. 2002. *The Civilizations of Africa: A History to 1800* (University Press of Virginia: Charlottesville).

Eisenman, Robert. 1998. *James the Brother of Jesus: The Key to Unlocking the Secrets of Early Christianity and the Dead Sea Scrolls* (Penguin Books: London).

Ekelund, Robert B. Jr., Robert F. Herbert, Robert D. Tollison, Gary M. Anderson, and Audrey B. Davidson. 1996. *Sacred Trust: The Medieval Church as an Economic Firm* (Oxford University Press: New York).

El-Swaify, S. A., E. W Dangler, and C. L. Armstrong. 1982. *Soil Erosion by Water in the Tropics* (University of Hawaii: Honolulu).

Eltis, David. 1986. "Fluctuations in the Age and Sex Ratios of Slaves in the Nineteenth-Century Transatlantic Slave Traffic," *Slavery and Abolition,* 7: 257–72.

1987. *Economic Growth and the Ending of the Transatlantic Slave Trade* (Oxford University Press: New York).

2000. *The Rise of African Slavery in the Americas* (Cambridge University Press: New York).

Eltis, David, and Stanley L. Engerman. 1992. "Was the Slave Trade Dominated by Men?" *The Journal of Interdisciplinary History,* 23: 237–57.

2000. "The Importance of Slavery and the Slave Trade to Industrializing Britain," *The Journal of Economic History,* 60: 123–44.

Eltis, David, and Lawrence C. Jennings. 1988. "Trade between West Africa and the Atlantic World in the Pre-Colonial Era," *American Historical Review,* 9: 936–59.

Eltis, David, and David Richardson. 2004. "Prices of African Slaves Newly Arrived in the Americas, 1673–1865: New Evidence on Long-Run Trends and Regional Differentials." In David Eltis, Frank D. Lewis, and Kenneth L. Sockoloff (eds.), *Slavery in the Development of the Americas* (Cambridge University Press: Cambridge).

Equiano, Olaudah, and Robert J. Allison. 1995. *The Interesting Narrative of the Life of Olaudah Equiano* (Bedford Books: New York).

Esteban, Javier Cuenca. 1999. "Factory Costs, Market Prices, and Indian Calicos: Cotton Textile Prices Revisited, 1779–1831," *Economic History Review*, 52: 479–755.

Falconbridge, Alexander. 1788. *Account of the Slave Trade on the Coast of Africa* (J. Phillips: London).

Fauvelle, Francois-Xavier. 2013. *The Golden Rhinoceros: Histories of the African Middle Ages* (Princeton University Press: Princeton).

Feinberg, Harvey M. 1989. *Africans and Europeans in West Africa: Elminans and Dutchmen on the Gold Coast during the Eighteenth Century* (The American Philosophical Society: Philadelphia).

Fenoaltea, Stephano. 1984. "Slavery and Supervision in Comparative Perspective: A Model," *The Journal of Economic History*, 44: 635–68.

1999. "Europe in the African Mirror: The Slave Trade and the Rise of Feudalism," *Rivista Di Storia Economica*, 15: 123–65.

Fenrich, Jeanmarie, Paolo Galizzi, and Tracy E. Higgins (eds.). 2011. *The Future of African Customary Law* (Cambridge University Press: New York).

Fenske, James. 2010. "The Causal History of Africa: A Response to Hopkins," *Economic History of Developing Regions*, 25: 177–212.

2012. "Land Abundance and Economic Institutions: Egba Land and Slavery, 1830–1714," *The Economic History Review*, 65: 527–55.

Fenske, James, and Namratta Kala. 2015. "Climate and the Slave Trade," *Journal of Development Economics*, 112: 19–32.

Findlay, Ronald. 1975. "Slavery, Incentives, and Manumission: A Theoretical Model," *Journal of Political Economy*, 83: 923–34.

1990. "The "Triangular Trade" and the Atlantic Economy of the Eighteenth Century: A Simple General-Equilibrium Model." In *Essays in International Finance* (Princeton University Press: Princeton).

Findlay, Ronald, and Kevin H. O'Rourke. 2007. *Power and Plenty: Trade, War, and the World Economy in the Second Millennium* (Princeton University Press: Princeton).

Finley, Moses I. 1973. *The Ancient Economy* (The University of California Press: Berkeley).

1980. *Ancient Slavery and Modern Ideology* (The Viking Press: New York).

Fogel, Robert, and Stanley L. Engerman. 1974. *Time on the Cross: The Economics of American Slavery* (Little, Brown: Boston).

1977. "Explaining the Relative Efficiency of Slave Agriculture," *American Economic Review*, 67: 275–96.

Fortunato, Laura. 2012. "The Evolution of Matrilineal Kinship Organization," *Proceedings of the Royal Society*, 279: 4939–45.

Fourie, Johan. 2021. *Our Long Walk to Economic Freedom: Lessons from 100,000 Years of Human History* (Cambridge University Press: Cambridge).

Frank, Andre Gunder. 1998. *ReOrient: Global Economy in the Asian Age* (University of California Press: Berkeley).

Frankema, Ewout, and Morton Jerven. 2014. "Writing History Backwards or Sideways: Towards a Consensus of African Population, 1850–2010," *Economic History Review*, 67: 907–31.

Fynn-Paul, Jeffrey. 2009. "Empire, Monotheism and Slavery in the Greater Mediterranean Region from Antiquity to the Early Modern Era," *Past and Present*, 205: 3–40.

Galor, Oded. 2022. *The Journey of Humanity: The Origins of Wealth and Inequality* (Dutton: United States of America).

Garenne, Michel, and Etienne Van De Walle. 1989. "Polygyny and Fertility among the Sereer of Senegal," *Population Studies*, 43: 267–83.

Garrard, Timothy F. 1980. *Akan Weights and the Gold Trade* (Longman Publishing Group: London).

Gebregziabher, Solomon, Abdul Mounem, Hendrik Van Brussel, Herman Ramon, Jan Nyssen, Hubert Verplancke, Mintesinot Bahailu, Jozef Decker, and Josse De Barerdemaeker. 2006. "Animal Drawn Tillage, the Ethiopian Ard Plough, *Maresha*: A Review," *Soil and Tillage Research*, 89: 129–43.

Geggus, David. 1989. "Sex Ratio, Age and Ethnicity in the Atlantic Slave Trade: Data from French Shipping and Plantation Records," *The Journal of African History*, 30: 23–44.

Gemery, Henry, and Jan Hogendorn. 1974. "The Atlantic Slave Trade: A Tentative Economic Model," *Journal of African History*, 15: 223–46.

1990. "Evidence on English/African Terms of Trade in 18th Century," *Explorations in Economic History*, 27: 157–77.

Getz, Trevor R. 2004. *Slavery and Reform in West Africa: Towards Emancipation in Nineteenth Century Senegal and the Gold Coast* (Ohio University Press: Athens).

Giblin, James. 1990. "Trypanosomiasis Control in African History: An Evaded Issue?" *The Journal of African History*, 31: 59–80.

Global Runoff Data Center. 2007. "Major River Basins of the World." The Global Runoff Data Centre. "Discharge Data." 56068 Koblenz, Germany. https://grdc.bafg.de/data/data_portal/index.html.

Gomez, Michael A. 1998. *Exchanging Our Country Marks: The Transformation of African Identities in the Colonial and Antebellum South* (The University of North Carolina Press: Chapel Hill).

2008. *African Dominion: A New History of Empire in Early and Medieval West Africa* (Princeton University Press: Princeton).

Goody, Jack. 1971. *Technology, Tradition and the State in Africa* (Oxford University Press: London).

Goody, Jack, and S. J. Tambiah. 1973. *Bridewealth and Dowry* (Cambridge University Press: Cambridge).

Graeber, David, and Marshall Sahlins. 2017. *On Kings* (Hau Books: Chicago).

Graeber, David, and David Wengrow. 2021. *The Dawn of Everything* (Farrar, Straus and Giroux: New York).

Green, Toby. 2012. *The Rise of the Trans-Atlantic Slave Trade in West Africa, 1300–1589* (Cambridge University Press: New York).

2019. *A Fistful of Shells: West Africa from the Rise of the Slave Trade to the Age of Revolution* (Penguin Random House: London).

Greif, Avner. 1989. "Reputation and Coalition in Medieval Trade: Evidence from the Maghribi Traders," *The Journal of Economic History,* 49: 857–82.

1994. "Cultural Beliefs and the Organization of Society: A Historical and Theoretical Reflection on Collectivist and Individualist Societies," *Journal of Political Economy,* 102: 912–50.

2006. *Institutions and the Path to the Modern Economy: Lessons from Medieval Trade* (Cambridge University Press: Cambridge).

Grollemund, Rebecca, Simon Branford, Keon Bostoen, Andrew Meade, Chris Venditti, and Mark Pagel. 2015. "Bantu Expansion Shows That Habitat Altered the Route and Pace of Human Dispersal," *Proceedings of the National Academy of Sciences,* 112: 13296–301.

Guinnane, Timothy W. 2023. "We Do Not Know the Population of Every Country in the World for the Past Two Thousand Years," *Journal of Economic History,* 83: 912–38.

Hall, Bruce S. 2011. *A History of Race in Muslim West Africa, 1600–1960* (Cambridge University Press: Cambridge, New York).

Hamilton, A. 2005. *The Niger River: A Lecture Delivered at the Bromley Literary Institute, Tuesday, 25th March, 1862* (Black Classics Press: Baltimore).

Harari, Yuval Noah. 2015. *Sapiens: A Brief History of Mankind* (HarperCollins Publishers: New York).

Harley, C. Knick. 1998. "Cotton Textile Prices and the Industrial Revolution," *Economic History Review,* 51: 49–83.

Harms, Robert. 1981. *River of Wealth, River of Sorrow: The Central Zaire Basin in the Era of the Slave and Ivory Trade, 1500–1891* (Yale University Press: New Haven).

Harwood, Phil. 2013. *Canoeing the Congo: The First Source-to-Sea Descent of the Congo River* (Summersdale: West Sussex).

Haskell, Thomas L. 1979. "Explaining the Relative Efficiency of Slave Agriculture in the Antebellum South: A Reply to Fogel-Engerman," *American Economic Review,* 69: 206–07.

Hawthorne, Walter. 1999. "The Production of Slaves Where There Was No State: The Guinea-Bissau Region, 1450–1815," *Slavery and Abolition,* 20: 97–124.

2001. "Nourishing A Stateless Society during the Slave Trade: The Rise of Balanta Paddy-Rice Production in Guinea-Bissau," *The Journal of African History,* 42: 1–24.

2003. *Planting Rice and Harvesting Slaves: Transformations along The Guinea-Bissau Coast, 1400–1900* (Heinemann: Portsmouth).

2010. *From Africa To Brazil: Culture, Identity, and an Atlantic Slave Trade, 1600–1830* (Cambridge University Press: Cambridge).

Heath, William. 2014. *The Children Bob Moses Led: A Novel of Freedom Summer* (NewSouth Books: Birmingham).

Heblich, Stephan, Stephen J. Redding, and Hans-Joachim Voth. 2022. "Slavery and the British Industrial Revolution." National Bureau of Economic Research Working Paper.

Henrich, Joseph. 2016. *The Secret of Our Success: How Culture is Driving Human Evolution, Domesticating Our Species, and Making Us Smarter* (Princeton University Press: Princeton).

2020. *The WEIRDest People in the World: How the West became Psychologically Peculiar and Particularly Prosperous* (Farrar, Straus and Giroux: New York).

Herbst, Jeffrey. 2000. *States and Power in Africa: Comparative lessons in Authority and Control* (Princeton University Press: Princeton).

Heywood, Linda M. 2009. "Slavery and Its Transformation in the Kingdom of Kongo: 1491–1800," *The Journal of African History*, 50: 1–22.

Hilt, Eric. 2017. "Economic History, Historical Analysis, and the 'New History of Capitalism,'" *The Journal of Economic History*, 77: 511–35.

Hoffman, Philip T. 2015. *How Did Europe Conquer the World?* (Princeton University Press: Princeton).

Hogendorn, Jan S., and Marion Johnson. 1986. *The Shell Money of the Slave Trade* (Cambridge University Press: Cambridge, New York).

Hopkins, Anthony. 1973. *An Economic History of West Africa* (Columbia University Press: New York).

Hornbeck, Richard, and Trevon Logan. 2023. "One Giant Leap: Emancipation and Aggregate Economic Gain." National Bureau of Economic Research. Working Paper 31758. Cambridge, MA.

Horton, Mark, and John Middleton. 1988. *The Swahili: The Social Landscape of a Mercantile Society* (Blackwell Publishers: Malden).

Howard-Hassmann, Rhoda. 2008. *Reparations to Africa* (University of Pennsylvania Press: Philadelphia).

Hsieh, Change-Tai, Erik Hurst, Charles I. Jones, and Peter J. Klenow. 2019. "The Allocation of Talent and U.S. Economic Growth," *Econometrica*, 87: 1439–74.

Iliffe, John. 2007. *Africans: The History of a Continent* (Cambridge University Press: New York).

Inikori, Joseph. 1977. "The Import of Firearms into West Africa 1750–1807: A Quantitative Analysis," *Journal of African History*, 18: 339–68.

2002. *Africans and The Industrial Revolution in England: A Study in International Trade and Economic Development* (Cambridge University Press: Cambridge).

2009. "English Versus Indian Cotton Textiles: The Impact of Imports on Cotton Textile Production in West Africa." In Giorgio Riello, and Tirthankar Roy (eds.), *How India Clothed the World* (Brill: Leiden).

Jobson, Richard. 1932. *The Golden Trade* (Penguin Press: London).

Johnson, Marion. 1966. "The Ounce in 18th Century West African Trade," *The Journal of African History*, 7: 197–214.

Johnson, Marion, J. Thomas Lindblad, and Robert Ross. 1990. *Anglo-African Trade in the Eighteenth Century: English Statistics on African Trade, 1699–1808* (Centre for the History of European Expansion: Leiden).

Johnson, Walter. 2013. *River of Dark Dreams: Slavery and Empire in the Cotton Kingdom* (Harvard University Press: Cambridge).

Kea, Ray A. 1971. "Firearms and Warfare on the Gold and Slave Coasts from the Sixteenth to the Nineteenth Centuries," *The Journal of African History*, 21: 185–213.

1982. *Settlement, Trade, and Politics in the 17th Century Gold Coast* (The John Hopkins University Press: Baltimore).

Kelley, Robin D. G. 2002. *Freedom Dreams: The Black Radical Imagination* (Beacon Press: Boston).

Kelly, Morgan. 2021. "Persistence, Randomization, and Spatial Noise." UCD Center for Economic Policy. Discussion Paper No. DP16609.

Kenny, Joseph O. P. 1982. *The Catholic Church in Tropical Africa, 1445–1805*. Ibadan University Press and Dominican Publications. https://scispace.com/papers/the-catholic-church-in-tropical-africa-1445-1850-1qdjbx4hd0.

Kiros, Teodros. 2005. *Zara Yacob: Rationality of the Human Heart* (Africa World Press: London).

Klein, Martin A. 2001. "The Slave Trade and Decentralized Societies," *The Journal of African History*, 42: 49–65.

Koyama, Mark, and Jared Ruben. 2022. *How the World Became Rich: The Historical Origins of Economic Growth* (Polity Press: Cambridge).

Kremer, Michael. 1993. "Population Growth and Technological Change: One Million BC to 1990," *Quarterly Journal of Economics*, 108: 631–716.

Kuczynski, R. R. 1948. *Demographic Survey of the British Colonial Empire, Vol. 1: West Africa* (Oxford University Press: London).

1949. *Demographic Survey of the British Colonial Empire, Vol. II* (Oxford University Press: London).

Kyrtatas, Dimitris J. 1993. "The Western Way to Freedom," *New Left Review*, 197: 85–95.

Laitin, David, and Joachim Moortgat. 2012. "Geographic Axes and the Persistence of Cultural Diversity," *Proceedings of the National Academy of Sciences USA*, 109: 10,263–10,268.

Landes, David. 1983. *Revolution in Time: Clocks and the Making of the Modern World* (Harvard University Press: Cambridge).

LaTorre, Joseph Raymond. 1978. "Wealth Surpasses Everything: An Economic History of Asante, 1750–1874," PhD dissertation, University of California at Berkeley.

Law, Robin. 1980. *The Horse in West African History* (Oxford University Press: Oxford).

Lawrence, Benjamin N., and Richard L. Roberts. 2012. *Trafficking in Slavery's Wake: Law and the Experience of Women and Children in Africa* (Ohio State University Press: Columbus).

Le Goff, Jacques. 2005. *The Birth of Europe: 400–1500* (Blackwell Malden).

Legg, S. J. 1985. "Comparisons of Different Methods of Load Carriage," *Ergonomics*, 28: 197–212.

Levine, Ross, Chen Lin, and Wensi Xie. 2020. "The African Slave Trade and Modern Household Finance," *Economic Journal*, 130: 1817–41.

Ligon, Richard. 2011. *True and Exact History of the Island of Barbados* (Hackett Publishing: London).

Livingstone, David. 1858. *Missionary Travels and Researches in South Africa; Including a Sketch of Sixteen Years' Residence in the Interior of Africa, and a Journey from the Cape of Good Hope to Loanda on the West Coast; thence across the Continent, Down the River Zambesi, to the Eastern Ocean* (Harper & Brothers: New York).

Locke, John. 1690. *Two Treatises of Government* (Awnsham Churchill: London).

Logan, Carolyn. 2011. "The Roots of Resilience: Exploring Popular Support for African Traditional Authorities." *Afrobarometer Working Paper No. 128.*

Lovejoy, Paul E. 1983. *Transformations in Slavery: A History of Slavery in Africa* (Cambridge University Press: Cambridge).

1987. "The Role of the Wangara in the Economic Transformation of the Central Sudan in the 15th and 16th Centuries," *The Journal of African History*, 19: 173–93.

1988. "Concubinage and the Status of Women Slaves in Early Colonial Northern Nigeria," *The Journal of African History*, 29: 245–66.

2005. *Slavery, Commerce and Production in the Sokoto Caliphate of West Africa* (Africa World Press, Inc.: Trenton).

2016. *Jihad in West Africa during the Age of Revolutions* (Ohio University Press: Athens).

Lovejoy, Paul E., and David Richardson. 1995. "British Abolition and Its Impact on Slave Prices along the Atlantic Coast of Africa, 1783–1850," *The Journal of Economic History*, 55: 22.

2001. "The Business of Slaving: Pawnship in West Africa, c. 1600–1810," *The Journal of African History*, 42: 23.

Lovejoy, Paul, and Toyin Falola (eds.). 2003. *Pawnship, Slavery and Colonialism in Africa* (Africa World Press: Trebton).

Lowes, Sara. 2020. "Kinship Structure and Women," *Daedalus*, 149: 119–33.

2022. "Kinship Structure and the Family: Evidence from the Matrilineal Belt." National Bureau of Economic Research Working Paper.

Macaulay, Vincent, Catherine Hill, Alessandro Achilli, Chiara Rengo, Douglas Clark, William Meehan, and James Blackburn. 2005. "Single, Rapid Coastal Settlement of Asia Revealed by Analysis of Complete Mitochondrial Genomes," *Science*, 305: 1034–36.

Maddison, Angus. 2003. *The World Economy: A Millennial Perspective* (OECD: Paris).

Mann, Kristin, and Urano de Cerqueira Andrade. 2023. "Manumission Papers, Bahia, 1831–1840," *Journal of Slavery and Data Preservation*, 4: 18–29.

Manning, Patrick. 1990. *Slavery and African Life: Occidental, Oriental, and African Slave Trades* (Cambridge University Press: Cambridge).

2010. "African Population Projections, 1850–1960." In K. Ittmann, D. D. Cordell, and G. H. Maddox (eds.), *The Demographics of Empires: The Colonial Order and the Creation of Knowledge* (Ohio University Press: Athen).

Markoff, Shira, David Radcliff, and Darrick Hamilton. 2024. "A Bright Future with Baby Bonds: How States and Cities Should Invest in Our Kids." The New School: Institute on Race, Power and Political Economy. https://racepowerpolicy.org/2024/02/a-brighter-future-for-baby-bonds/.

Martin, Peter J. 1991. "The Zanzibar Clove Industry," *Economic Botany*, 45: 450–59.

Martinez, Jenny S. 2012. *The Slave Trade and the Origins of International Human Rights Laws* (Oxford University Press: Oxford).

Mattoso, Kátia de Queirós, Herbert S. Klein, and Stanley L. Engerman. 1986. "Research Note: Trends and Patterns in the Prices of Manumitted Slaves: Bahia, 1819–1800," *Slavery and Abolition*, 7: 59–67.

Maxwell, John Franceis. 1975. *Slavery and the Catholic Church* (Barry Rose Publishers: London).

Mayaux, Philippe, Etienne Bartholome, Steffen Fritz, and Alan Belward. 2003. "A New Landcover Map of Africa for the Year 2000," *Journal of Biogeography*, 31: 861–77.

Mayshar, Joram, Omer Moav, and Luigi Pascali. 2022. "The Origins of the State: Land Productivity or Appropriability," *Journal of Political Economy*, 130: 1091–144.

McCann, James C. 2005. *Maize and Grace: Africa's Encounter with a New World Crop, 1500–2000* (Harvard University Press: Cambridge).

McCloskey, Deirdre N. 2010. *Bourgeois Dignity: Why Economics Can't Explain the Modern World* (University of Chicago Press: Chicago).

2016. *Bourgeois Equality: How Ideas, Not Capital or Institutions, Enriched the World* (The University of Chicago Press: Chicago).

McCloskey, Deirdre N., and Art Carden. 2020. *Leave Me Alone and I'll Make You Rich: How the Bourgeois Deal Enriched the World* (The University of Chicago Press: Chicago; London).

McEvedy, Colin, and Richard Jones. 1978. *Atlas of World Population History* (Penguin: Harmonsworth).

McIntosh, Susan Keech. 1981. "A Reconsideration of Wangara/Palolus, Island of Gold," *The Journal of African History*, 22: 145–58.

Meillassoux, Claude. 1991. *The Anthropology of Slavery* (The Athlone Press: London).

Metcalf, George. 1987a. "Gold, Assortment and the Trade Ounce: Fante Merchants and the Problem of Supply and Demand in the 1770s," *A Journal of African History*, 28: 27–41.

1987b. "A Microcosm of Why Africans Sold Slaves: Akan Consumption Patterns in the 1770s," *The Journal of African History*, 28: 377–94.

Meyer, Marvin (ed.). 2008. *Tha Nag Hammadi Scriptures: The Revised and Updated Translation of Sacred Gnostic Texts* (HarperOne: New York).

Michalopoulos, Stelio, and Elias Papailoannou. 2013. "Precolonial Ethnic Institutions and Contemporary African Development," *Econometrica* 81: 113–52.

2020. "Historical Legacies and African Development," *Journal of Economic Literature*, 58: 53–128.

Miers, Suzanne, and Martin Klein (eds.). 1999. *Slavery and Colonial Rule in Africa* (Routledge: London).

Miers, Suzanne, and Igor Kopytoff. 1977. *Slavery in Africa: Historical and Anthropological Perspectives* (University of Wisconsin Press: Madison).

Miller, George A., and P. N. Johnson-Laird. 1976. *Language and Perception* (Cambridge University Press: Cambridge).

Miller, Joseph C. 1988. *Way of Death; Merchant Capitalism and the Angolan Slave Trade, 1730–1830* (Wisconsin University Press: Madison).

Mintz, Sidney, and Richard Price. 1992. *The Birth of African American Culture; An Anthropological Perspective* (Beacon Press: Boston).

Miotto, Martina, and Luigi Pascali. 2022. "Solving the Longitude Problem: A Story of Clocks, Ships and Cities," *Journal of International Economics*, 155. https://doi.org/10.1016/j.jinteco.2025.104067.

Miracle, Marvin P. 1966. *Maize in Tropical Africa* (University of Wisconsin Press: Madison).

Moes, John E. 1960. "The Economics of Slavery in the Ante Bellum South: Another Comment," *Journal of Political Economy*, 68: 183–87.

Mokyr, Joel. 1977. "Supply vs. Demand in the Industrial Revolution," *Journal of Economic History*, 37: 981–1008.

1990. *The Levers of Riches: Technological Creativity and Economic Progress* (Oxford University Press: Oxford).

2017. *A Culture of Growth: The Origins of the Modern Economy* (Princeton University Press: Princeton).

Morgan, Edmund S. 1972. "Slavery and Freedom: The American Paradox," *The Journal of American History*, 59: 5–29.

1975. *American Slavery, American Freedom* (W. W. Norton and Company: New York).

Morris, Christopher. 2020. "With "the Economics-of-Slavery Culture Wars," It's Déjà Vu All Over Again," *Journal of the Civil War Era*, 10: 524–57.

Moscona, Jacob, Nathan Nunn, and James Robinson. 2020. "Segmentary Lineage Organization and Conflict in Sub-Saharan Africa," *Econometrica*, 88: 1999–2036.

Moses, Robert P. 2001. *Radical Equations: Civil Rights from Mississippi to the Algebra Project* (Beacon Press: Boston).

Murdock, George P. 1949. *Social Structure* (Macmillan Co.: New York).

1959. *Africa: Its Peoples and their Culture History* (McGraw-Hill: New York).

1967. *Ethnographic Atlas* (University of Pittsburgh Press: Pittsburgh).

Niane, D. T. 1965. *Sundiate: An Epic of Old Mali* (Pearson Education Limited: Edinburgh Gate).

Nieboer, Herman Jeremias. 1900. *Slavery as an Industrial System: Ethnological Researches* (Martinus Nijhoff: The Hague).

Nohara, Daisuke, Akio Kitoh, Masahiro Hosaka, and Taikan Oki. 2006. "Impact of Climate Change on River Discharge Projected by Multimodel Ensemble," *Journal of Hydrometeorology*, 7: 1076–89.

North, Douglas, and Robert Thomas. 1971. "The Rise and Fall of the Manorial System: A Theoretical Model," *Journal of Economic History*, 31: 777–803.

North, Douglass. 1982. *Structure and Change in Economic History* (W. W. Norton and Company: New York).

North, Douglas C., John Joseph Wallis, and Barry R. Weingast. 2009. *Violence and Social Order: A Conceptual Framework for Interpreting Recorded Human History* (Cambridge University Press: Cambridge).

Northrup, David. 1978. *Trade without Rulers: Pre-Colonial Economic Development in South-Eastern Nigeria* (Clarendon Press: Oxford).

2002. *Africa's Discovery of Europe: 1450–1850* (Oxford University Press: New York).

Nunn, Nathan. 2008. "The Long Term Effects of Africa's Slave Trades," *Quarterly Journal of Economics*, 123: 139–76.

2009. "The Importance of History for Economic Development," *Annual Review of Economics*, 1: 65–92.

Nunn, Nathan, and Diego Puga. 2012. "Ruggedness: The Blessings of Bad Geography in Africa," *Review of Economics and Statistics*, 94: 20–36.

Nunn, Nathan, and Leonard Wantchekon. 2011. "The Slave Trade and the Origins of Mistrust in Africa," *American Economic Review*, 111: 3221–52.

Nwokeji, G. Ugo. 2010. *The Slave Trade and Culture in the Bight of Biafra* (Cambridge University Press: Cambridge).

2011. "Slavery in Non-Islamic West Africa, 1420–1820." In David Eltis, and Stanley L. Engerman (eds.), *The Cambridge World History of Slavery* (Cambridge University Press: Cambridge).

O'Brien, Patrick, and Stanley L. Engerman. 1993. "Exports and the Growth of the British Economy from the Glorious Revolution to the Piece of Amiens." In Barbara Solow (ed.), *Slavery and the Rise of the American System* (Cambridge University Press: Cambridge).

Oakes, James. 1990. *Slavery and Freedom: An Interpretation of the Old South* (Vintage Books: New York).

Obikili, Nonso. 2016a. "The Impact of the Slave Trade on Literacy in West Africa: Evidence from the Colonial Era," *Journal of African Economics*, 25: 1–27.

2016b. "The Trans-Atlantic Slave Trade and Local Political Fragmentation in Africa," *The Economic History Review*, 69: 1157–77.

Officer, Lawrence H. and Samuel H. Williamson. 2025. "The Price of Gold, 1257–Present." Measuringworth.com. http:www.measuringworth.com/gold/.

Olmstead, Alan L., and Paul Rhode. 2018. "Cotton, Slavery, and the New History of Capitalism," *Explorations in Economic History*, 67: 1–17.

Olson, Mancur. 1993. "Dictatorship, Democracy, and Development," *American Political Science Review*, 87: 567–76.

Olsson, Ola, and Douglas A. Hibbs Jr. 2005. "Biodiversity and Long Run Economic Development," *European Economic Review*, 49: 909–38.

Oriji, John. 1987. "The Slave Trade, Warfare and Aro Expansion in the Igbo Hinterland," *Transafrican Journal of History*, 16: 151–66.

Ozak, Omer. 2018. "Distance to the Pre-industrial Technological Frontier and Economic Development," *Journal of Economic Development*, 23: 175–221.

Pandolf, K. B., B. Givoni, and R. F. Goldman. 1977. "Predicting Energy Expenditure with Loads While Standing or Walking Very Slowly," *Journal of Applied Physiology*, 43: 577–81.

Park, Mungo. 2000. *Travels in the Interior Districts of Africa* (Duke University Press: Durham).

Patterson, Orlando. 1982. *Slavery and Social Death: A Comparative Study* (Harvard University Press: Cambridge).

1991. *Freedom in the Making of Western Culture* (Basic Books: New York, NY).

2021. "Ancient Slavery and the Creation of Freedom." In Toby Buckle (ed.), *What Is Freedom?* (Oxford University Press: Oxford).

Phillips, Anne. 1989. *The Enigma of Colonialism: British Policy in West Africa* (London).

Pierce, Lamar, and Jason Snyder. 2018. "The Historical Slave Trade and Firm Access to Finance in Africa," *Review of Financial Studies*, 31: 142–74.

Pijper, Frederick. 1909. "The Christian Church and Slavery in the Middle Ages," *The American Historical Review*, 14: 675–95.

Piketty, Thomas. 2014. *Capitol in the 21st Century* (Harvard University Press: Cambridge).

Pillai, Manu S. 2015. *The Ivory Throne: Chronicles of the House of Travancore* (HarperCollins: India).

Polanyi, Karl. 1964. "Sorting and "Ounce Trade" in the West African Slave Trade," *The Journal of African History*, 5: 381–93.

Pomerantz, Kenneth. 2000. *The Great Divergence: China, Europe, and the Making of the Modern World Economy* (Princeton University Press: Princeton).

Posnansky, Merrick. 1976. "New Radiocarbon Dates for Northern and Western Africa," *The Journal of African History*, 17: 161–95.

Prak, Maarten, and Jan Luiten van Zanden. 2023. *Pioneers of Capitalism, The Netherlands, 1000–1800* (Princeton University Press: Princeton).

Price, Gregory N., and Warren Whatley. 2021a. "Did Profitable Slave Trading Enable the Expansion of Empire? The Asiento de Negro, the South Sea Company and the Financial Revolution in Great Britain," *Cliometrica*, 15: 675–718.

2021b. "L'Asiento de Negros, la Compagnie des mers du Sud, les profits de la traite d'esclaves et la révolution financière en Grande-Bretagne," *Revue d'économie financière*, 0: 231–37.

2023. "Did the African Slave Trades Reduce the African Population?" Unpublished paper.

Quirk, Joel. 2009. *Unfinished Business: A Comparative Survey of Historical and Contemporary Slavery* (United Nations Educational, Scientific and Cultural Organization: Paris).

Raboteau, Albert J. 1978. *Slave Religion: The "Invisible Institution" in the Antebellum South* (Oxford University Press: Oxford).

Rattray, R. S. 1929. *Ashanti Law and Constitution* (Oxford University Press).

1969. *Ashanti* (Negro Universities Press: New York,).

Rediker, Marcus. 2008. *The Slave Ship: A Human History* (Penguin Books: New York).

Reniers, Georges. 2011. "Malthus, the 18th Century European Explorers and the Principles of Population in Africa," *Etude Popul Africa*, 25: 181–93.

Reyes-Centero, Hugo. 2016. "Out of Africa and into Asia: Fossil and Genetic Evidence on Modern Human Origins and Dispersals," *Quaternary International*, 416: 249–62.

Rhode, Paul. 2024. "What Fraction of Antebellum US National Product Did the Enslaved Produce?" *Explorations in Economic History*, 91. https://doi.org/10.1016/j.eeh.2023.101552.

Richards, W. A. 1980. "The Import of Firearms into West Africa in the Eighteenth Century," *The Journal of African History*, 21: 43–59.

Richardson, David. 1979. "West African Consumption Patterns and their Influence on the Eighteenth Century English Slave Trade." In Jan Hogendorn, and Henry Gemery (eds.), *The Uncommon Market: Essays in the Economic History of the Atlantic Slave Trade* (Bogle-L'Ouverture Publications: London).

Richardson, David. 1991. "Prices of Slaves in West and West Central Africa: Towards an Annual Series, 1698–1807," *Bulletin of Economic Research*, 43: 21–56.

Ridgeway, R. 1929. "Summarized Data of Gold Production." In *Economic Paper.* Washington, DC: Washington Bureau of Mines.

Rio, Alice. 2021. "Slavery in the Carolingian Empire." In Craig Perry, David Eltis, Stanley L. Engerman, and David Richardson (eds.), *The Cambridge World History of Slavery* (Cambridge University Press: Cambridge).

2023. *Slavery after Rome, 500–1100* (Oxford University Press: Oxford).

Roberts, Richard L. 1980. "Production and Reproduction of Warrior States: Segu Bambara and Segu Tokolor, circa 1712–1890," *The International Journal of African Historical Studies*, 13: 389–419.

1987. *Warriors, Merchants, and Slaves: The State and the Economy in the Middle Niger Valley, 1700–1914* (Stanford University Press: Stanford).

Robertson, C., and M. Klein (eds.). 1983. *Women and Slavery in Africa* (University of Wisconsin Press: Madison).

Rodney, Walter. 1970. *A History of the Upper Guinea Coast, 1545–1800* (Clarendon Press: Oxford).

1972. *How Europe Underdeveloped Africa* (Bogle-L'Ouverture Publications: London).

Rossi, Pauline. 2019. "Strategic Choices in Polygamous Households: Theory and Evidence from Senegal," *Review of Economic Studies*, 86: 1332–70.

Ryder, Alan F. 1969. *Benin and the Europeans, 1485–1897* (Humanities Press: New York).

Satia, Priya. 2018. *Empire of Guns: The Violent Making of the Industrial Revolution* (Penguin Press: New York).

Schaefer, Donald F., and Mark D. Schmitz. 1979. "The Relative Efficiency of Slave Agriculture: A Comment," *American Economic Review*, 69: 97–105.

Schumpeter, Elizabeth. 1960. *English Overseas Trade Statistics, 1697–1808* (Oxford University Press: London).

Sen, Amartya. 1997. *Human Rights and Asian Values* (Carnegie Council on Ethics and International Affairs: New York).

1999. *Development as Freedom* (Anchor Books: New York).

Sheleff, Leon. 1999. *The Future of Tradition: Customary Law, Common Law and Legal Pluralism* (Frank Cass: London).

Sheridan, Richard B. 1958. "The Commercial and Financial Organization of the British Slave Trade, 1750–1807," *Economic History Review*, 11: 249–63.

Sheriff, Abdul. 2010. *Dhow Cultures of the Indian Ocean: Cosmopolitanism, Commerce and Islam* (Columbia University Press: New York).

Smith, Adam. 1776. *The Wealth of Nations* (Methuen and Co., Ltd: London).

Smith, Robert. 1970. "The Canoe in West African History," *The Journal of African History*, 11: 515–33.

Sobel, Dava. 1995. *Longitude: The True Story of a Lone Genius Who Solved the Greatest Scientific Problem of His Time* (Walker Books: London).

Solow, Barbara L. 1985. "Caribbean Slavery and British Growth: The Eric Williams Hypothesis," *Journal of Development Economics*, 17: 99–115.

St. Clair, William. 2006. *The Door of No Return: The History of Cape Coast Castle and the Atlantic Slave Trade* (Blue Bridge: New York).

Stanley, Henry Morton. 1878. *Through the Dark Continent, Vol. I* (Harper Brothers: New York).

1879. *Through the Dark Continent, Vol. II* (Harper Brothers: New York).

1891. *In Darkest Africa: Or the Quest, Rescue and Retreat of Emin Governor of Equatoria* (Charles Scribner's Sons: New York).

Stelzner, Mark, and Sven Beckert. 2023. "The Contribution of Enslaved Workers to Output Growth in the Antebellum United States," *The Economic History Review*, 77: 137–59.

Subrahmanyam, Sanjay. 2019. "Between Eastern Africa and Western India, 1500–1650: Slavery, Commerce and Elite Formation," *Comparative Studies in Society and History*, 61: 805–34.

Sutch, Richard C. 2018. "The Economics of African-American Slavery: Cliometrics Debate." National Bureau of Economic Research Working Paper Series, No. 25197. Cambridge: NBER.

Sweet, James H. 2003. *Recreating Africa: Culture, Kinship, and Religion in the African Portuguese World, 1441–1770* (University of North Carolina Press: Chapel Hill).

Táíwò, Olúfémi. 2010. *How Colonialism Preempted Modernity in Africa* (University of Indiana Press: Bloomington).

2021. *Can a Liberal Be a Chief? Can a Chief Be a Liberal: Some Thoughts on an Unfinished Business of Colonialism* (Prickley Paradigm: Chicago).

2022. *Reconsidering Reparations* (Oxford University Press: New York).

Temin, Peter. 2017. *The Roman Market Economy: What Modern Economics Can Tell Us About Ancient Rome* (Princeton University Press: Princeton).

Thomas, Hugh. 1997. *The Slave Trade: The Story of the Atlantic Slave Trade: 1440–1870* (Touchstone: New York).

Thornton, John K. 1977. "Demography and History in the Kingdom of Kongo, 1550–1750," *Journal of African History*, 18: 507–30.

1983. *The Kingdom of Kongo: Civil War and Transition, 1641–1718* (University of Wisconsin Press: Madison).

1998. *Africa and Africans in the Making of the Atlantic world, 1400–1800* (Cambridge University Press: Cambridge).

1999. *Warfare in Atlantic Africa, 1500–1800* (UCL Press: London).

Tobler, Waldo. 1993. "Three Presentations on Geographical Analysis and Modeling." National Center for Geographic Information and Analysis Technical Report 93-1. University of California, Santa Barbara.

Turchin, Peter, Jonathan Adams, and T. D. Hall. 2006. "East–West Orientation of Historical Empires and Modern States," *Journal of World-Systems Research*, 12: 219–29.

van Waijenburg, Marlous. 2018. "Financing the African Colonial State: The Revenue Imperative and Forced Labor," *The Journal of Economic History*, 78: 40–80.

van Zanden, Jan Luiten. 2009. *The Long Road to the Industrial Revolution: The European Economy in a Global Perspective, 1000–1800* (Brill: Boston).

Vansina, Jan. 2010. *Being Colonized: The Kuba Experience in Rural Congo, 1880–1960* (University of Wisconsin Press: Madison).

Verger, Pierre. 1964. *Bahia and the West African Trade, 1549–1851* (Published for the Institute of African Studies by Ibadan University Press: Ibadan).

1976. *Trade Relations between the Bight of Benin and Bahia from the 17th to 19th Century* (Ibadan University Press: Ibadan, Nigeria).

Visser-Maessen, Laura. 2016. *Robert Harris Moses: A Life in Civil Rights and Leadership at the Grassroots* (University of North Carolina Press: Chapel Hill).

Voigtlander, Nico, and Hans-Joachim Voth. 2013. "The Three Horsemen of Riches: Plague, War, and Urbanization in Early Modern Europe," *Review of Economic Studies*, 80: 774–811.

Walk Free. 2023. "The Global Slavery Index 2023." Minderoo Foundation. https://walkfree.org/global-slavery-index/.

Weisdorf, Jacob L. 2005. "From Foraging to Farming: Explaining the Neolithic Revolution," *Journal of Economic Surveys*, 19: 561–85.

West, Jenny. 1991. *Gunpowder, Government and War in the Mid-Eighteenth Century* (The Boydell Press: Rochester, NY).

Westermann, William L. 1955. *The Slave Systems of Greek and Roman Antiquity* (The University of Pennsylvania Press: Philadelphia).

Whatley, Warren. 2014. "The Transatlantic Slave Trade and the Evolution of Political Authority in West Africa." In Emmanuel Akyeampong, Robert Bates, Nathan Nunn, and James Robinson (eds.), *Africa's Development in Historical Perspective* (Cambridge University Press: Cambridge).

2018. "The Gun-Slave Hypothesis and the 18th Century British Slave Trade," *Explorations in Economic History*, 67: 80–104.

2022a. "How the International Slave Trades Underdeveloped Africa," *The Journal of Economic History*, 82: 403–41.

2022b. "Review of 'Priya Satia, Empire of Guns: The Violent Making of the Industrial Revolution,'" *Journal of British Studies*, 61: 483–84.

Whatley, Warren, and Rob Gillezeau. 2011a. "The Fundamental Impact of the Slave Trade on African Economies." In Paul Rhode, Joshua Rosenbloom, and David Weiman (eds.), *Economic Evolution and Revolution in Historical Time* (Stanford University Press: Stanford).

2011b. "The Impact of the Slave Trade on Ethnic Stratification in Africa," *American Economic Review*, 101: 571–76.

White, Lynn. 1962. *Medieval Technology and Social Change* (Oxford University Press: London).

1982. *Machina Ex Deo* (MIT Press: Cambridge).

Whitman, Stephen T. 1997. *The Price of Freedom: Slavery and Manumission in Baltimore and Early National Maryland* (The University Press of Kentucky: Lexington).

Wilkerson, Isabel. 2020. *Caste: The Origins of Our Discontent* (Random House: New York).

Wilks, Ivor. 1961. "The Northern Factor in Asante History: Begho and the Mande," *The Journal of African History*, 2: 25–34.

1962. "A Medieval Trade Route from the Niger to the Gulf of Guinea," *The Journal of African History*, 3: 337–41.

1975. *Asante in The Nineteenth Century: The Structure and Evolution of a Political Order* (Cambridge University Press: London; New York).

1982a. "Wangara, Akan and the Portuguese in the 15th and 16th Centuries. I. The Matter of Bitu," *The Journal of African History*, 23: 333–39.

1982b. "Wangara, Akan and the Portuguese in the 15th and 16th Centuries. II. The Struggle for Trade," *The Journal of African History*, 23: 463–72.

1993. *Forests of Gold: Essays on the Akan and the Kingdom of Asante* (Ohio University Press: Athens).

Wilks, Ivor, John O. Hunwick, and Nancy Ellen Lawler (eds.). 1996. *The Cloth of Many Colored Silks: Papers on History and Society, Ghanaian and Islamic in Honor of Ivor Wilks* (Northwestern University Press: Evanston, Ill.).

Wright, Gavin. 1978. *The Political Economy of the Cotton South: Households, Markets, and Wealth in the Nineteenth Century* (Norton: New York).

1979. "The Efficiency of Slavery: Another Interpretation," *American Economic Review*, 69: 219–26.

2006. *Slavery and American Economic Development* (Lousiana State University Press: Baton Rouge).

2014. "Review of River of Darkness," *Journal of Economic Literature*, LII: 877–79.

2020. "Slavery and Anglo-American Capitalism Revisited," *The Economic History Review*, 73: 353–83.

Yamauchi, Susumu. 1994. "Looting of Men and Legal Theories in Medieval and Early Modern Europe," *Journal of Law and Politics*, 23: 13–32.

Yamazaki, Dai, Fiachra O'Loughlin, Mark A. Trigg, Zachary F. Miller, Tamlin M. Pavelsky, and Paul D. Bates. 2014. "Development of the Global Width Database for Large Rivers," *Water Resources. Research*, 50: 3467–80.

Yasuba, Yasukichi. 1971. "The Profitability and Viability of Plantation Slavery in the United States." In Robert Fogel, and Stanley L. Engerman (eds.), *The Reinterpretation of American Economic History* (Harper Row: New York).

Zawaira, Tendai, Clance Matthew, and Carolyn Chisadza. 2022. "Social Institutions, Gender Attitudes and Female Labor Force Participation in Sub-Saharan Africa," *South African Journal of Economics*, 91: 186–213.

Zewde, Naomi. 2019. "Universal Baby Bonds Reduce Black–White Wealth Inequality, Progressively Raise Net Worth of All Young Adults," *Review of Black Political Economy*, 47: 3–19.

Index

Printed by Integrated Books International,
United States of America